KAMLOOPS

Cover is a pastel of a brace of Kamloops trout, by noted Canadian artist, Tommy Brayshaw. Art work courtesy of Alec Jackson.

About the Author

S teve Raymond was born in Bellingham, Washington, and has spent much of his life fishing the nearby Kamloops trout waters. His first book was the original edition of *Kamloops,* published in 1971. It was followed two years later by the award-winning *Year of the Angler,* hailed by many as a modern angling classic. Raymond also has contributed to numerous angling anthologies, including *Fishing Moments of Truth, The Masters on the Dry Fly* and *The Masters on the Nymph.* He was editor of *The Flyfisher* for six years and continues to write a column for that magazine. His articles also have appeared in *Fly Fisherman, Sports Illustrated, Field & Stream* and other publications. He introduced the Kamloops trout to television viewers on ABC-TV's *American Sportsman* series.

Raymond served as international secretary of the Federation of Fly Fishermen in 1970-71 and was voted the Federation's man of the year in 1977. He is a past president of the Washington Fly Fishing Club and currently is vice-president of the Museum of American Fly Fishing. Raymond, his wife and two children now live in Seattle where he is an editor on the staff of *The Seattle Times.*

ISBN 0-936608-09-9

KAMLOOPS

An Angler's Study
of the Kamloops Trout

by
Steve Raymond

Revised Edition, 1980

Frank Amato Publications
P.O. Box 02112
Portland, Oregon 97202

The author's father landing a Kamloops trout in
Hihium Lake, 1940.

In memory of my father

Lt. Col. FREDERICK R. RAYMOND

United States Army

He loved the Kamloops trout and its native country

and taught his son to do likewise.

8

Preface

The term "revised edition" is a publisher's euphemism. Usually it means that an old book has been republished with a new cover. Often there also is a new introduction or foreword which tries, in a few words, to bring everything up to date. The text itself is the same tired old type of the original, dusted off and run through the press again. It costs a lot less to do it that way.

But that is not the case here. In fact, "revised edition" may not be an adequate term to describe this volume. It has been completely rewritten, not only to bring it up to date, but also to add a significant amount of new material. So what you have here, essentially, is a new book. To be sure, readers of the first edition will find in this one much that is familiar, but they will also discover much that is new.

Why such an elaborate revision? In the decade since the writing of the first edition there have been many changes in the environment of the Kamloops trout, in management of the fishery, in the attitudes of fishermen and in fishing methods and equipment, and these alone seemed sufficient reason for major changes in the text. The section on the history of the Kamloops also has been expanded with the addition of new material, some new fly patterns have been listed and there are descriptions of many lakes not mentioned in the original edition.

The decision to rewrite the text also offered an opportunity to correct some unfortunate errors that appeared in the first edition. The publishing house responsible for the book somehow scrambled the captions of several photos — as those who recognized the scenes pictured undoubtedly quickly noticed. Other errors, typographical and otherwise, had been marked for correction on the galley proofs of the original edition, but the book went to press without the corrections being made. Now, at last, they have been.

Finally, this new edition reflects some changes in the author himself. One cannot spend a decade fishing and writing without learning a great deal more about both than he knew to begin with. I think the evidence of that will be apparent in the text that follows.

But one thing has not changed, and that is the character of the Kamloops trout, which originally inspired the writing of this book. The qualities of the Kamloops as a game fish remain unsurpassed and its reputation has grown as more and more anglers have gotten acquainted with it. Perhaps this new edition will lead others to a new or greater appreciation of the Kamloops trout and its native country; if so, then the book will have served its purpose.

Steve Raymond
October 1, 1979

Contents

Chapter One

A Brief History

The fragile warmth of a spring afternoon slowly melts the mounds of old snow hidden in the pine thickets and the runoff swells the headwater springs. The streams that flow from them quicken more each day, hurrying down the slopes to frozen lakes that lie waiting to receive them. The growing spate forces openings in the surface ice and the wind forces the openings wider; cracks spread out from them through the rotting ice until it fractures and the wind sweeps away the shards. At last, after the long stillness of winter, the lakes are free again to feel the touch and movement of the breeze.

Even as the ice retreats, mature Kamloops trout are drawn to the inlet streams by some mysterious instinct not yet fully understood by men. In ones and twos at first the trout enter the streams, pressing forward against the icy flow. As the streams gradually grow warmer and the last snow is flushed from the hills, the trout — large, hook-jawed males, precocious smaller males and great, dark females burdened with spawn — begin the run in earnest, driving themselves forward with a sudden urgency to fulfill their life's purpose.

While the trout press forward with the business of spawning, the changing season also stirs something in the blood of every angler. From desktop and dinner table, their eyes suddenly look far away while their minds take out memories of seasons past, turn them over and enjoy them: memories of rising trout and fluttering sedges, of days when the trout took eagerly and ran far across the flats and the afternoon air vibrated with the sounds of a fly reel under ultimate stress. Closet doors are opened and old cane is taken out after a winter's rest and handled lovingly again. The mothball fragrance of fur and feathers pervades the house as new flies are dressed and filed away in plastic boxes and metal fly books. Out come the tattered maps with the circled names, names like Peterhope and Plateau, Broken Hook and Hardcastle, and the mind races with furious plans for the dawning season.

Then, from nearly every compass point, the anglers begin their own migration to the Kamloops trout waters of British Columbia. From all over the earth they come to match their skills against one of the greatest game fish of the world.

Now these things are an accepted part of the life of the province, a seasonal event as certain as the autumn fall of leaves. But it was not always so. It was but a moment ago in the geological history of the land that the first trout of any kind made their way to its waters and the first men built their lodges there. The story of the Kamloops trout and the men who fish for it begins during the last glacial period, about 20,000 years ago. At that time most of the province of British Columbia lay beneath vast gleaming layers of ice that surrendered their grip upon the land with infinite slowness. But inevitably the great tentacles of ice retreated to the north, carving great canyons as they did so and leaving a vast array of rubble in their wake.

The runoff from the vanishing glaciers sought outlets to the sea, filling glacial chasms, spilling over to dig new channels, battering its way stubbornly to final release in the ocean. The watercourses thus formed gradually assumed the rough shape of the watersheds we know today, and as the rivers flooded out of the heart of the province fish and wildlife followed them upstream to their sources.

Among these fish were runs of salmon and steelhead from the Pacific which probed restlessly as far into the interior lakes and tributaries as the young rivers would let them go, planting the seeds of new generations in the glacial gravel of the river bottoms. To these places their progeny returned to spawn in their own time. But over time some of the offspring from the steelhead runs failed to join in the seaward migration of the young, remaining instead as permanent residents of the largest interior lakes. Others were landlocked when their exits to the sea were blocked as rivers changed course or geologic upheavals closed off migratory routes. Living, growing and breeding entirely in the fresh waters of the interior, these fish become the root stock for what is now called the Kamloops trout.

Somewhere from the mists of prehistory came tribes of Indians who settled among the pine forests, lakes and rivers of the young country. They trapped and speared the Kamloops trout on their spawning beds and dried them on crude wooden racks for food, just as they did with the salmon and steelhead in their seasons. But the Kamloops trout still grew in numbers and extended its range.

Then, a little more than 160 years ago, one of the first white settlements of the province was established at the point where the North and South Thompson Rivers converge in a broad, grassy valley surrounded by timbered ridges that are a part of what geologists call the Southern Interior Plateau. There, in 1812, Fort Kamloops was established, and in time the name Kamloops was also given to the nearby lake where the Thompson's mighty flow is stilled and widens to a great expanse of water.

These early British Columbians left few records of their angling accomplishments. In fact, more than three-quarters of a century would pass before the big silver trout they caught from Kamloops Lake would even have a name. Then, in 1892, samples of the trout from Kamloops Lake were sent to the renowned biologist Dr. David Starr Jordan of Stanford University for identification. T. W. Lambert, author of *Fishing*

14

in British Columbia, one of the earliest published accounts of angling in the province, recorded the event:

"For several years two Americans came every season to Savona's Ferry (on Kamloops Lake) to fish, and, becoming impressed with the beauty of the so-called silver trout, they sent a specimen to Professor Starr Jordan, of the Leland Stanford University of San Francisco. The first specimen did not arrive in good condition and another specimen was sent, in the preparation of which I personally assisted. It was a fish of about 1½ lb. in weight, a very beautiful specimen and a most typical example of the silver trout.

"Professor Jordan described this fish as a new species, under the name of *Salmo kamloopsii . . .*"

In arriving at his identification, Jordan noted the trout bore a strong resemblance in appearance, shape and color to the familiar rainbow trout and steelhead of the Western United States. But he also noted some differences, chiefly in the number of scale rows on the new trout, which Jordan observed was much higher than on the familiar rainbow trout (*Salmo gairdneri*). Under the taxonomic procedures followed in Jordan's time, such relatively small differences were considered sufficient evidence of a new species, and Jordan decided that was what he had on his hands. He chose the name *Salmo kamloopsii* in honor of the lake from which the sample trout had come.

The original natural range of *Salmo kamloopsii* was limited to Shuswap, Adams, Kamloops, Okanagan, Kootenay and a few other large lakes in the major watersheds of southern British Columbia. It was found in only a few of the many smaller lakes, most of which were isolated by natural barriers from the main watersheds. The great majority of the thousands of small lakes on the Southern Interior Plateau were barren of fish life.

The few large lakes where the Kamloops trout existed naturally were more than enough to handle the small amount of angling pressure that existed in the early days. Men were more interested in fur, gold, timber and other sources of wealth than fish, and the often harsh realities of frontier life left little time for fishing anyway – except when the catch was needed for survival. Transportation throughout the province, riven by great mountain ranges and deep canyons, was difficult and slow and the population remained small. There were no laws or regulations governing the taking of trout; there seemed no need for them. Yet those who had the time and the means to fish for sport sometimes found angling the like of which has seldom been seen elsewhere on earth.

Dr. Lambert was such a man. A surgeon attached to the Western Division of the Canadian Pacific Railway Company, his duties left him time to explore the angling possibilities of the region and, fortunately for posterity, he later related the results of many of these expeditions in his little book, published posthumously in 1907. Many remarkable catches are described

15

in this volume, but one far exceeds any of the others. Indeed, it may rank as the greatest fishing story of all. In Dr. Lambert's words:

"About twenty-three miles from Kamloops there is a lake known as Fish Lake, in which the fishing is so extraordinary as to border on the regions of romance, though locally it is considered a matter of course. For lake fishing, in point of numbers, it is impossible that this piece of water could be beaten; it is like a battue in shooting, the number to be caught is only limited by the skill and endurance of the angler; indeed, little skill is needed, for anyone can catch fish there, though a good fisherman will catch the most. Also fish can be caught on any day, some days being better than others, but a blank day is an impossibility.

"The lake is twenty-three miles south of Kamloops, and is reached by a good road, and there is now a small wooden house, where one can stop and hire boats. Ten years ago there was only a trail, which was rough travelling on horseback, with a pack horse to carry tent and provisions. The lake has been a fishing ground for the Indians from time immemorial, and fish used to be brought down by them to Kamloops from a fish trap built in the creek running out of the lake. I have also seen them fishing with bait and spearing fish at night; but the true bait for Fish Lake is the fly, and contrary to the usual case, the white man with a fly and modern tackle can make catches which far surpass any that the Indian ever made. The trap has now been abandoned, and the Indians do not fish on this lake any more.

"From time to time half-breeds and cowboys came into Kamloops with stories of big catches of trout made with a willow bough and a piece of string with a fly tied to it; sometimes 300 or 400 fish would be brought down which had been caught in this way.

"This stimulated the sporting instinct of the inhabitants, and a few visits were paid to the lake and good catches were made, but the fishermen who went there were of a very amateur kind. In the summer of 1897 an American proposed to me that we should go up and try what good tackle could do; in fact, he proposed that we should go up and try to make a record.

"We went up in the first week of August, and the result far surpassed our wildest imagination. We fished three full days, and brought back 1,500 trout, which weighed 700 lb., cleaned and salted. The first day we caught 350, for some time was wasted in finding the best places. The second day a start was made at 5 a.m., and we fished till long after dark, about 9:30 p.m., catching 650; the third day we caught about 500 . . .

"Flies were abundant, and the fish were ravenous for both real and artificial; they almost seemed to fight for our flies as soon as they touched the water. Even when almost every feather had been torn off they would take the bare hook. We fished with three flies, and often had three fish on at one time . . . Our fish were cleaned and salted each day

16

by some Indians, so that none were wasted, and no fish were returned to the water except the very smallest.

"We had estimated our catch on the best day to be over 700 fish; but, owing to exhaustion and the necessity of cooking our supper, after being seventeen hours on the water, we did not feel equal to removing our fish from the boat, and during the night a raid was made on them by mink, which are very plentiful round this lake. Though it was impossible to say how many had been carried off, 650 was the exact total of fish counted on the following morning. If allowance is made for a rest for lunch, and time taken off for altering and repairing flies and tackle, it will be easily seen that this number of fish caught by two rods in one day on the fly constitutes a record which would be very hard to beat on this lake or any other. The best I was ever able to do again, with another rod, was a little over 300 . . ."

It is hardly surprising that Lambert could never equal his remarkable record on Fish Lake, now known as Lac le Jeune. No lake could long withstand catches of such magnitude, and such grand catches soon tempted men whose motives were not related to sporting instincts. The biologist Dr. J. R. Dymond later wrote "that commercial fishermen have made as much as $500 in a single month trolling for Kamloops trout, which were sold at 27¢ a pound." Overharvesting by both sport and commercial fishermen soon began to make serious inroads into the trout populations of various lakes so that it became obvious that some form of regulation would be necessary in order to preserve the fishery.

The need for regulations led to establishment of a provincial game commission in 1905. The commissioner's post was given to Arthur Bryan Williams, who was born in Lismany, Ireland, December 9, 1866. Williams held the post for many years and, under his administration, the range of the Kamloops trout was to be increased a thousandfold while regulations were promulgated to protect it.

As a fly fisherman, Lambert was an exception in the early history of angling for Kamloops trout. Trolling was the method used most often, and it was a method well suited to the large, deep lakes where Kamloops trout were native. Francis C. Whitehouse, another early writer on British Columbia, described tackle consisting of long greenheart rods which were secured to a boat with six-foot lengths of rope and used for trolling. Two rods normally were fished from each boat and each rod was fitted with a heavy reel and 600 feet of line. Lures were attached to leaders made of wire or gut. The ropes attached to the rods prevented their loss if a heavy trout should strike while the angler was busy with the oars.

Compared with the light, sophisticated tackle in use today, White-house's heavy trolling outfit seems pretty awkward. But unquestionably it was well suited for fishing the large, deep lakes that were the typical habitat of the native Kamloops trout.

KAMLOOPS

Very little was known about the Kamloops trout or its life history when the Fish Cultural Service began experiments with trout at the salmon hatchery on Granite Creek near Shuswap Lake. In 1908, eggs were obtained from Kamloops trout spawning in a tributary of Shuswap Lake and fry from these eggs were planted in two previously barren lakes northeast of Kamloops — Paul and Pinantan. Lying in the same watershed, these lakes drain into the North Thompson River, but falls in the outlet below Paul Lake had prevented trout from making their way upstream from the river. But Paul and Pinantan were barren only in terms of a fish population; over uncounted centuries, they had developed a swarming abundance of insect life and fresh-water scuds and plankton. In this respect they were typical of hundreds of small lakes scattered across the Southern Interior Plateau — fishless lakes whose rich, sunwarmed waters throbbed with tiny, teeming life and gave birth to great hordes of hatching insects in the spring evenings.

Paul Lake received the initial plant of 5,000 fry, and the little fish fed eagerly on the great untouched stocks of food that nature had slowly built. In a short time they grew fat and strong and the word went out among local anglers that Paul Lake was a place to try. And even as Paul Lake's reputation was spreading, its fish population was growing. Mature fish from the first planting had found its tributaries and had spawned in them, sending new generations of trout down from the spawning creeks to forage in the rich shallows of the lake.

In 1922 a hatchery was built to take advantage of the spawning run that had developed. Eggs were collected from the mature trout that flocked upstream and these were hatched into fry for planting other lakes. In 1924 a good road was punched through to Paul Lake, making it more readily accessible to anglers.

Other hatcheries also were being established. One was built at Gerrard on the Lardeau River above Kootenay Lake in 1914 and eggs were stripped from the huge Kootenay Lake trout when they reached their spawning grounds in the river. Another was established on fertile Pennask Lake, in the high country between Merritt and Kelowna.

From these sources, dozens of previously fishless lakes received their first trout. Like those in Paul Lake, the fish usually grew rapidly and provided spectacular fishing within a few years of the first planting.

In addition to the formal stocking program carried out by the government, there were many informal, unofficial and often unrecorded plantings made by local anglers. More often than not, these were the work of one or two fishermen who would trap a few fry in a spawning tributary, put them in a bucket of water and carry them to some new and virgin lake for release. And in this often haphazard way, the range of the Kamloops trout was extended.

Of all the lakes that received their first trout in this way, Knouff Lake is probably the outstanding example. A beautiful, island-dotted lake lying in the rolling, timbered hills northeast of Kamloops, Knouff was, if anything, richer than all the other lakes around it, with broad shoals and weedbeds and enormous sedge hatches in the spring. If ever a lake was ripe and waiting to receive a supply of trout, Knouff was the one. And Len Phillips, a local resident, and his son decided to give it the trout it lacked.

The Phillipses trapped 10 ripe trout in the stream between Paul and Pinantan Lakes and placed them in a barrel filled with water. It took them five days to haul the barrel to Knouff Lake, stopping at streams and springs along the way to change the water. One of the trout died during the journey, but on May 20, 1917, the nine survivors were released in Knouff Lake and left to find its inlet stream and spawn.

For three years the lake was left undisturbed and then, on May 20, 1920 — exactly three years after the first fish were released — it was opened for fishing. According to one account, 28 anglers travelled to the lake, unsure what they would find there — or whether they would find anything at all. What they found was angling of a kind to stagger the imagination. One trout of 17½ pounds was landed that day, and several weighing more than 15 pounds were caught.

The fame of Knouff Lake spread quickly and it went on to become known as one of the world's greatest dry-fly waters within the next few years. It supported incredible hatches of "traveling sedges," large, clumsy insects that fluttered for long distances across the surface after hatching, bringing even the very largest trout to the top to feed. For more than a decade, Knouff Lake offered superlative fishing, and at its peak in 1930 a 17¼-pound Kamloops trout was taken there on a dry fly, and 8- and 10-pound fish were common.

In large measure it was the fame of Knouff Lake that first drew the attention of anglers from outside British Columbia and brought them to the province to sample its newly productive Kamloops trout waters. And the successes of the early plantings of trout in Paul, Pinantan, Knouff and other lakes encouraged additional efforts. However, little was yet known of the life history of the Kamloops trout, and even less was known about the relation of the fish to its environment, so that the stocking program went on in ignorance of what was necessary to achieve desirable results and with little regard for the varying characteristics of the different lakes. Because of this ignorance, the results achieved ranged from spectacular successes to utter failures.

But if one thing had become clear it was that the Kamloops trout was a resource of growing value and importance to the province. Accordingly, the government decided it needed to know more about these fish in order to manage them properly, and in 1925 Dr. J. R. Dymond was asked to begin an investigation of the Kamloops trout and other game fish of British Columbia. Two years later he was joined in this work by Dr. Charles McC. Mottley, a scientific assistant for the Biological Board of Canada.

In 1931 Mottley reached Paul Lake and began a study of the Kamloops trout that was to last five years. Mottley was an imaginative scientist whose work pushed forward the frontiers of fisheries knowledge and largely filled in the gaps of what was known about the life cycle of the Kamloops trout. He developed the first stocking formula based on the carrying capacity of the Kamloops trout lakes and also set the record straight once and for all as to exactly where the Kamloops belonged on the trout family tree.

Noting that Jordan had based his identification of the Kamloops trout as a separate species primarily on its higher number of scale rows, Mottley set out to find whether that difference was due to heredity or some difference in the environments of the Kamloops and rainbow trout. He conducted an ingenious experiment to determine the answer: "The eggs from a single female Kamloops trout, fertilized by the milt from a single male, were divided into two lots, one of which was raised at the ordinary hatchery temperature at Nelson, B. C., the other being kept for five weeks following the eyed-egg stage at a temperature about 9 degrees F. higher. The fish were reared to a size of three inches, when they were killed and scale counts were made on a sample of 100 from each lot. Those raised at the higher temperature had an average of five rows less than those raised at the ordinary hatchery temperature.

"This experiment led to the conclusion that the number of scale rows could be modified by changing the temperature at the time of early development."

Mottley had demonstrated that the lower water temperatures of the spawning tributaries of the Interior lakes were responsible for the difference in the number of scale rows between Kamloops and rainbow trout — in other words, that the difference was due to environmental factors rather than heredity. His experiment proved conclusively that genetically the Kamloops was no different from *Salmo gairdneri,* the rainbow trout. He reclassified the Kamloops as a variety of the rainbow which he decided to call *Salmo gairdneri kamloops.*

The matter of classification was of little interest outside the scientific community, but it did reveal one important thing: The Kamloops trout could not be exported and still remain a Kamloops trout. Its characteristic appearance, growth and behavior were tied inextricably to the environmental conditions of its native country; where those conditions were not present, the Kamloops would be indistinguishable from any other variety of rainbow trout.

This lesson was not to be learned quickly. For many years after Mottley's experiments, attempts were made to plant Kamloops trout in the coastal waters of British Columbia and several Western states where the climate and environment were much different from those of the British Columbia Interior. With few exceptions — notably Pend Oreille Lake in Northern Idaho — these attempts met with failure. The transplanted fish failed to show the growth, appearance and game qualities expected of Kamloops trout, and sometimes they died out altogether. Gradually anglers outside the province began to understand that they would have to go to British Columbia to fish for Kamloops trout; the trout could not be brought to them.

The introduction of the Kamloops trout to the smaller, shallower Interior lakes had made it available for the first time to fly fishermen. It quickly proved itself a willing fly-rod fish, responding avidly to wet flies and rising well to floating imitations when a hatch was on. Knouff Lake clinched the Kamloops' reputation as a fly fisherman's fish, and anglers began to flock from outside the province to take advantage of the new opportunities offered. The growing sport fishery and the increasing tourist trade that was based on it quickly founded a new industry. Resorts were built to accommodate the visiting anglers and local anglers hired themselves out as guides.

One of the first resorts was built at Paul Lake, and others soon followed on Pinantan, Knouff, Lac le Jeune and other waters. In 1927, James D. Dole of the Dole pineapple family began construction of a private lodge on Pennask Lake which was to house the famous Pennask Lake Fishing Club, a private fishing lodge whose membership included (and still includes) Canadian and American businessmen. Throughout the years since the lodge opened in 1929, the pages of its guest register have been inscribed with the names of many well-known and well-to-do visitors, capped by Her Majesty, Queen Elizabeth II.

Among the early Kamloops trout guides, the name of one stands out far above the rest: Arthur William ("Bill") Nation was born in Bristol, England, on June 29, 1881, but spent much of his adult life in the Kamloops country, and to many veteran B. C. anglers his name is still synonymous with the Kamloops trout.

Nation was a lean man with a Hoover haircut and a hawkish nose on which he balanced a pair of steel-rimmed spectacles. He began his career as a Kamloops trout guide on Little River, but when Echo Lodge was built on Paul Lake Nation made it his headquarters. From Echo Lodge he guided anglers on Paul Lake and dozens of other waters. His knowledge gained from years of observation of the Kamloops trout was not surpassed for years, and his legacy is a series of fly patterns that bear his name: Nation's Fancy, Nation's Special, Nation's Silvertip and others, of which we will see more later.

A day with Bill Nation usually began with a leisurely breakfast at Echo Lodge, after which the soft-spoken guide would consult the barometer. Through some special formula known only to him, the barometer would determine where the day's fishing would be spent, or whether it

WILLIAM NATION

ANGLERS' GUIDE

Specializing in
Fly Fishing

for

KAMLOOPS RAINBOW TROUT

Headquarters
at
ECHO LODGE,
PAUL LAKE,
KAMLOOPS, B. C.

Wm. Nation, with day's catch of trout on flies tied by himself. Taken with a client from Hong Kong, August, 1934, in one of the number of high altitude lakes fished from Paul Lake in July and August only.

Fishing Paul Lake and day trips to Knouff, LeJeune, Pillar and Pinantan Lakes, and the Thompson, Adams and Little Rivers—all within easy distance on the car road.

Hyas Long, Pemberton, Devick and Beaver Lakes are reached by car and from four to six miles on horseback in day trips, or stay a few days in cabins. Jewel, Winfield Beaver, Dee, Canim, and Big Bar Lakes can be reached by car, and are from four to six day trips.

Hi-Hiume Lake, especially good for fly fishing from mid-July to end of August, is a two hour run by car and a ten-mile pack, with comfortable cabins at the lake.

A guarantee of at least 100 trout a week. Each season I net for clients up to 70 trout a day in number, and of larger fish, up to 60 lbs. weight of trout a day, all on the fly.

Season April 16th to November 16th. Bookings, in advance, $35.00 a week. Special flies tied for Kamloops Rainbow, guaranteed to kill, $2.50 a dozen.

Taupo and Rotorua Lakes in New Zealand in their season.

For further information or reservations, WRITE OR WIRE

WILLIAM NATION
Echo Lodge, Paul Lake, Kamloops, B. C.

Photo courtesy of *Fish and Game in British Columbia* by A. Bryan Williams.

was even worth going fishing at all. When a lake had been selected, Nation would hand out some of his own flies to his clients and they would set out to fish together. Talking incessantly, Nation would row the boat and watch for rises, telling his client where to cast and how to retrieve. With the knowledge gained from countless days on the water, Nation seldom failed to find fish or show his clients how to catch them.

When the day's fishing was done, the party would return to the lodge where Nation would dress the catch. If the customer wanted fresh fish sent home, Nation would pack them carefully, stuffing them with moss so that the fish were in the round and placing them in boxes among layers of moss covered with ice. Then they were taken to Kamloops to be dispatched by railway express.

Nation fished until the last week of his life. His last customer, in October, 1940, was Dr. Bill McMahon of Seattle. "I arrived in Kamloops in the evening and went out to Paul Lake," McMahon recalls. "Nation met us there that evening. I had borrowed two bamboo rods and Nation went through my tackle after we'd had dinner. As I remember, it was dusk or dark when he stepped outside. He strung up the rods and took one and laid out the line in the air, just feeling it in the dark. 'Yes, this balances well,' he said, and then tried the other one and said they were satisfactory.

"So the next day we started fishing with Bill. My guide was a big Scotsman named Alec. He was one that Bill pressed into service when he had occasion to. He, too, was a very knowledgeable fisherman, but not of the caliber of Bill Nation." Nation himself accompanied McMahon's wife.

"It was a ritual with Bill. There was none of the hurly-burly early morning things. You had your breakfast and then he consulted the barometer. And it was a very considered judgment on the barometer because it determined where you would fish. And under certain circumstances, unfortunately, even though I had only 10 days to fish, he would say: 'Can't fish today.'

"I think there were two such days, and of course I was just screaming to go fishing, so on these days he would troll. He'd go out into the lake with these spoons, multiple long things, if you insisted on fishing. I guess they were baited with worms or something, so he wasn't a purist, but I think that was almost like a form of a little chastisement if you were going to be so stupid as to insist on fishing on a day like this. The gods and the fates did not ordain that you fish on those days; the barometer was off.

"I didn't know the formula, but we would go from the high lakes — Peterhope and some of the others — to Paul Lake itself and all the varying stages in between. We fished Lac le Jeune which was then noted for the fact that there were more fish in the air at one time on that lake than

23

Bill Nation, famous Kamloops guide and fly tyer, poses with a trout taken by one of his clients. The handwritten inscription reads: "Rainbow trout on fly rod from a high altitude lake — Mr. H. G. Sheldon, of Hong Kong with Wm. Nation, guide. June 10th, 1935."

one had ever seen in his life. You'd look over the lake and the lake was alive with big, rising, lunging, leaping rainbows.

"My wife had never — never in her life — held a fly rod in her hand. She actually fished, she threw a fly the first day under his tutelage.

"He had a wonderful sense of humor. We went by horseback into one lake. We stopped at a ranch and got horses and Bill — he had done this many times, so he was prepared for it — put the rods in a golf bag and carried it over the pommel of his saddle. The day was absolutely miserable, it was really a wet, cold, rainy day. So we rode into this lake and — poor Bill — his great invention had failed, there was a hole in the bottom of the golf bag and one of the rod tips had fallen out. But he rode back over the trail and found the tip and about an hour later he came along and we fished in the driving rain.

"We always had fine fishing with Bill. He knew he was dying and I think he purposely picked different areas each day, even though the barometer might have said so. He wanted to show us his country and more or less relive his own life.

"He had been in the hospital in Kamloops and the diagnosis was well known (cancer of the esophagus), but he had then left the hospital and come back to Paul just a couple of weeks before we arrived there. And, as we learned, we were the last people that he fished with.

"I left a rod, one of the rods that I had borrowed, so I wrote to Bill after we got home. There was a bit of a delay and then I received a letter from the lady who managed the lodge telling me that Bill had died. She was so sorry, but they had just gathered together all of his tackle and sold it to get some money to take care of his funeral expenses. He didn't have much to show for his lifetime of effort.

"So I've always felt kind of happy that maybe I did help a bit, and I got another rod to replace the one I had left there."

Bill Nation's death ended an era in the history of Kamloops trout fishing. He tried unceasingly in dozens of ways to improve the fish and the fishing in his beloved lakes and he introduced the Kamloops trout to many anglers who would later write about it or carry word of it to the far corners of the earth. He died a pauper, but few others have lived a life as rich as his, and he left a legacy that will forever be a part of the lore and mystique of the Kamloops trout.

But if Nation is the best remembered of the early Kamloops fishermen and guides, he was by no means the only one. Others — Colonel Ashton, Colonel Flint and Colonel Carey; Dr. Lloyd Day, Tommy Brayshaw among them — also made lasting contributions. Their names remain a part of the tradition of Kamloops trout fishing, and tales of their exploits are still shared over campfires or when anglers gather around a convivial bottle after a day of sport.

Kamloops trout fishing reached its golden age in the 1930s. The Depression made times difficult for owners of the new resorts that had been built in optimism only a few years before, but often the owners of these establishments were from pioneer stock accustomed to facing hard times. They made the best of things and hoped for better times, and those fortunate enough to visit them in those difficult years often found the warmest hospitality and incredible angling for great wild trout in new lakes just coming into their prime. In the years after they were first stocked, before the trout consumed their superabundance of feed, these lakes often produced fish that averaged 8 or 10 pounds or even more. Fighting their way through the clinging muck of roads freshly cut through the wilderness, the Kamloops trout anglers of the '30s found wild adventure in virgin lakes.

The Kamloops trout quickly earned for itself the reputation of being something apart from other trout. It fought with unparalleled strength and stamina and a special reckless violence not found in other trout, and anglers discovered it was a fish to test their skill to new limits. When hooked, the first response of a bright, well-conditioned Kamloops trout is likely to be a long, swift run that pulls great lengths of line from the reel, followed by a series of violent leaps; and then the performance is repeated. Slow to tire, the Kamloops may sulk or sound or run straight at the angler, a sudden tactic that has brought many battles to a quick conclusion in favor of the trout.

It was this special strength and vigor of the Kamloops trout that won the affection of multitudes of anglers. Among them was Bryan Williams. Asked to compare the Kamloops trout with the noble summer-run steelhead, Williams said, "I think the Kamloops trout is the more active of the two. I have had them make as many as 14 clean jumps out of the water, some of these jumps being to great heights. I am inclined to think that the Kamloops trout is a harder fish to handle than the steelhead, though both require considerable skill to land."

An example of the Kamloops trout's capacity for speed and violence was described by the British angler W. A. Adamson in his book, *The Enterprising Angler.* On an early trip to Hihium Lake, Adamson was fishing from a boat when he hooked a 7-pound Kamloops on the fly. The trout stripped nearly all the backing from Adamson's reel and, fearful of losing the fish and perhaps his line and backing as well, the angler plunged into the water and followed the fish on foot across a shallow shoal. Finally the trout was subdued and Adamson regained his drifting boat. In three hours' fishing, Adamson caught more than 30 trout from 2½ to 7 pounds — an adventure that was not at all beyond the ordinary for that time.

In fact, the diaries of anglers who fished the Kamloops trout lakes during the '30s and '40s are filled with accounts of catches that seem incredible to us today, and their photo albums contain pictures showing dead trout by the score. To modern anglers, influenced by a growing conservation ethic and a spreading catch-and-release philosophy, such

26

This was one day's catch for four rods at Hihium Lake in 1940. By modern standards, such a catch would be considered outright slaughter, but the 50 trout shown in this photo still were 30 less than the daily limit for four anglers in 1940.

catches seem shocking and shameful and it is hard to understand why anyone would want his picture taken amid the evidence of such slaughter. But it must be remembered that the climate of the times was much different then, and even large catches were within the legal limits then existing. Attitudes, too, were different; the number of anglers was relatively small and the number of fish was large, and the resource seemed limitless. So those who would criticize these anglers of the past should realize that it did not seem to them that they were taking more than their rightful share of fish, and under the conditions then existing they could not foresee the day when such catches could threaten the future of the sport.

By the late 1930s, improved means of transportation had made it possible for more anglers to reach the Interior lakes. The journey along the Fraser Canyon remained an exhausting, frightening trip by auto, but the railroads made it relatively quick and easy to reach the fishing grounds and more and more roads were being built into lakes that had been isolated previously. New resorts were built and as economic times turned slowly for the better the business of sportfishing became increasingly important to the local economy.

Typical of the resorts was the one built at Big Bar Lake in pleasant country north of Clinton. The lake is a transparent gem of water, rimmed by mountains and surrounded by pine forest, aspen groves and meadows. While not an especially rich lake compared with the others around it, Big Bar nonetheless produced its share of large trout that were noted for their beauty. An advertisement placed by the resort in 1935 offered "Special rates to Business Girls during July and August." One who was not a "business girl" could stay at the lodge for $4 a week or rent a cabin for $7 a week. The accommodations were log cabins with wood stoves and outdoor plumbing and offered a more primitive style of life than many anglers would accept today; but it was a good life, perhaps made better by the fact that its pleasures did not come so easily, and there was something memorable about rising in the cold, clean morning air to await the pleasant scent of woodsmoke from the cook stoves.

The largest trout ever taken on hook and line may have been a Kamloops caught by a troller in Jewel Lake in 1932. Various weights, ranging up to 56 pounds, have been given for this fish, but its weight never was recorded officially so that it never has been recognized as a world's record (although published photographs of the fish show a monster trout that indeed could have weighed as much as 56 pounds). Some dispute whether the fish actually was taken by trolling; the late Tommy Brayshaw commented sardonically that it more likely was caught "with a manure fork."

Jewel Lake produced another giant trout in 1933, a fish that weighed 48 pounds three days after it was taken. Because it was not weighed reliably when caught, this fish also never has been acknowledged as a record.

But a 51-pounder taken from Jewel Lake in the mid-1940s was weighed and authenticated as the winner of a local fishing derby. *Field and Stream* magazine, then recognized as the arbiter of world records, refused to accept the fish because it failed to receive a notarized affidavit attesting to the weight of the trout and the circumstances of the catch.

Fisheries officers stripping spawning trout from Kootenay Lake recorded one of 52 pounds in 1930. And Premier Lake, near Cranbrook, yielded a trout of 35½ pounds in 1933.

Bryan Williams recorded the catch of a Kamloops trout of 18¾ pounds on a wet fly, and there probably have been larger fish taken that went unreported. The dry-fly record is better documented because it was established so recently. It was a 25-pound, 2-ounce Kamloops trout that rose to a No. 8 Royal Coachman dry fly at Balfour on the West Arm of Kootenay Lake. The angler, Tom Durkop, a tourist from West Germany, fought the fish 2½ hours and landed it only after another angler towed Durkop's boat out of the path of an oncoming ferry boat. The date was September 10, 1977.

But even during the halcyon days of the 1930s, such giant fish were the exception rather than the rule. Still, the lakes were generous with their yield of trout from 2 pounds up, and so were the rivers connecting lakes that held Kamloops trout — especially those streams shared by the great runs of sockeye salmon that annually penetrate far into the Interior. The best of them was the Little River, a swift 2½-mile stretch between Big and Little Shuswap Lakes where Kamloops trout gathered to feed on sockeye alevins emerging from the gravel in the spring. Lee Richardson, in his fine book *Lee Richardson's B. C.*, tells of the fly fishermen who gathered annually at Little River in anticipation of the fry emergence and the frenzied response of the trout. Bryan Williams, Frank Whitehouse, Letcher Lambuth and Tom Mesdag were among the well-known regulars who came often to match their skills against the trout.

In his diary, Richardson recorded a conversation with Bryan Williams about a day in 1913 when Williams, in four hours fishing on the river, hooked ten trout and landed eight — the smallest 4 pounds and the largest 12¾. Williams called it his most memorable day of angling, and Richardson goes on to say that the Little River also presented him with his most exciting angling moments. He wrote:

"Within minutes the mergansers and gulls telegraphed the approach of another school (of fry), and I began false casting in anticipation of their arrival. This time, amidst the welter of silver and crimson, I managed to hook a 4-pounder. . .Eventually we brought it to net in the calm of the lake. Mike (Richardson's guide) then rowed back around the main thrust of the river, dropping down to a point opposite the cottonwoods, there to await the next rush of events." Another school of fry

29

appeared, "and as the fingerlings came through the slot with trout all around, I managed to pin a 7-pounder that took us far into the lake and deep into the backing before it could be brought to net. Two more schools ran the gauntlet before the run came to an end, and from each we took one fish. There was time for only one, possibly two, casts before the young sockeyes were gone and the trout with them; yet it was my finest hour in angling." That was a typical reaction to the wild, furious excitement that prevailed when the river was filled with big Kamloops trout slashing wildly through schools of fry.

A stonefly hatch preceding the sockeye emergence also provided exciting spring angling in the Little River, and some fishermen favored the autumn days when sockeye salmon crowded into the river to spawn and the Kamloops trout gathered to feast on loose eggs swept down by the current from the spawning redds.

Little River and the mouth of the nearby Adams River truly were in a class by themselves, but there were other streams that produced spectacular fishing even though some lacked the wealth of the Little River sockeye run. Many memorable catches were made in the Canim River and the Kootenay; Whitehouse, for example, wrote of taking as many as 15 trout up to 3 pounds in a single day of fishing on the latter.

The Kamloops trout waters gave generously of themselves to the anglers of the 1930s. Much of the wonderful fishing they provided came about almost by accident — a combination of fortuitous natural circumstances and introductions of trout carried out largely in ignorance. But the good days were numbered, and by the end of the decade it was growing obvious that many of the better lakes had passed their prime. Many lakes with natural inlet streams where trout could spawn had quickly become overpopulated, and the exploding trout populations consumed the surplus food stocks that nature had so patiently built up in these waters. Sometimes the predation of the trout became so fierce that insect stocks were reduced to the point they could no longer sustain themselves. Trout grew thinner even as they became more numerous, and lakes that had produced immense fish in the years immediately after they were stocked for the first time began instead to produce large numbers of small, poorly-conditioned trout.

In other lakes where only limited spawning could take place, the trout populations remained in a natural balance with the food stocks, and these waters continued to produce large fish. But this often led to the mistaken supposition by anglers that these lakes naturally were capable of producing big fish under any circumstances and that no matter how many trout were planted in them they would all grow up to imposing size. So fishermen demanded that more trout be stocked in these waters. Responding to the pressure, provincial authorities did stock some of them heavily, with the inevitable result that the food stocks and the average size of the trout both declined rapidly.

Knouff Lake was among the first to fall victim to these circumstances. With only limited spawning water, especially in dry years, the lake had been able to sustain a natural balance that kept food supplies at an abundant level and still produced good numbers of large fish. Even the big, vulnerable traveling sedges that made Knouff a mecca for dry-fly fishermen continued to hatch in prodigious numbers, despite predation by the trout.

The angling diaries of Tommy Brayshaw record that Brayshaw fished Knouff Lake from 1928 to 1933, a period in which the trout population was wholly sustained by natural spawning and the lake was never stocked. He recorded that the average size of the fish caught in the 1933 season was 5 pounds, 2 ounces.

"Then," Brayshaw wrote, "the Kamloops club brought pressure to bear on the new (resort) owner and some 150,000 fry, or fingerlings, I do not know which, were introduced. The following year I went there and was shown a trout of 1 lb. 6 oz. as a 'fine fish.' I fished for an hour or two, catching a number of half-pounders, and then I packed up and left.

"There was a first-class lake ruined by overstocking, but there was another factor in its downfall that I do not think has ever been brought out, and that was that an old chap at the south end of the lake put in a sawmill and raised the level of the lake some two or three feet, giving the small fish access to the shallows where the sedge used to hatch in the millions; I believe these young fish cleaned out the sedge."

Together, the impacts of the additional stocking and the raising of the water level were disastrous. The decline in the average size of the trout was immediate and drastic, and within a single year, or two at most, the traveling sedges were reduced to the point of extinction. A lake perhaps unique in all the world had been destroyed, and it has been impossible to restore it to its original character, even under modern management practices. And Knouff Lake was only one of a number of fine, productive lakes that were ruined, either temporarily or permanently, by such ignorance and carelessness.

Other forces also were taking a toll on some of the best lakes. The growing population of the province led to increased angling pressure and development. Mining and agricultural pollution damaged or destroyed trout lakes. Irrigation practices sometimes proved harmful to Kamloops trout waters, although some impoundments created for irrigation also became excellent fisheries in their own right.

There are thousands of lakes in the British Columbia Interior and by the end of the 1930s most of them still were without fish life, virgin waters waiting with their vast supplies of food to receive the first plants of trout. But it was apparent that the popular lakes that had given the Kamloops trout its reputation among anglers, and which formed the basis for a growing sportfishing economy, were in need of help. A large-scale effort was needed to restore the Kamloops trout fishery, but Canada and most of the rest of the world found itself at war within a year or two — an all-consuming war that took all the men, money and material the nation could produce. There was no money left over to pay for research or management of the fishery, and with the populace largely preoccupied with other matters the fishery was left to fend for itself. Things got worse instead of better.

Paul Lake had been under careful management according to Mottley's formula, but sometime around 1945 the redside shiner was introduced into the watershed, probably by an ignorant angler using shiners for bait. The full effects of this were not observed until about 1948 when the shiner population had exploded and there were literally millions of them in Paul Lake, competing with the trout for the lake's limited food resources. Often the shiners proved more efficient in this competition, and whatever forage value the smaller shiners may have had for trout was more than offset by their consumption of the lake's natural food supply; the trout population showed sharply reduced growth, both in size and numbers.

Similar introductions of the redside shiner occurred in other lakes. Faced with poor management, increasing angling pressure and the abuse and pollution that are inevitable byproducts of development, the Kamloops trout was forced to cope with a new, more efficient and rapidly multiplying competitor. And the fishery continued to suffer.

But gradually, in the years after the war as the world began slowly to return to normal pursuits, men and money to manage the fishery began to become available once more. It had been a long war, and many of the men who had fought in it were anxious to make up for a lot of postponed fishing trips. Suddenly there was time to think of fishing again, and again there was support for the management necessary to produce good sport. Together these circumstances began to bring about a reversal of the deterioration of the fishery.

The British Columbia Game Department, as it was known then, established a Fisheries Research Group to study sport fisheries problems and decide what management practices would be necessary to restore the lakes to full production. The group was specifically directed to examine the relationship between the productivity of lakes and the quality and quantity of sport fish they could produce — the key to proper management.

The flow of research papers, shut off for the better part of a decade, began again. Surveys were made of waters in which the Kamloops trout had been introduced to determine the growing capacities of different lake environments. Inventories of lakes were compiled with evaluations of their productivity. A study was begun of the shiner population of Paul Lake and its impact on the trout. The British Columbia Resources Conference began to convene annually to discuss the future of resource management in the province, including its sport fisheries. Studies were made of the spawning habits of Kamloops trout and the relative merits of wild and domestic strains of trout. As the results of these research efforts were published, they were applied to management programs.

Lakes that had contained species of scrap fish were poisoned and replanted with trout. These and other lakes were stocked according to a more detailed and exacting formula than that devised by Mottley, a formula calculated to achieve a close balance between trout populations and food stocks. Stocking of barren lakes began again and new angling frontiers began to open even as old waters returned to production. The great days of the 30s would never be restored — there were now too many fishermen for that — but superb angling in virgin waters became available again to those willing to make the effort to find it.

The rebirth of the fishery led to a boom in the sportfishing industry. Fishing resorts again flourished and many new ones were built. Continual improvements were made to the Fraser Canyon highway and other Interior arterial routes, making the Interior lakes readily accessible to anyone with an automobile. New names were added to the list of famous waters: Roche, Lundbom, Leighton and Tunkwa, the Meadow and Aurora Lake chains, and many others. Old names like Paul and Pinantan were restored as angling meccas. Quality fishing was again available to anyone who cared to seek it out, and increasing numbers of anglers from within and without the province flocked to the Interior to do so.

For more than a decade the fishery grew and prospered, and as some lakes peaked and then declined, other new ones came along to take their place. In the cyclical history of the Kamloops trout, the postwar era was one that produced remarkable fishing, and if the fishery was never quite so generous as it had been during the '30s, it still produced many memorable catches for growing legions of anglers.

But like an angry storm brooding on the distant horizon, a combination of circumstances was brewing that again was destined to plunge the Kamloops trout lakes into an abrupt decline. In the late 1960s the storm began to break with fearful suddenness and effect.

One circumstance was the rapid growth of the population of the province and of the Northwest region as a whole. And as the numbers of people grew, so did the leisure time available to them and the means they had to spend it. The increasing affluence of the populace allowed many of them to purchase recreational vehicles that soon filled the backwoods roads on their way to campsites on countless lakes. Fishermen came in greater numbers and stayed longer than before, testing the resource to unprecedented limits. Many of these were newcomers to the outdoors, with no appreciation or understanding of the delicate ecological balances of the Kamloops trout lakes and their surroundings. They cut trees from the shoreline to fuel their campfires and their campsites wore away the grass to expose the bare soil to erosion. Infatuated with mechanical devices, they ran motorbikes up and down the hillsides, digging deep ruts into the fragile soil, removing ground cover and contributing to still more erosion — and the noise of their machines chased away the wildlife that once abounded around the margins of the lakes.

They even came in the winter, on noisy snowmobiles that gave them access to frozen lakes where they cut holes in the ice and caught the ripe trout that would have spawned in the spring, literally exterminating whole year classes of fish in some lakes. And when they left, their garbage often remained behind on the ice, waiting to pollute the water when the ice melted in the spring. Inevitably, many lakes suffered acutely from this year-round onslaught of anglers, many of them completely uneducated in the wiles, ways and manners of the outdoors.

All this would be bad enough in itself, but the attitude of the provincial government made matters even worse. Indifference toward fisheries and wildlife was the most that anyone could expect from the conservative government that held power during all but a few years of the '60s and '70s; more often, the attitude was one of outright hostility. The government's policy has been and remains one of ruthless exploitation of the timber, water and mineral resources of the province, with no thought for the impact on fish and wildlife populations. Dams, strip mines and enormous logging clearcuts have scarred the province from one end to the other, creating sweeping ecological changes of the most brutal kind, with incalculable damage to fish and wildlife populations. The Kamloops trout waters have not escaped these depredations.

While pursuing its policy of exploitation, the government has cut funds for management of fish and wildlife, and these cuts came at a time when rapid inflation made management even more costly than it had been. The result was reduced programs in research, management and enforcement and an inevitable deterioration of the fishery.

So some of the Kamloops trout lakes have been damaged or totally destroyed as productive fisheries; others have been so damaged aesthetically that fishing is no longer enjoyable in them. Fisheries managers have been forced to adopt a defensive policy, reducing limits and imposing restrictions to accommodate the growing pressure and abuse. Such a policy is geared to buying time, protecting as much as possible of what remains in hopes that in the future public enlightenment may produce a more enlightened government that will take the lead in the necessary work of restoration and protection.

It is difficult at this point to be very optimistic about the future of the Kamloops trout. But even with all that has happened in the past decade, it is obvious that the limits of the resource are far from being reached. Even considering all the mistakes that have been made, and all the pressures and abuses which many lakes have endured, there still remain many that are much as they always have been. For the most part, they lie off the beaten track, accessible only on foot or by the most difficult roads, filled with strong trout that rise willingly to sedges fluttering across the shoals in the spring sunshine. So the story of the Kamloops trout still has some chapters yet untold, and these are the lakes on which those chapters will be written. But present trends must be soon reversed if the tale is not to have a premature ending.

It would be incorrect to imply that all the developments of the past decade have been harmful. Some positive things have occurred. The defensive posture management authorities have been forced to assume has led to the classification of some waters as trophy fisheries, with restrictions on tackle and bag limits, and others as fly-fishing-only waters. Such management will ensure the protection of these waters for at least the immediate future. Fly fishermen benefit most from these classifications, but traditionally it has been the fly fishermen who have taken the lead in working to protect and conserve the fishery, so such benefits are well earned.

Ten years ago there were only two small fly fishing clubs in the province; now there are half a dozen or more, banded together in the B. C. Federation of Fly Fishing Clubs, a growing organization that is beginning to have more weight and influence on management decisions from which all fishermen will benefit. A strong and active member club in Kamloops has experimented with aerating devices to keep trout alive in shallow lakes where oxygen depletion is a problem. The same club carried out an exemplary land-use study of the important Roche Lake region near Kamloops, recommending intelligent policies and restrictions for the future management of the lakes within the region and the lands surrounding the lakes. The government's lack of response to these recommendations can only be regarded as a temporary defeat; their logic must ultimately become clear even to the most shortsighted and stubborn bureaucrats.

The B. C. Federation has allied itself with the much larger international Federation of Fly Fishermen, which has provided financial assistance and advice to the B. C. clubs. Last year the B. C. Federation held the province's first conclave for fly fishermen, drawing anglers from all over the Northwest to a meeting at Kamloops. Such events are significant in that they provide tangible evidence of the growing interest and support for quality fishing, and offer a chance for biologists and managers to mingle shoulder-to-shoulder with the anglers who are their constituents. Inevitably, there is a cross-pollination of ideas that are later translated into action at the management level.

The growing number of Kamloops trout fly fishermen also has fostered some departures from the traditional approach to angling for these splendid fish. It is most evident in the establishment of a "scientific school" of fly tying, a studied approach to the proper imitation of the insects and crustacea of the Kamloops trout lakes that has resulted in a

Three Kamloops trout from Lundbom Lake, 2 to 2½ pounds each.

whole new generation of fly patterns. These are much different from the bright, attractor patterns of Bill Nation and his compatriots of the 1930s; they tend to be sparsely tied and made of somber-colored materials that are a much closer match for the natural hues of the insects that are the mainstay of the Kamloops trout diet. There has been a concurrent increase in the average level of skill of Kamloops trout fly fishermen, partly due to increasingly sophisticated tackle and partly to the educational programs of the province's fly fishing clubs. These clubs also are a constant source of new recruits to the ranks of fly fishermen and the conservation philosophy that is an inherent part of the sport. All these things augur well for the future.

Fly fishermen have not been alone in their efforts to organize and lobby for the continued existence of their sport. Fifty of the most important resorts and fishing camps have joined to form the B. C. Interior Fishing Camp Operators Association. Part of the purpose of the organization is to publicize the services and accommodations offered by its members, but an even more important part of its program is to work for better management and control of the lakes and fisheries that provide the resort operators their livelihood. The resort owners and the organized sportfishermen share many common goals and one hopes they will choose to work together.

The past decade also has seen significant developments in the literature of the Kamloops trout, and perhaps this is an opportune time to go back and trace the growth of that literature from its origin. The Kamloops trout has not inspired a particularly large or impressive body of literature compared with the vast array of general angling titles in print, but it does comprise an important historic record of the methods and traditions of Kamloops trout fishing.

Lambert's *Fishing in British Columbia* may truly be said to be the first book about the Kamloops trout, since it described the identification and naming of the fish, in which Lambert played a role. Published in London by Horace Cox in 1907, the book — like many that would follow it — did not concern itself solely with the Kamloops trout, but also described fishing for steelhead and salmon in British Columbia waters and even included a chapter on tuna fishing at Santa Catalina Island. Its primary importance today is in its descriptions of the Kamloops trout fishery as it existed before man began his manipulation of it.

Bryan Williams' *Rod and Creel in British Columbia,* published in Vancouver in 1919, also included chapters on the early Kamloops trout fishery. It is a scarce volume today, commanding a price many times its original worth on the rare-book market. More common, but still not easy to find, is Williams' *Fish and Game in British Columbia,* published in 1935 by the Sun Publishing Co., Vancouver. Although hardbound, it was the prototype for many softcover fishing guides that would follow in later years, offering capsule descriptions of many of the most important Kamloops trout lakes. It also carried advertising for a number of resorts and fishing camps, including a full-page ad placed by "William Nation, Angler's Guide, Specializing in Fly Fishing for Kamloops Rainbow Trout." The ad features a photo of the old master seated in the rear of a boat loaded with a day's catch. About two dozen trout are visible in the photo, none appearing to weigh less than 5 pounds. The book is of historic interest mostly for its descriptions of the Kamloops trout lakes as they were in the 1930s (see page 22).

In 1932, J. R. Dymond published *The Trout and Other Game Fishes of British Columbia,* a slim little volume that was the work of F. A. Acland, Ottawa. The book included handsome (if slightly exaggerated) paintings by E. B. S. Logier of the species described. A chapter was devoted to the Kamloops trout, which Dymond identified as *Salmo kamloops Jordan,* and although Dymond wrote that "Little is known about the life-history of the Kamloops trout," he did provide interesting and revealing records of the growth of trout stocked in previously barren lakes and of the angling methods that had been developed for them. Dymond also described the Mountain Kamloops trout, *Salmo kamloops whitehousei,* which Dymond himself had named, apparently in honor of

37

KAMLOOPS

F. C. Whitehouse. The Mountain Kamloops is a small alpine variety of trout, a strain of rainbow whose appearance and habits have been shaped by the harsh environment in which it is found. Today it is seldom recognized as a separate subspecies or variety of either the rainbow or the Kamloops.

Perhaps the most significant event in the history of Kamloops trout literature was the publication in 1939 of *The Western Angler*, by the late Roderick Haig-Brown. It was a most impressive book, published in two handsome volumes by the Derrydale Press of New York in a numbered edition limited to 950 copies. It provided a thorough inventory of the habits and habitat of the game fish of British Columbia and included several chapters on the Kamloops trout, offering the most complete and detailed description of the fishery to appear in print up to that time. There were seven chapters in all, including discussions of Mottley's experiments on Paul Lake and the fly patterns of Bill Nation. One chapter was devoted to fly patterns and another was entitled "Some Fauna of Interior Lakes," which contained the first popularly published observations on the entomology of Interior waters.

Logier's paintings from *The Trout and Other Game Fishes of British Columbia* were included along with black-and-white photos for illustrations. The frontispiece included a color plate labeled "Interior Flies" that showed a dozen of Nation's patterns, "Mr. Brayshaw's sedges for interior lakes" and "Mr. Brayshaw's large wet flies for Little River fishing." In addition to its value as an unprecedented description of the Kamloops trout fishery, *The Western Angler* also revealed the eloquent writing style that eventually would make Roderick Haig-Brown British Columbia's most beloved man of letters — as well as its most revered angler and conservationist. Today copies of *The Western Angler* are extremely rare and those in good condition seldom change hands for less than $500.

A revised trade edition of *The Western Angler* published in 1947 offered a condensed version of the chapters on Kamloops trout, but was important for another reason: It contained a color painting and many drawings by Tommy Brayshaw, whose graceful, lifelike fish portraits and carvings would one day make him the province's most respected angling artist.

In 1944, Haig-Brown published what many consider his finest book, *A River Never Sleeps*, which also included a brief chapter on the Kamloops trout and the personalities of Mottley and Nation. A year later, W. A. Adamson's *The Enterprising Angler* was published by William Morrow & Co. in New York with the author's description of his fishing on Hihium Lake.

Sport Fishes of Western Canada and Some Others, by F. C. Whitehouse, was published privately in Vancouver in 1946. It contained one chapter on trolling for Kamloops trout in the early days, another on fly fishing, among other chapters on steelhead, salmon, char, grayling, black bass and other species. Two years later it was published again in a different version entitled *Sport Fishing in Canada.* This edition, also published privately by the author and limited to 1,200 copies, contained added chapters on "Eastern Canada Fishing," tuna and broadbill swordfish. The chapters on Kamloops trout were unchanged from the original version of the book.

In 1950, Holt, Rinehart & Winston published Bruce Hutchison's *The Fraser,* an entertaining history of the exploration and settlement of the Fraser River watershed. There is a chapter entitled "For Anglers Only" that describes fishing on Kelly Lake and includes references to Nation and some of his fly patterns. But Hutchison never referred to the Kamloops trout by that name, preferring instead to call it a rainbow and using the long-outmoded scientific name *Salmo irideus.* He also wrote of an epic battle between Bryan Williams and a Kelly Lake trout that finally broke Williams' leader but died of exhaustion before it could escape. Hutchison says it weighed 16 pounds, but one cannot help but question his veracity; Williams' written version of what apparently was the same incident places the weight of the fish at slightly less than 4 pounds.

Haig-Brown again touched briefly on the Kamloops trout in his delightful series of brief essays published in 1951 as *Fisherman's Spring.* Ten years later he would list the Kamloops trout again in an inventory of British Columbia game fish compiled for *The Living Land,* a scholarly dissertation on the natural resources of British Columbia. The book also contained some of the finest examples of Tommy Brayshaw's art, and altogether it remains a model for all future works of its kind. Sadly, Haig-Brown's words of caution about wasteful exploitation of resources and the hazards of hasty development were not well received by the provincial government and have gone largely unheeded.

In 1970 Jim Kilburn began the first of a series of articles on the entomology of British Columbia waters that was published in *Western Fish & Game* magazine. The series continued irregularly for several years, during which the magazine changed its name to *Western Fish and Wildlife.* Kilburn's series offered the most complete and accurate listing of the keys to identification of the insects of Interior lakes yet to appear in print, along with descriptions of their behavior and fly patterns designed to imitate them. His well-researched articles played a major role in stimulating the rise of the "scientific school" of fly tying in British Columbia. The magazine, now unfortunately defunct, offered many other articles on fly patterns and angling techniques that were of interest or use to Kamloops trout anglers.

The first edition of *Kamloops* made its appearance in 1971 as the first book devoted entirely to Kamloops trout.

Catch of Trout
Made in Paul Lake
near Kamloops, BC

The past few years have witnessed an increasing number of titles dealing at least in part with Kamloops trout fishing. Jack Shaw's *Fly Fish
the Trout Lakes* appeared in 1976, a soft-cover volume published by the
Mitchell Press of Vancouver. Shaw, a well-known fly tyer, offers practical advice on fishing the Kamloops trout lakes, something at which he
is an acknowledged expert. His little book is filled with color photos of
natural insects and fly patterns, and — although he lacks formal training
in entomology — Shaw draws upon extensive personal experience in the
observation and filming of aquatic insects to describe their behavior.
His book contains much information that is useful for the Interior angler.

The following year saw the publication of *The Ardent Angler-Artist,*
a brief biography of Tommy Brayshaw by Stanley E. Read, professor
emeritus at the University of British Columbia. Published in a limited
edition of 2,000 copies by the University of British Columbia Press, the
book is mainly a showcase of Brayshaw's paintings, drawings and carvings, many reproduced in color. It includes a foreword by Lee Straight,
a tribute from Roderick Haig-Brown, Read's biography of Brayshaw and
some excerpts from Brayshaw's own correspondence and diaries, some
of them touching briefly on his experiences on Kamloops trout waters.
The Ardent Angler-Artist will remain as an important acknowledgement
of Brayshaw's artistic contributions to the angling traditions of British
Columbia.

Finally, *Lee Richardson's B. C.* made its appearance late in 1978 as a
warmly nostalgic collection of anecdotes acquired from many productive

days on B. C. waters. Richardson, an outdoor photographer and accomplished raconteur, fished with all the famous B. C. angling names on virtually all the famous waters of the province, often when those waters were at their peak. His book, a limited edition published by the Champoeg Press of Forest Grove, Oregon, presents glimpses of Pennask Lake, Little River, Devick's Beaver Lake and TaWeel as they were in days gone by.

The growth of the literature surrounding the Kamloops trout is a healthy sign; it is one measure of the regard that anglers have for this fish and the value they attach to it. Books about the Kamloops trout will assure perpetuation of the traditions that have grown up around it. More important, they will convince more and more people of the need to preserve the fishery resource.

The increasing strength and numbers of organized sportfishermen, particularly fly fishermen; the banding together of resort and fishing camp owners, and the growth of the literature devoted to Kamloops trout − all these are positive signs. But they are not yet very significant compared to the severe pressures that exist on the fishery and the habitat of the Kamloops trout. While it is true that the Kamloops trout has more friends, and more important friends, than perhaps ever before in its history, it is equally true that it has more enemies, and they are more powerful enemies, than ever before.

The Kamloops trout is a complex creature whose survival depends equally upon its fragile environment and public support for the preservation of that environment. That the Kamloops trout survives today in the face of all the brutal damage that has been done to its habitat is an indication of the inherent toughness of the species. But its toughness alone is no longer enough to assure survival; the future of the Kamloops trout now depends largely on the attitudes of the people with whom it shares its native country. Its life history and habits are worth knowing, not only because they add much to the pleasures of angling, but also because such knowledge is essential among anglers − and the public − if the fishery is to be preserved.

And that is the ultimate purpose of this book: To acquaint the reader with the Kamloops trout, its life, its habits and all the subtle interrelationships of nature that make it what it is; and to foster an understanding of its role as a vital part of the heritage of British Columbia and a resource whose value extends far beyond the borders of the province. For the Kamloops trout has become a citizen of the world, a great game fish whose name stirs excitement far beyond the borders of its homeland. If those responsible for its stewardship are equal to the task, then for uncounted future seasons anglers will still come to test their skills against the special challenge that only the Kamloops trout can give.

Chapter Two

Life History

The Kamloops trout begins its existence as a tiny spark of life buried in the cold, dark gravel of a stream bottom. Typically, it is a stream fed by a small spring and swollen by the icy waters of melting snow. The eggs are deposited in nests scooped out by the female parent, fertilized by the male and then covered with a layer of coarse, protective gravel. Water, bearing life-sustaining oxygen, filters through the gravel to the developing embryos.

By the end of May the spawning run is finished and the eggs, with their precious cargo of developing life, are left alone. The earth, overburdened with water from the melted snows and spring rains, gives up its moisture readily, and the spawning tributaries rise and sometimes spill over their banks, their swift currents carrying down tufts of pine and grass, last year's decaying leaves and all the tiny flotsam of the forests.

Sometimes there is too much water, too much current for the little spawning streams to carry, and the force of falling water digs new channels, leaving the buried eggs to die, or sweeps away the loose gravel of the spawning redds and the precious eggs along with them. Sometimes, where loggers have cut away the surrounding timber, the unprotected soil melts under rain and is carried by the runoff to the streams, so that they run thick and heavy, the color of an old and ugly bruise. The silt from the clear-cuts settles in the crevices of the redds, blocking the free passage of oxygen-bearing water so that the eggs suffocate and die. And if that is not enough, the cut-over land gives up its water too quickly, so that the streams quickly drop and clear and go dry before their time, and any embryos that still live are left to rot beneath the sun-dried gravel of the stream.

But when all the floods and freshets have passed, and the streams unaffected by loggers have settled back to their normal depth and flow, some eggs still live in them. The water now is clear and warm, and all around in the forest there are signs of new growth. Shoots of green lengthen the lodgepole tips and fir limbs; wild strawberries show the first small traces of the sweet fruit they will later bear; the skunk cabbage unfolds its waxy leaves and yellow blooms in black-bottomed bogs, and the twilight flickers with the movement of hatching insects. The sun dries out the land and warms the lakes, and great high thunderheads roll quickly past in the afternoon sky, flashing and rumbling and bursting briefly with rain that makes the world fresh and gleaming until the sun returns to dry it once again.

KAMLOOPS

The days grow longer as they pass, and the bright red-gold eggs buried in the gravel show the twin dark spots of a new pair of eyes, as yet unseeing. As the days become weeks, there is visible through the eggs' translucent shells the developing shape of tiny tadpole forms. All the while, the water drops, the current slows, the temperature climbs higher and the embryos develop faster and faster in a race to hatch before there no longer is water enough to serve them with oxygen in their buried place. For some, the race is lost, and they die on the threshold of life. But others still live until their membranous eggshells begin to split and tiny trout emerge, all eyes and reddish yolks.

Some spawning streams flow out of lakes or from one lake into another, and in them the embryos develop even faster in water warmed before it left the lake. These eggs always are the first to hatch, and the emergent trout — or alevins — are given a head start in the competition that will determine which of the year's young will survive. The emergent alevins are only 10 or 12 millimeters long, lacking scales and bearing little evidence of the fins or tails they will later grow. In shape they still resemble a tadpole, except for the yolk that remains attached to provide them with nourishment through their first few days of life.

The alevins remain concealed in the gravel where they hatched, slowly absorbing the yolk sacs, gaining strength and growing. In three weeks at most the yolk is gone and the tiny trout have grown to a length of about 20 millimeters. But now they must leave the relative safety of the gravel to search for food in the open stream.

By the hundreds they come forth, wriggling up through the gravel crevices into the full flow of the current. Immediately they begin to feed, and immediately they are fed upon, becoming prey for watchful kingfishers and patient herons and sometimes for the larger of their own kind. Of those that survived nature's whims to begin life in the gravel, few will pass the tests that now begin.

By day the trout — no longer alevins but fry — school up in the center of the stream, shifting back and forth but never moving far, casting an occasional glint of reflected sunlight from their tiny turning sides. When the long summer twilight dies and only starlight falls upon the stream, the schools edge nervously toward the streambanks. There, apparently in response to some instinct triggered by the cool temperature of the inlet streams and the absence of light, the schools split up and some begin to slip downstream, the beginning of their migration to the lake that lies below.

The fry headed downstream collide with schools still holding near the banks, and fry from both schools dart excitedly in all directions, some fleeing to the center of the stream where new schools form and turn, scatter and reform, and drop downward toward the lake. All this occurs during the darkest hours of the night, and when daylight returns the fry take up new positions in the center of the stream and resume their feeding, holding steadily in the current, a tiny, swarming host pausing in the first step of their life's journey.

While the fry of the inlet streams are beginning their downstream migration, their counterparts in outlet streams remain residents of the pools in which they hatched. Shifting position little, they forage on the stream's microscopic life, holding, feeding and growing in the warmer and more stable flow of the outlet, waiting for some secret signal to start them on an upstream journey, against the current, to the lake where they will spend their lives. Finally it comes, in the warm August days when stream temperatures reach their peak, and the tiny trout begin to move. Unlike the fry of inlet streams, their migration is greatest during the middle of the day when the water temperature and light are greatest. Moving upstream by day, holding position by night, the schools of fry move haltingly against the flow until they reach its origin and pass from the current into the calm, clear waters of the lake.

Although it peaks in August, this upstream movement may begin as early as July. There is a second peak in September, and then the movement quickly subsides to a few frantic stragglers. And when it is finished, there are still fry left in the streams. With all the thousands of fry that hatch in the inlet and outlet streams, there always are some that do not respond to nature's signals, that do not migrate, but stay in their natal streams throughout the heat of summer, the change of fall and the bitterness of winter.

The fry — both migrant and non-migrant — find a limited diet in the small streams. Their first food after emergence is tiny two-winged insects, taken drowned or on the surface, and the tiny nymphs of stoneflies and mayflies and small caddis larvae. Outlet streams below rich lakes often provide more substantial fare, with plankters and scuds washed down from the lake. Competition for this meager food supply is fierce, and there is never enough to sustain even the relatively few trout that remain in the streams after migrations have taken place. Starvation and death await the losers of the competition; the survivors are stunted.

By August, most of the fry are an inch long or better, and they have begun to grow their first scales. A series of thin, parchment-like plates, the scales grow in overlapping fashion like shakes on a roof. As growth occurs, fresh material is added in concentric rings to the outer edge of each scale, and when growth is rapid these rings are thick and widely spaced. When it is slow, as it always is in winter, the rings and the spaces between them are thinner. The life and growth of the fish is documented in these rings, and biologists trained to read the scales can determine whether the trout that grew them migrated immediately after hatching or wintered over in the stream. The trout's age also can be determined from its scales, as surely as the age of a tree may be determined from the rings of its trunk.

Fry remaining in the streams after the summer migrations have passed must face the stern tests of a long and rugged winter. Only those streams fed by lakes or relatively warm springs remain free-flowing through the winter, and even in these the trout may face the threat of ice jams that scour the streambottoms. There is little movement by the fry, either upstream or downstream; the small fish cling to survival mainly by tenacity until spring's advent finally sets them free. And then most of the survivors will begin the migration that passed them by the year before, entering the lake as fingerlings much smaller than their brethren of the earlier migration. Still, there always are a few that do not migrate at all, that spend their entire lives in the relatively infertile environment of the stream, feeding, breeding and dying there without ever reaching a length of more than a few inches.

But the trout that migrate to the lakes waste little time in feeding on the abundant life they find in them, and by the time of their second spring they have grown to a length of several inches. They are, by this time, handsome little fish, bright silver with prominent parr marks — a series of dark bluish bars along their flanks that they will wear until they are eight or nine inches long. They range freely through the rich pastures along the shoreline or over the shoals and flats in search of food, consuming *Daphnia,* the water flea, and copepods and aquatic insects and scuds and terrestrial insects blown onto the surface.

Even here they are vulnerable to a host of predators. Ospreys, eagles, herons, loons, kingfishers and mergansers find them and eat them, and although predation among Kamloops trout is relatively rare, they may sometimes fall victim to a larger, hungry member of their own species. And some lakes harbor other fish species that take a toll of the young trout. More insidious is the threat of disease and the stress of competition, but the results are just as deadly. Through ruthless selection, nature weeds out first the fry, then the fingerlings, until only those most fitted for survival — the quickest and most wary, the strongest and the best — still survive.

In two years, given a relatively favorable environment, the Kamloops trout may reach a length of 12 to 15 inches and weigh a pound or more. The speed of growth and the ultimate size attained are limited only by the richness of the environment, or lack of it, and the length of time it takes the trout to reach sexual maturity. By the time it has grown to 10 or 12 inches, the Kamloops trout begins to forage in deeper water and for the first time begins to enter the angler's catch, though many fishermen release such small trout in the hope of finding bigger game.

By this time the Kamloops trout is a small model of the great fish it will later be. The parr marks have disappeared and the fish wears a coat of bright armor or the bronze dress of trout that live in lakes with dark, amber-colored water. Already they are strong and active fish, swift in their feeding and determined in their fight against the angler.

In May and June the trout feed on the surface for hatching sedges, midges and mayflies and the emerging nymphs of dragonflies and damsel-flies. This is the time when all the teeming life of the lake reaches a peak of feeding, breeding and movement; it is the best time of all for the fly fisherman, the time when many come to test their skills against the strong and wary trout. But the orgy of surface feeding tapers off quick-ly as the hatches diminish in July. Then the trout go deep, and beneath the sun-warmed waters of late July and August they forage for scuds or seek out slow and awkward snails clinging to the underwater weeds or intercept the leeches that swim leisurely through the depths.

Summer in the Kamloops trout country is apt to be very warm. Day after day the sun climbs to its zenith in an empty sky and sucks the freshness from the meadows and the forests. Squadrons of sunflowers on the slopes turn their faces obediently to trace the sun's track across the summer sky and the rich green grass of spring turns yellow-dry. The warm surface air, heated to a hundred degrees or more, shimmers with heat waves, and dragonflies and yellowjackets buzz lazily over the steamy, gunmetal surfaces of the lower lakes. Lightning strikes trigger fiery explosions in the dry pine forests and the fires clot the sky with yellow-brown smoke that obscures the sun like fog and holds the heat like a blanket.

In some lakes, particularly smaller ones, the hot, still summer days lead to stratification, and the water forms in stable layers, each with its own temperature and oxygen level. Sometimes the warm water and reduced oxygen level cause the trout to fall into a lazy lethargy in which they feed little, if at all. The rapid growth of spring comes quickly to a halt, and an expert reading the scales of these fish will recognize the "summer check" of growth.

The August heat gives way to September's shorter days and changing weather. Strong winds begin to stir and cool the surfaces of the Interior lakes and the trout return to the shallows to feed. Again they turn to aquatic insects, feeding now on their subsurface forms, but now terres-trials, such as the flying ant, are added to their diet and the trout rise to them eagerly during the fall flights on the warm September afternoons.

The long, lingering Indian summer days of late September are among the best times to fish for Kamloops trout. The nights begin to bear a hint of Arctic chill and the forest leaves flame with color, then softly die away to become faint glowing coals and disappear. The day-time air is often hot and tense and still, poised for the first blast of im-pending winter; finally it comes, a sudden violent gust, sweeping hard gray clouds across the pinetops, blowing the first big spattering drops of cold rain. The trout are fat and strong and they feed eagerly to store up strength for the coming winter and the rigors of spawning that will come afterwards.

Then, on a cold, gray late October morning, the first snow falls, a swirling swarm of large wet flakes that covers the ground briefly but

47

melts almost as quickly as it came – a rehearsal for the storms that will soon begin in earnest. Sometimes the smaller trout, caught in a last feverish desire to feed, will rise vainly to the snowflakes as they spiral gently to the surface and disappear.

Now the days are short and dark and the high-country nights are crackling cold. In the mornings the lakes are rimmed with thin layers of ice that match the silver frost along the shore. Finally there is a fall of snow that does not leave, and the hills gleam whitely with it in the soft winter light. More and more it comes, slanting out of a slate-colored sky to be driven by the wind into drifts along the ridgetops and the valleys in between. At last the lingering suspense of autumn is ended and the beautiful white agony of winter has begun.

The trout in the lakes continue feeding until the last possible moment, but each morning the ice reaches out farther from the shore. Finally there is a long, clear night when the air is still and cold and the sky is lit with the frozen light of countless stars; and silently the ice tentacles reach out to touch and join, covering the lakes with a frozen layer of fantastic crystal patterns. Now each lake is shut off from the air and the earth around it, a world unto itself that will remain locked away until the return of spring.

Below the surface layer of ice the water temperature hovers barely above the freezing point. The trout's metabolism falls along with the temperature and the trout move little and feed even less. Their lives and the lives of the creatures with them are reduced to a slower pace, a time when life and strength and energy are carefully conserved. If they feed at all it is to forage slowly on the bottom organisms that are present now in much smaller numbers than before, and again scuds remain the primary source of food. They live on oxygen already present in the water, plus whatever is provided by photosynthesis when weak winter sunlight penetrates through the ice to the sparse aquatic plants of winter.

Because their life now is sluggish and slow, their need for oxygen is less, and it is well that this is so. If snow covers the surface ice of the smaller, sheltered lakes, the sun is shut out for long periods so that there is no light for photosynthesis. The age-old process of organic decay goes on, and even though the rate is slower, it uses its share of the oxygen on which life depends. Sometimes the demand for oxygen is too great to supply all the living organisms of the lake, and the trout begin to die. Each year, unless the winter is unusually short and mild, some lakes are "winter-killed" in this subtle, secret way, and the spring thaw reveals them to be barren of the trout that frolicked in their shallows the year before.

But if nature is kind, the trout will survive the season. There is a slow, imperceptible lengthening of the days, an occasional strong, warm wind that rots the drifts on the south-facing slopes, and the snow squalls become mixed more and more with rain. Occasionally the sun breaks through the scudding clouds and the snow-laden forest limbs begin to drip away the weight that holds them down. Patches of the surface ice begin to melt and form puddles on the frozen layers beneath. And then, suddenly, spring comes with a great rush; the sun's growing warmth dissolves the snow and the ice begins to decay and break.

Patches of open water appear and the wind finds them and stirs the surface into riffles that lap against the remaining ice. Fractures spread through the ice and grow wider and the wind drives the splintering shards of ice into one another so that they split into even smaller pieces that melt and rapidly disappear. Together, the sun and wind triumph over the ice, and gradually the lakes are swept clear of it, the last stubborn bits carried like broken panes of glass to languish and melt upon the shore. Released from their cold prison, the mature trout are summoned urgently to the inlet streams to spawn, and the others are seized with the desire to resume feeding. Suddenly the lakes are filled with renewed life and in the first few days or weeks after ice-out the trout feed with special vigor.

As the spring insect hatches move toward the peak of their cycle, the trout fall again into their familiar routines of feeding, seeking the maturing nymphs and pupae and then, finally, the adult insects as they struggle through the surface film to take their initial flight. If the trout share the lake with other species of fish, the time inevitably comes when they will begin turning to these other species as a source of food. Generally the Kamloops trout is at least two years old and at least 15 or 16 inches long before it begins to prey upon other fish, but there are exceptions to this rule and trout as small as 10 inches have been found with fish in their stomachs.

The victims of these predations usually are shiners, kokanee, suckers or other forage-sized species, introduced naturally or artificially. In the rivers or the large lakes through which sockeye salmon smolts must pass large Kamloops trout feed eagerly on their schools, driving the little fish to the surface in frantic bursts of spray. Where forage fish are abundant, the Kamloops trout feeds upon them eagerly and rapid growth results.

By its third year, a typical maiden Kamloops trout is a thing of real beauty, with strength apparent in every line of its shape. Its color is carefully calculated by nature to make it unobtrusive in its environment, and in clear-water lakes its back is a deep blue-green punctuated by a fine spray of black spots. This dark color, which protects the Kamloops trout from predators above, gives way to a bright nickel finish on the flanks and a snow-white belly underneath. The caudal fin is blue-gray and spotted heavily, with the spots following the lines of the fin rays. The pectoral and ventral fins are pale lavender and the tips of the ventral and anal fins are edged in cream. In lakes with dark or amber-colored water, the Kamloops trout is more likely to be heavily spotted and its flanks distinctly bronze.

49

Kamloops trout on their spawning redds. The trout at left and center weigh between 3 and 4 pounds each; a smaller, precocious male fish is at right.

As the Kamloops trout approaches its first spawning, gradual changes in color and form take place. The maturing male develops a long, deep head and the maxillary bone along the upper jaw grows long and hard. The body thickens, the snout becomes longer and the trout begins to wear the familiar badge of the male, a pronounced hook at the tip of the lower jaw. The female, too, shows the changes that are taking place deep within her, growing thick through the body, sometimes with a small protuberance on the lower jaw.

A faint, iridescent rose tint spreads along the lateral line of both sexes, at first visible only when light strikes it at the proper angle. But as the trout ripens, the stripe becomes thicker and brighter until the fish wears a deep carmine sash along its sides. The gill plates turn crimson, then deep purple and the once clean white belly turns a dark, dirty gray as the act of spawning nears.

The changes of form and color of the Kamloops trout at various stages of its life have been the cause of much confusion. As with the Pacific salmon, the early white settlers mistakenly believed that these were characteristics of different species rather than changes that came to the same species at different stages of its life. Dymond discovered and recorded some of this confusion when he interviewed residents around Kootenay and Okanagan Lakes. "The small, heavily-spotted, greenish-colored fish, often found in streams flowing into these lakes, are called brook trout," he wrote. "The large, blue-backed, lightly-spotted silvery fish are called silver trout, or silver salmon; the fish with distinct lateral bands are called rainbow trout, and the very dark-colored ones, black trout." Other local names were Kootenay trout, Stit-tse and Mountain trout. The Kamloops sometimes has been mistakenly called a golden trout and a land-locked salmon or, during spawning, a black salmon. But as the life cycle of the Kamloops trout became generally known, anglers and local residents alike began to realize the fish to which they had applied this host of local names was one and the same, and now it is uniformly known throughout the province and far beyond by its only proper name: The Kamloops.

The changes associated with the first spawning generally come to the Kamloops trout at the age of three or four years. Often males mature a year or two before females, a characteristic of all the anadromous species of salmon and trout. Some precocious males may spawn at the age of two years, and mature male trout of only six or seven inches are seen often in the spawning runs. In some populations, maturation comes late and the trout may be five years old before they spawn for the first time, and at least one strain, the Gerrard or Lardeau strain that spawns in the Lardeau River, does not mature until it is six or seven years old.

By the time it is ready to spawn the Kamloops trout has known the rich feeding of several summers and the lean months of several winters. The exact mechanism that causes it to suddenly break out of its careful pattern and draws it almost unerringly to its natal stream is not yet fully understood. The prevailing theory is that the changes brought about by sexual maturation trigger an instinct within the trout to seek out the characteristic odor of the stream that gave it birth. Each stream has its own unique scent, a combination of the chemical constituents of its water, and it is believed this odor is "imprinted" on the trout before they migrate from the stream. To the trout it means nothing until sexual maturation suddenly impels the fish to use its keen olfactory sense to seek the source of the familiar scent. It is a neat theory and one that goes farther than any other to explain the intricacies of the spawning run; but even it is unable to account fully for all the variations that occur. Part of the difficulty is that the homing mechanism, however it works, is not perfect; the return of spawning fish to their home streams is not 100 percent, and always there are a few individuals that stray to other streams. In some cases, trout that hatched in outlet streams may even stray to an inlet to spawn, and vice versa. Some of the Kamloops trout lakes have both inlet and outlet streams and spawning runs to both are common. Apparently there is no genetic difference between these runs; trout from

51

a single source stocked in previously barren lakes have quickly established runs to both inlet and outlet streams.

The first ripe trout seek the outlet streams even before the ice has left the lake. Their journey to spawning is relatively easy compared to that of the inlet spawners because they are able to move with the current, not against it. Because it begins so much earlier, the spawning run to the outlet may be nearly at its end when the inlet runs are only just beginning. The outlet spawners dig their nests and deposit their eggs in water that is extremely cold; only later when the sun has warmed the lake that is the source of the outlet will the stream temperature rise enough to accelerate the development of the buried embryos.

The beginning of the inlet spawning run seems much more dependent on the weather. If the spring is late and the ice is slow to leave, the run may be delayed; usually the ice is breaking up or altogether gone and the inlet temperatures are rising before the first trout appear offshore. As the temperature of each inlet continues to rise, the first ripe fish begin to move tentatively into the stream. Their upstream migration takes place during the warmest part of the day, and they seek sheltered places to rest when darkness falls and the temperature plummets. A sudden frosty night may retard the migration temporarily and a quick thunderstorm also often brings a temporary halt. But in this slow, uncertain way, the trout struggle upstream against the weight of the warming spring runoff.

Males and females enter the stream together, although in some years the numbers of one sex will be greater than the other. But always a portion of the run consists of small, precocious males, nature's way of ensuring there always will be at least some male fish to fertilize the precious eggs. The trout seek beds of coarse gravel to make their redds. The very largest of them, such as the huge trout that spawn below Trout Lake in the Lardeau River, are capable of turning over stones six or seven inches in diameter in their nest-digging activities. Areas of stable flow and comfortable current velocities are chosen.

Male fish pair up with females, usually in ratios of a single male fish to five or more to each female. The hen fish begin digging the nests, scooping out a safe hollow in the gravel with broad beats of their powerful tails. Several times the female settles into the nest as if to test its size, then resumes digging until the nest finally meets her approval. The digging goes on around the clock, with the big females tearing and ripping their tails on the sharp stones, pausing briefly to rest, then resuming their urgent task. The male fish, meanwhile, begin fighting one another for the favor of the females. Big trout chase their smaller rivals, slamming into them, biting them and pursuing them in furious rushes across the gravel bars and through the pools. The greater the number of males attending a single female, the fiercer the combat is likely to be — and there is no quarter.

It is a sight to remember — great, dark, hook-jawed fish ranging through the pools, tearing their flanks and bellies on the stones, slamming into one another, twisting and turning and snapping at their foes. In larger streams a single male trout may try to defend several hundred feet of streambed against its challengers, with round-the-clock vigilance and determination.

When at last the nest is ready, the female settles into it and the victorious male, scarred from his struggles, settles alongside. Then, with her mouth stretched wide in exertion, the female shudders convulsively and spills her eggs onto the gravel; simultaneously the male, its mouth also spread in a huge, straining yawn, covers them with milt. For each pound of her weight the female bears about a thousand eggs.

At the last moment the smaller males dart in again in a last-ditch effort to spill their own cargo of milt upon the eggs, but the dominant male turns quickly to defend the nest with all his remaining strength. The hen, meanwhile, moves quickly on to dig another nest upstream, and the gravel dislodged by her fresh digging settles over the fertilized eggs in the nest she left behind, forming a loose protective layer that shields them from the light and from hungry predators. This cycle is repeated until the fish are spent. Even then, the male stays on, guarding the nests after the female has left to seek quiet water in which to rest before starting the downstream journey to the lake, or perhaps to die. The male, after guarding the nests for a time, will move on in search of another female, fighting and spawning until his sperm is gone and his strength nearly used up. And of them all, not every fish is able to expend its full supply of eggs or milt; for physiological reasons, the reproductive materials sometimes become bound up, gradually to be absorbed back into the bodies of the trout after they have returned to the lake.

For many trout, spawning is the last act of life. They do not all die, as do the Pacific salmon, but some expend the last ounce of energy on which life depends. Lacking strength to hold position in the flow, they are carried away downstream and swept up into the shallows, there to gasp out their last remaining life on a gravel bar. Alive or dead, spawning trout in the small, shallow streams of the high country are especially vulnerable to the predations of hungry lynx or bear, and the banks of the spawning streams are often littered with the decomposing remains of trout slain by these animals.

But even after death, the trout serve a purpose. Their decomposing remains add to the fertility of the stream and contribute to its strict economy, helping to provide the food that will sustain the offspring the trout will never see. Their passage and their sacrifice is grimly marked

53

by the sight of vultures soaring high over the spawning creeks in the last weeks of May.

If the spawning ordeal means death for many fish, there are always at least some that will survive. The stronger trout return to the lakes to feed again and, perhaps, to spawn a second time, or even a third. Mortality in spawning is highest among the older, larger fish, and among the males, with their furious combat. But many of the small, precocious males survive to spawn again.

When the spawning run is very large the mortality is greater. Trout overcrowd the redds and the competition between the males is even greater. With so many fish digging, spawning and fighting together in a small area, the number of survivors is bound to be proportionally less. When the runs are small and the spawning trout are fewer in number, the competition is less and the percentage of survivors is greater. In such years as many as half the ripe fish that enter the streams at the beginning of the run may survive at the end of it.

The spent survivors, known as kelts, show little evidence of their former elegance and grace. They are thinner, still dark, and some show the dead white spots of fungus growth. Their fins are ragged and worn, their bellies scarred and bruised. The females have lost a quarter of their weight and the males nearly as much, part of it in the expenditure of eggs or milt, part in the great exertions of spawning. Spent fish in the outlet streams must be in especially good condition to regain the lake. They must swim against the current at a time when the flow is often at its height. Those without the strength to fight the flow are trapped in the eddies, easy prey for hungry animals or birds. And even if they escape the fate of being eaten, their strength ebbs quickly and their death is only a matter of time.

But those which still are strong enough to swim against the flow begin their upstream migration in the warmest hours of the day, resting during darkness to resume their struggle when the sun returns. The survivors of the inlets follow no such pattern, holding station in the current as they drop down with it toward the lake.

The time spent by trout in their spawning depends upon the size of the runs. In years of very large runs the intensive combat weakens the trout quickly and shortens their stay over the spawning redds. In normal years or in years when the run is small the trout spend a longer time in the stream, sometimes stretching their stay to six or seven weeks.

When the surviving kelts return to the lakes, they feed voraciously, trying to regain their strength. They are especially vulnerable to anglers, but a fresh kelt is always a disappointment. It is too weak to provide much sport and its appearance seldom is pleasing. The energy it expends in contest with the angler may be its last reserves, so that even if it is released it will not recover. And if the angler, in ignorance of what he has

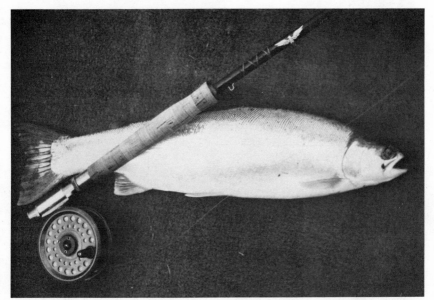

A typical Kamloops trout, clean and bright and built for speed and power. This three-pounder was fooled by a floating sedge pattern on a sunny morning early in July.

caught, kills the fish and attempts to eat it, he will find its flesh soft and white and tasteless.

But if the kelt survives to feed through the summer it gradually regains a semblance of its prior form and beauty. It may regain its former weight, but usually will not grow much beyond it unless the lake is exceptionally rich or forage fish are abundant. There is a common misconception among anglers that trout, once having spawned, will grow larger than their former weight; but this is untrue in the great majority of cases.

The recovering kelts gradually take on some of the silvery shine they had as maiden fish, but the skin along their bellies remains dark and the spawning scars are slow to heal. The kelt retains a hint of its deep purple spawning dress along its flanks and gill covers, and an experienced angler will know immediately when he has caught a trout that has spawned before.

Some Kamloops trout may live for six or seven years (or, in the case of the Gerrard strain, even longer), spawning two or three times during their lives. But they will be a very small minority, having survived the disastrous effects of flood or drought, the exhaustive rigors of spawning and the deadly predations of birds, animals, other fish and man. They will have been parent to several thousand offspring, at most of which a few hundred will have survived. They will have drawn their strength and nourishment from the other creatures of the lake, from the tiniest ani-

55

mals in their teeming thousands to the large, conspicuous and vulnerable nymphs of the damselfly and dragonfly, the pupae of sedges and midges, the ubiquitous scud and the sinuous leech.

You may see them at twilight, great old trout, wise to the ways of anglers, rolling in the shadows for a fluttering sedge. By daylight they will be gone, prowling the depths in search of scuds or forage fish. They have met all the tests that man and nature can contrive, and they have survived. And in the world of the Kamloops trout, that is all that matters.

Yet finally the vigor and strength, the quickness and keenness that has brought them so far must inevitably begin to fail. Their eyesight weakens, and as it does the quick, unerring thrust to capture an insect or a tiny fish is no longer true. Now the energy that must be expended in feeding no longer matches the worth of the reward, and the old trout begins to lose its weight and strength. The deterioration is gradual but sure, as certain as it is that man's own faculties begin to fail him in his latter years. No longer swift and sure in its movements, no longer certain of its sensory perceptions, the trout feeds less and its strength quickly ebbs away. Finally it becomes an effort for the trout to keep its now-emaciated body in trim and it knows that it must rest. It seeks a shallow place, perhaps the edge of a weed-covered shoal where sheltering deep water is close at hand, and settles into the soft vegetation. There it remains, its gills working slowly, sustaining a tired life a little longer.

The impatient scavengers of the lake do not wait for the trout to die. The snails begin to tear at its flesh while the trout's heart still beats. The end comes slowly and without dignity until eventually some final point is reached, the gills open and close a final time, the stout heart is finally still. Even in death and decay the trout will add sustenance to the lake, and those creatures which consume its flesh will in turn be consumed by the trout's own offspring. And then the ancient cycle will be complete, and renewed.

Mountain Kamloops Trout

There is another trout that bears the Kamloops name. This is the so-called Mountain Kamloops trout, a small alpine rainbow found in lakes at high elevations where the growing season is short and aquatic food stocks are limited both in number and variety.

The Mountain Kamloops once was considered a subspecies of the Kamloops when the latter was thought to be a distinct species in its own right. Then it was learned that the characteristics of the Mountain Kamloops, like those of the Kamloops, resulted from environmental factors and not from any genetic differences. While it still was recognized as a subspecies it was known as *Salmo kamloops whitehousei,* as described earlier.

As described by Dymond, the distinguishing characteristics of the Mountain Kamloops trout included its color — olive green on the back, yellowish green on the flanks and a profuse array of spots on the head, back and sides and on the dorsal, adipose and caudal fins. Bluish parr marks generally are worn by the fish throughout its life, even during spawning. Dymond reported that some of these trout also display a conspicuous orange tip on their dorsal fins, and the ventral and anal fins are edged in white along their trailing edges. The crimson markings typical of rainbow trout make their appearance during spawning.

The Mountain Kamloops trout is a small fish, seldom reaching a foot in length. Their heads are quite large in proportion to their bodies, as is commonly the case with trout living in high-elevation waters with short growing seasons and limited food stocks. The Mountain Kamloops has very small scales, averaging 150 to 155 diagonal rows, with a variation from 140 to 164.

The Mountain Kamloops spawns in June when the ice goes out of the mountain lakes. It is not unusual for these trout to reach maturity and spawn at a length of only six inches. These fish are living proof of the ability of trout to adapt to a wide variety of conditions, but in most respects they are no different from rainbow trout found in any high-elevation waters. Their small size and relative inaccessibility to anglers makes them unimportant as a game fish and they are mentioned here only because they once were thought to be a subspecies of the Kamloops trout.

Hybrid Trout

Any angler experienced in fishing for Kamloops trout probably would argue that there's no point in trying to improve it through cross-breeding. The native Kamloops trout is swift and strong, hardy and fast-growing, vigorous and sometimes violent and in perfect harmony with its environment. From an angler's viewpoint, it seems to have every desirable characteristic for a trout, and it has them in greater measure than any other known stock or strain or species. So what possibly could be gained by experiments in hybridization?

The answer is: not very much. Nevertheless, it probably was inevitable that some fish culturists — being the curious creatures that they are — would try it. A number of hybridization experiments have been recorded. One was in the hatchery at Cranbrook, B. C., where Kamloops and cutthroat trout were crossed and the resultant offspring were called Cranbrook trout. These fish grew to large size, as hybrids often do, but they lacked the sporting characteristics of both the Kamloops and the cutthroat.

It has been a good many years since these experiments were carried out and the work has not been continued. The Kamloops trout has since become firmly established in its own right as a game fish of unparalleled quality, a unique resource whose preservation is in the best interest of both anglers and fisheries managers. The hybridization experiments are but a minor footnote in the history of the Kamloops trout and it is all to the good that the work has been discontinued.

Chapter Three

The Resource

The Kamloops trout is one of nature's most perfect works, the product of a union between the water and the land, the end result of countless eons of evolution and upheaval, of endless experimentation and change. Its strength comes from the minerals leached secretly from the soil of the surrounding hillsides by the melting snow and the spring rains, and its life is shaped by the cycle of the seasons. It is tied to the land as firmly as the roots of the lodgepole pines that shelter its spawning streams, and it is an integral part of a complex but fragile scheme that includes all the plants and animals with whom it shares its lakes, and all the others that live on, around or over them.

Except for those that feed in the open sea itself, few trout are so favored as those of the British Columbia Interior, where the richness of land, water and climate have combined in an intricate web of life that is difficult to understand but deceptively easy to disturb.

It begins with the very shape of the land itself.

Topography and Geology

The gentle rolling hills of the Southern Interior Plateau today hold little evidence of the land's violent past. In long-ago epochs whose story is written in the rock, the mountains of the province were lifted up out of ancient sedimentary layers; subterranean volcanic fires seared the crevices and exploded through the surface vents, spilling lava on the deformed sediments. Then glaciers reached down from the north to scratch and claw the surface rock. For successive ages the glaciers advanced and retreated, leaving the marks of their violent passage on the face of the land. Mountaintops were ground into rubble and ancient rivers were dammed; inlets from the prehistoric sea were closed off to become frozen lakes of salt water, and great canyons were carved by the abrasive weight of the ice. In each retreat, the glaciers left behind a wake of rubble and silt and a landscape dotted with glacial cirques and tortured folds.

Slowly life returned to the wounded land. Scrub trees and grass took fragile root in the rubble and the silt and slowly spread. Wild flowers, their seeds carried by the wind, sprouted in silty soil moistened by the melt from the last retreating glaciers. From the more hospitable valleys the colonies of plants spread up the slopes to the windswept heights of the ridgetops. Through the eons they dropped their leaves and limbs to decay and add themselves to the developing soil, and erosion played its part by cutting through the lava to the calceous sedimentary rock, and as the soil grew richer so did the plants that drew their sustenance from it. Animals came to feed upon the plants and other animals came to feed upon them; waterfowl stopped to nest and feed in the young lakes and ponds, and fish from the sea followed the brawling rivers to their sources.

A prominent feature of the new landscape was the Southern Interior Plateau. Wedged between the Coast Range and the Columbia Mountains at the southern end of the province, the plateau is a high range of gently rolling hills on a bed of sedimentary and volcanic rock, covered with a layer of glacial silt. After ages of erosion, growth and change, it has a deceptively gentle appearance, its slopes now thickly covered with green or golden grass, with stands of aspen, fir and pine clustered in the draws and along the ridges. Only in the tortured rock of the canyon walls is the evidence of past upheavals plainly visible.

Except for the deep valleys, the elevation of the plateau ranges from 3,000 to 6,000 feet. Runoff and natural drainage from the highlands collects in the glacial folds and cirques and the Southern Interior Plateau has many lakes. Most are quite small; some are too shallow or too alkaline to support fish of any kind, and some do not even exist year-round. Some are large and deep enough to challenge the stoutest boat and the most knowledgeable boatman. It was in these lakes, draining to the rivers that flow out of the province, that the Kamloops trout evolved, and it was these lakes that provided the stock that has since been introduced to the smaller, higher lakes. And it is in these smaller, higher lakes of the Southern Interior Plateau that the Kamloops trout has grown and prospered and made a name for itself among anglers.

Climate and Elevation

The growing season and productivity of these lakes are determined in large measure by the climate and the elevation at which they lie. These factors also influence the behavior of trout, determining where they are likely to be found at different seasons.

Elevation and climate are interrelated. Air temperature declines with elevation and precipitation increases. The Southern Interior Plateau is in the rain shadow of the Coastal Range and thus is spared the heavy rainfall of the coastal valleys. Its summer climate is warm and dry, and most areas receive less than 30 inches of rainfall annually, with the deeper valleys receiving only a third of that amount.

March and April usually are the driest months, but the late spring brings rain and June is the wettest month. Snowmelt and the spring rains fuel the springs and inlet streams that feed the lakes. High-elevation lakes where precipitation is heaviest frequently may be "flushed" by the inflow of water, making them less productive than lakes where this does not occur so often. Much depends upon the soil surrounding each lake; if it is hard and insoluble the runoff will be mostly on the surface, carrying little of value that the lake may use to add to its productivity. If the soils are soft and soluble, the runoff will penetrate and leach the chemical wealth from the soil and rock, adding it to the nutrients in the lake. Then, if the precipitation rate is low and the evaporation rate is high, the lake will be rich in nutrients and capable of supporting large crops of aquatic life. This is the fortunate situation that exists in most of the lakes of the Southern Interior Plateau.

The sun provides light for the photosynthesis of aquatic plants and a source of heat to warm the water and regulate the speed of the living and growing processes. The air temperature of the Interior valleys often exceeds 100 degrees during the summer, but the average summer temperature of the high country varies from 65 to 75.

The climate appears to have more overall influence on the length of the growing season that on the rate of growth itself, though it also is important to the latter. The long, warm summers, dry climate and relatively short winters are ideal for growing trout.

It would appear from all this that lakes lying at lower elevations would be the most productive. They should have the longest growing seasons, the highest evaporation rates, the least precipitation. However, the problem is not that simple. The larger lakes in the deep valleys of the Southern Interior Plateau are mostly of such depth that sunlight cannot penetrate to the growing areas of aquatic vegetation and their capacities for producing trout food are thus somewhat limited. But a happy medium is reached in the smaller, shallower lakes that dot the higher slopes. There the sun is able to reach with its light to the weedy lake floors and, if other factors are favorable, these lakes are rich in aquatic life.

Excessive blooms of algae may occur in the shallower lakes during the warm summer months. The decay of this algae removes much of the oxygen from the water, and sometimes too little is left for the trout to survive, resulting in a "summer kill" of fish. These kills usually are not total, as "winter kill" is almost invariably, but they may significantly reduce the population of trout and they may occur in lakes at any elevation, depending upon their depth, fertility and the warmth of the season.

The climate also is responsible for the thermocline, a phenomenon of great importance to trout fishermen. In the spring, after the ice goes out, the slightly warmer water at the bottom of the lake rises to the surface and this "turnover" leads to a condition in which temperature and oxygen saturation are uniformly constant throughout the lake. But the warming temperature and stabilizing weather of late spring and summer quickly upsets this equilibrium. Water is a poor conductor of heat, and the warm weather quickly causes a layer of warm water to form near the surface of most lakes. This layering effect inhibits circulation so that stagnation results, and the oxygen supply in the cooler bottom layer of water is quickly depleted to the point that virtually no oxygen remains. Between these two extremes is a layer where the temperature of the

61

water is less than that of the surface but more than that of the layer beneath, and the oxygen content is marginal.

The boundary between the upper and middle layer, where it exists, or between the upper and lower layer where it does not, is called the thermocline. Above it circulation occurs regularly, oxygen content is high and the temperature is warm and likely to be nearly uniform; below it, temperature and oxygen saturation drop off quickly. The significance of this is that trout are likely to seek the zone of greatest comfort to themselves, and this usually will be at or near the thermocline. By patiently taking the temperature of the water at various depths the angler can determine with considerable accuracy where this point is, then fish his imitations at the appropriate depth.

There is no hard and fast rule for determining which lakes are affected by the thermocline. The large, deep lakes of the lower valleys often are free of it, possibly because many of them have rivers of significant size flowing into them, maintaining circulation throughout the summer months. But most of the smaller lakes at elevations between 3,000 and 4,500 feet become stratified more often than not, and when they do not it may be due to an unusually cool, wet summer season and a lack of shelter from the wind. A wise fly fisherman will carry a thermometer with him to sample the temperature at various depths in July and August.

Stratification ends with the cooler temperatures and winds of autumn. The surface layer cools until it is no warmer than the water below it, and the thermocline disappears, permitting circulation to be restored until eventually the lake again reaches a point of equilibrium where temperature and oxygen saturation is constant throughout.

It is precisely because of the thermocline that fly fishermen enjoy their greatest success in the spring and fall when trout are scattered randomly from the top to the bottom of a lake. But many lakes near the 5,000-foot level or above remain cool enough through the summer to fish effectively with flies at any time.

Soil and Nutrients

The richness of the food chain in any lake depends upon the nutrients dissolved in its water. The Kamloops trout lakes receive their water from seepage, springs, runoff or a combination of these. But regardless of where it comes from, the water comes in contact with at least one type of soil and usually several before it reaches the lake. Water is a great natural solvent, and as it flows over or through different types of soil it dissolves many basic chemical compounds and minerals contained in them.

But even if the water flows through very rich and soluble soil, the nutrients it carries will be present only in extremely minute quantities by the time the water reaches the lake. It is then that the evaporation rate becomes important; evaporation removes the water but leaves the nutrients behind in a less dilute solution. Over a long period, the lake becomes a "nutrient trap," accumulating a rich supply of salts, chemicals and minerals which are vital to the production of aquatic life.

Water flowing from springs generally carries with it a larger share of dissolved minerals than water from streams carrying mostly surface runoff. Springs often are fed by subterranean seepage, which allows the water more time and contact with the soil. Runoff streams flow rapidly over the very top layer of soil and absorb much less of value. Thus, all other things being equal, a spring-fed lake is likely to be somewhat more productive than one that gets most of its water from direct runoff.

Biologists surveying the Kamloops trout waters have used a unit of measurement that expresses the number of dissolved solids per million parts of water as an indication of productivity. This unit is expressed as TDS, for "total dissolved solids." Most of the lakes of the Southern Interior Plateau have been found to have a TDS well in excess of 200 parts per million, which is relatively high for lakes. Some have a TDS of more than 1,000 parts per million, and some shallow lakes or ponds range all the way up to 100,000 parts per million — although the latter are far too alkaline to support trout. The ocean, by comparison, has a TDS of 33,000 to 37,000 parts per million.

The dissolved solids are used in the manufacture of proteins, the basic building blocks of life. The oxygen, hydrogen, nitrogen and carbon dioxide necessary for this to occur already are present in the water. Carbon, another essential element, is available from the byproducts of animal and plant metabolism. Phosphorous is present in the form of phosphates, and sulfur comes from the oxidation of the iron found in the igneous rocks of the Southern Interior Plateau.

Calcium is extremely important. It is needed by nearly all the aquatic plants; crustaceans require it to build their outer skeletons, and snails utilize it in the manufacture of their shells. It also neutralizes the acidity that is a product of accumulated organic material on the bottoms of some lakes. It is leached from the soil or from soft limestone rock and carried by tributary waters to the lakes. The marl bottoms characteristic of many Kamloops trout lakes are caused by the high calcium content of the water, the marl itself the product of certain types of calcium-dependent algae. The *Chara* weed common to most of these lakes often is coated with crusts of marl, and its common name — stonewort — is derived from these rock-like deposits.

Plants and most animals also require potassium, and magnesium is needed by aquatic plants for the photosynthetic process. Manganese also is needed by many plants. These elements also are leached from the surrounding soils. Water flowing into the lakes also carries iron salts, and the iron is a component of the blood of animals and is used by some insect forms and green plants.

The TDS measurement is an expression of the relative concentration

63

of these materials in the water of a lake. It follows that waters with a high TDS will be able to produce more plankton, more algae and fixed plants, more insects, crustaceans and other forms of trout food and, ultimately, more and larger trout. This usually is the case, although local factors may sometimes intervene.

The amount of dissolved solids in a lake is not constant. Changes in the season change the evaporation rate, the rate of photosynthesis and the amount of runoff, and these in turn affect the concentration of dissolved solids in the lake. Pulses of aquatic life or heavy algae blooms remove dissolved solids from the water for varying lengths of time, but the waste products or decaying remains of these animals eventually return most of them to the water, and every hard rain helps to replenish the supply.

All these things are outside the thoughts of most anglers. They are not easily observed or readily understood, but the slow leaching of the hidden wealth of the soil and its transference into the constituents of aquatic life is at the very heart of the process that leads to the silver, gleaming trout called Kamloops.

Surrounding Vegetation

From the lowly lichens clinging to the rocks to the tallest stately pine, the plants that dwell in the margins of the Kamloops trout lakes and the slopes above them play an ecological role of extreme importance.

The valley floors of the Southern Interior Plateau are windswept and dry, carpeted with bunch grass and sage. In the folds where water collects, groves of aspen grow, along with cottonwood, scrub willow and wild rose. The vegetation remains much the same until the timberline is reached, between 2,000 and 3,000 feet on north-facing slopes and higher on slopes facing toward the south. At its lowest level the forest typically consists of pine, fir and larch in open stands with little undergrowth. At higher elevations the lodgepole pine predominates with a scattering of spruce and alpine fir and a dense layer of undergrowth.

It is the root structures of all these plants that hold rainwater and snowmelt, releasing it slowly to the earth to fuel the springs that feed the lakes and their tributary streams. When the trees are cut, or the land is cleared for roads, or defoliated for power lines, or the surface layers are shoveled away in mining, the earth loses its capability for holding and cooling the water. The runoff then is quick and warm and weighted with silt, making tributaries unsuitable for spawning and causing turbidity in lakes. Lacking the capacity to store and cool water, the land has none left to release during the critical summer months when streamflows are at their lowest and lake temperatures are highest. Springs or streams that once flowed throughout the year dry up in summer, setting off a drastic chain reaction throughout the ecological system of the entire watershed.

The Kamloops trout lakes have suffered less of this sort of abuse than waters in other areas of the province. Still, damage has occurred and is still occurring. Destruction of forests and ground cover has come from poor logging practices and forest fires (which often are the result of poor logging practices). Road-building and clearing for summer homes or subdivisions has hurt, too, and so has the indiscriminate routing of power lines near a number of lakes. The slopes around many lakes have been badly overgrazed by cattle, the grass cropped down to its roots or worn away altogether so that the water-holding capacity of the soil is severely depleted. At the very worst extreme, at least one lake has been used as a repository for the drainage from mine tailings, rendering it an ugly, murky biological desert.

Vegetation surrounding the lakes also plays a more subtle role in the ecology of the fishery. The vegetation provides areas of shelter and rest for the adult mayflies and sedges after their initial flight from the surface and before their mating rituals, and it offers essential habitat for important terrestrial species such as the flying ant. Without it, there is no fall of flying ants, and the mating cycles of the sedges and mayflies are disrupted; more of them fall prey to foraging birds and, without shelter, many are carried by the wind away from the lake. The decline of hatches is slow but inexorable.

The vegetation surrounding the Kamloops trout lakes is a part of the grand design, an integral component of the ecological web that has the Kamloops trout as one of its most important members. The effects of removing this vegetation may be drastic and sudden or subtle and slow, but all have one thing in common: They are seldom recognized by man until it is too late to easily repair the damage that has been done.

Types of Lakes

Lakes that are rich in dissolved solids and, consequently, rich in life, usually are designated eutrophic. A characteristic of eutrophic lakes is heavy sedimentation on the lake bottom, caused by the accumulation of dead organisms and the waste products of living creatures. In a typical eutrophic lake there is so much of this material that decomposition cannot proceed fast enough to remove it all and put the trapped nutrients back into the production cycle. Some nutritive materials in the sediment are therefore lost and the lake's production is inefficient; it must receive additional nutrients from outside sources in order to maintain production of plant and animal life.

Eutrophic lakes have a tendency toward thermal stratification and bottom stagnation during summer because the decay of organic sediment extracts the oxygen from the bottom layer of water. In lakes where thermal stratification and oxygen depletion are especially severe, the amount of productive bottom area may be reduced sharply during the warm summer months when stratification is at its peak. This, too, contributes to the relative inefficiency of the ecosystem of the lake.

KAMLOOPS

The tremendous fallout of dead organisms and wastes in these shallow lakes accelerates their life cycle and brings on an early "death." Because the sediment accumulates faster than the rate of decay, the lakes slowly fill up with it, becoming ever shallower. Tules and rushes encroach upon the shallows, establishing thriving colonies, and silt and blowing soil become trapped in their root systems until eventually what once was part of the lake has become dry land, and the tules and rushes encroach further into the lake and the process is repeated. Eventually the lake shrinks to become a shallow pond and then, finally, a meadow.

This process normally takes many centuries, but in some lakes it proceeds rapidly enough so that drastic changes are visible within the short span of a human lifetime. Any unnatural addition to the fertility of the lake, such as that caused by human or animal sewage leaching into it, accelerates the process. The majority of the Kamloops trout lakes are eutrophic, and throughout the Southern Interior Plateau it is possible to see lakes at all stages of development, from those that are yet young in limnological terms to those that are in the very last stages of eutrophication. And finally there are the lush meadows that are the grave markers of former lakes.

But while they exist, most eutrophic lakes are rich producers of trout. In addition to the usual complement of aquatic insects, certain fauna are characteristic of eutrophic waters. These include the larvae of the red chironomid, known as "bloodworms," and the fascinating larvae of *Chaoborus,* the so-called "phantom midge."

The other broad classification of lakes is designated by the word oligotrophic. These lakes have fewer dissolved solids and a smaller population of plant and animal life. In oligotrophic lakes, the decomposition of organic material or waste is about equal to the production of them so that the nutrients in the water are recycled back into the system and the production cycle is efficient; the lake therefore is able to sustain production without receiving nutrients from an outside source.

Oligotrophic lakes are less likely to show evidence of bottom stagnation during the summer months because they have less decaying sediment to extract oxygen from the water. These lakes seldom have heavy algae blooms, and colorless midge larvae are characteristic of them. Because the fallout of organic material is matched by the decay rate, they do not fill in, as do eutrophic lakes, and thus they may remain stable over long periods. They tend to be deeper to begin with, often lying in steep-walled canyons or deep, narrow folds in the earth. Because the surrounding topography usually is steep, the water flowing into these lakes tends to be mostly rapid surface runoff, carrying a minimal supply of dissolved solids and nutrients. Usually these lakes lack the extensive shallows or shoal areas that are commonly associated with eutrophic waters. Large lakes also tend to be oligotrophic because the concentration of dissolved solids is more dilute in them than it is in lakes with a smaller volume of water.

In surveying the lakes of the Kamloops country, biologists have used the term "littoral development" to mean that portion of the lake bottom which lies less than 10 meters below the surface. The measurement usually is expressed in percentages; a littoral development of 50 percent means that half the lake is less than 10 meters deep. These shallow areas are most important because they are exposed to the sunlight essential for photosynthesis and plant growth, and they usually support large populations of aquatic life. Eutrophic lakes are more likely to have a high percentage of littoral development, but that alone is not enough to make a lake eutrophic.

Most anglers are accustomed to thinking of a lake as a hole full of water with fish in it, but a lake is something very much more than that. Each lake is a dynamic system that produces and sustains life, a system that is ever changing with peaks and pulses of life and movement prompted by the cycle of the seasons and the days. The size and shape and depth and volume of a lake help determine how well it is able to make use of the salts and solids that flow into it, and — of most importance to the angler — what comes out of it.

Requirements of Trout

The introduction of Kamloops trout to the many once-barren Interior lakes is a relatively recent development. Most or all of the better lakes have now been stocked, but a few virgin waters may yet remain, awaiting their first plants of trout. The earliest introductions very often were carried out in ignorance, with no cohesive pattern or control; more often than not they were the private projects of individual anglers or small groups.

The results of these informal planting programs varied widely; some lakes produced very large trout in small numbers; others produced very small trout in large numbers, and some produced no trout at all. The reasons for this were little understood at the time, and as we have seen they sometimes led to false and very damaging conclusions. But since those early days, fish culturists have learned much about the survival requirements of Kamloops trout, and much about the waters themselves.

There is a certain set of minimal requirements necessary for the survival of Kamloops trout. The most obvious of them are the need for cool, clean water and a certain degree of oxygen saturation throughout the year. Those factors alone eliminate many of the Interior lakes; some are so shallow they become too warm in the summer; others experience stagnation and oxygen depletion in summer and/or winter so that trout could not survive throughout the year, and some are too alkaline for trout to live in. But it is not always easy to make a judgment on the suitability of a certain lake for trout; the circumstances are not always clear, and where the probability of survival is uncertain the only sure way to see if fish can survive is to put them in the lake and see what happens. Nowadays, however, there is rarely ever surplus stock available for experiments where the likelihood for success is marginal.

Some lakes are subject to summer or winter kill only in extreme years and may be safe for trout for years on end. These lakes usually are valuable producers that contribute substantially to the fishery, and it is well worth the risk to plant them again even after a kill. The growth rate in these lakes usually is rapid, fed by the decay of the previous population and the reprieve from predation that is granted to aquatic insects by the die-off. Within a remarkably short time the lakes are able to return to full production.

Aside from the inhospitable and marginal waters and those lakes periodically affected by seasonal kills, there are hundreds of lakes that are capable of indefinitely producing a large standing crop of trout. But the quality and quantity of the standing crop in each lake may vary radically, depending upon any number of circumstances.

Once introduced in a lake with tributaries suitable for spawning, the Kamloops trout will quickly establish a spawning run and reproduce. This is not always desirable; in lakes with extensive tributary spawning areas the population often increases so rapidly it soon exhausts the available food resources of the lake, and a large population of very small fish is the inevitable result. There is not always very much that can be done about this. It is difficult, if not impossible, to block off the spawning tributaries and attempt to manage the lake without natural spawning. And measures taken to increase the angling harvest from such lakes, including a reduction in the legal size limit and a waiver of the catch limit, have likewise seldom been successful because anglers usually ignore lakes containing smaller fish when larger ones may be available nearby. Even with relaxed limits, there has never been enough angling pressure to substantially reduce the numbers of fish in these overpopulated lakes, and for the most part they have remained overpopulated, contributing little of value to the overall sport fishery.

But while the problem of overpopulation remains beyond the control of fisheries managers, it has occasionally been solved by the beaver. Where natural spawning has occurred in the tributaries of Kamloops trout lakes, beaver dams have often put an end to it. This is desirable in lakes where overpopulation is a chronic problem, but as often as not the beavers have done their work on waters where it is not. This, too, has added to the problems of management, necessitating the stocking of lakes that formerly maintained themselves in balance with limited natural spawning.

Most of the Kamloops trout lakes lack tributaries where trout can spawn successfully, and some have them only in years of heavy runoff. Lakes of the latter type may provide different fishing from year to year, with small numbers of large fish in the years following dry seasons and larger numbers of smaller or medium-sized fish in the years after a wet spring. From an angler's viewpoint they are perhaps the most interesting waters because of the variety they offer. One of the best-known examples was Peterhope Lake, a beautiful lake above timberline in the hills between Kamloops and Merritt. Peterhope has a single tributary where fish may spawn in years of heavy runoff, and an outlet from which it is possible for recovering kelts and their offspring to reach the lake only in high-water years. This set of circumstances combined to produce a good crop of fry in some years while in others there were few fry or none at all. Since Peterhope is a rich lake to begin with, it is capable of producing some very large fish when the population is relatively small over a period of two or three years. In 1968, for instance, one trout of 16 pounds was taken on the fly and good numbers in the 8-pound class were caught, many on dry flies. But in other years, the average size of the trout was much smaller. These natural variations in the size of the population and the size of individual trout kept anglers interested in the lake, so that many returned to it season after season. Unfortunately, in recent years a number of factors — not all of them yet identified — have caused the fishery to deteriorate and the average size of the trout in Peterhope now is smaller than perhaps ever before. One hopes this is only a temporary condition, for Peterhope is an extremely important lake — especially to the fly fisherman.

Lakes such as Peterhope sometimes are stocked to supplement natural production when the trout population falls to unacceptably low levels. Because the natural spawning success is unpredictable it sometimes happens that supplemental stocking results in temporary overpopulation of the lake, but this problem usually works itself out if the lake is left alone long enough for it to do so.

Lakes that are totally lacking in areas where trout may spawn are completely dependent upon stocking. They are the easiest to manage because the size of the trout populations in them can be controlled within fairly narrow limits, so long as there is reasonably reliable data on the harvest by anglers. With this data, and a measurement of the productivity of the lake, the manager can control the population well enough to produce trout of a certain average size.

The majority of Interior lakes fall in this category. They include such well-known waters as Jacko and Pass Lakes near Kamloops and Lundbom and Marquart Lakes near Merritt. Stump Lake, on the highway between Merritt and Kamloops, is another of these lakes; it became famous for its huge trout, which resulted from limited stocking of this large, productive body of water.

Of particular interest is the remarkable strain of Kamloops trout known interchangeably as the "Gerrard" or "Lardeau" strain (most often the former). The names are derived from the Lardeau River, where the

69

trout spawn, and Gerrard, a community near the spawning area.

The Lardeau River is about 30 miles long, flowing from the southeast end of Trout Lake into the north end of Kootenay Lake. To spawning trout from Kootenay Lake it is an inlet, but its waters are warmed in Trout Lake before entering the river. A number of cold tributaries reach the Lardeau below Trout Lake so that by the end of its course the river's water temperature has been lowered considerably. The warmest part of the stream is just below the outlet from Trout Lake, and it is there that the Gerrard trout spawn.

The Gerrard fish are very slow to reach sexual maturity. A few ripen for the first time at the age of four or five years, but the majority do not become sexually mature until the sixth or seventh year of life, and there are records of some fish that spawned for the first time at the age of eight. Kootenay Lake has a large population of kokanee and in about their third year the Gerrard fish begin to feed on them. The trout's rate of growth is rapid after this point, and by the time they reach maturity they have had several years of rich feeding. This plentiful food source and the unusually long time the trout have to enjoy it combine to produce some fish of exceptional size – 20 to 30 pounds or more.

G. F. Hartman, who studied the reproductive biology of these fish, found that the spawning area chosen by the Gerrard trout has several things in its favor that are not found together elsewhere. First, the warm water flowing out of Trout Lake allows faster development of the trout embryos and a shorter incubation period. The fry emerge well ahead of those spawned in cooler waters downstream, giving them a competitive advantage. Second, the flow of water over the spawning redds is relatively stable because the lake is its source, and this protects the developing embryos from the possible effects of floods and freshets.

A third factor is the strength of the flow, which normally is so swift below the lake that only larger fish are able to easily maintain station in it. This selects against the possibility of successful spawning of smaller trout that may have matured at an earlier age. The river bottom at this point consists of very coarse gravel and only the largest females can successfully dislodge the rock to prepare a nest. This selects against the survival of eggs deposited by smaller, younger females. Finally, the largest males are more capable of defending the redds from the efforts of young, precocious males to join in the fun. This ensures that most of the eggs will be fertilized by larger males. Together these factors select strongly in favor of successful spawning by only the oldest, largest fish, and the genetic characteristics of late maturation are passed on to the succeeding generation.

Other long-lived strains of trout are known, but there are few that live so long before their first spawning or grow so large as the trout that spawn at Gerrard. But it is a fragile resource; in one year the number of trout counted spawning at Gerrard totaled only 16. But the run gradually has built up again so that now the spawning run averages several hundred fish a year.

These fish represent a resource of inestimable worth to the province — indeed, to the whole world, since there is no other like them. One would think that every possible effort would be made to preserve them and look after their welfare. But it is a sad reflection on the attitudes of the provincial government that this has not always been the case.

An old wooden bridge, built more than 40 years ago, spans the river at Gerrard. Over the years the bridge has fallen into disrepair so that it was judged unsafe for logging trucks to cross. Kootenay Forest Products, Ltd., which operates a mill at Nelson, B. C., needed road access to its logging operations on the far side of the river, and so a new bridge was proposed — right through the area used by the Gerrard trout for spawning. The provincial Fish and Wildlife Branch and many sportsmen's groups protested the bridge, arguing that its construction would disrupt spawning, damage the river and conceivably destroy the Gerrard strain of trout. Wrangling over the bridge went on for years and many times it appeared that those who argued for the fish would lose and an irreplaceable resource might be destroyed for the sake of short-term profit. That certainly would have been in keeping with the recent pattern of resource-management decisions in British Columbia.

But at last the defenders of the fish won their fight and the provincial government killed plans for the new bridge. Arrangements were made to barge the logs across Trout Lake and the trout spawning area was preserved. Now, when the giant trout arrive to spawn in May, hundreds of people come out to watch them and a park has been planned to include the spawning area.

There have been a few attempts to transplant Gerrard strain trout to other waters in the hope that they would retain their long-lived characteristics and produce fish of trophy size. Generally, these attempts have been unsuccessful — with one notable exception. Gerrard trout were the source of stock in Pend Oreille Lake in Northern Idaho, where they also found an abundant population of kokanee on which to feed. This combination produced some very large trout, including one of 37 pounds caught in 1947 which generally is recognized as the official world's record for a landlocked rainbow trout taken on angling gear. But for various reasons, including a lack of the circumstances that exist in the spawning area at Gerrard, the size of the trout in Pend Oreille Lake has declined in recent years.

Threats to the Resource

There are a number of natural hazards that sometimes pose threats to the environment of the Kamloops trout. These include floods, forest fires and landslides. But these are threats that always have existed, and although they may have meant temporary setbacks for isolated parts of

71

the fishery, the Kamloops trout always has been able to survive and pros-
per in spite of them.

The greatest threat to the future of the resource is man and his activities. Until recent years, the population of British Columbia grew relatively slowly, especially in the Interior. The rugged terrain, difficulty of access and relatively long distances between established settlements were
natural inhibitors to population growth. But all that has changed in the
past two decades. Improved highway, rail and air transportation has
brought the Interior within easy reach of the centers of population and
commerce on the Lower Mainland. The Interior now is the playground
for those who live and work in Vancouver and its suburbs. In the Interior
itself, many new businesses have been founded to serve the needs and
pleasures of those who come to play or visit, and these have led to a
startling increase in the local population. At the same time there has
been tremendous growth in the forest products and mining industries,
bringing even more people and problems to the Interior. Kamloops has
grown from a village to a major city, and lonely little junctions like
Cache Creek have grown into ugly little strip towns, their main streets
lined with fast-food franchises.

Despite efforts to control them, pollution and severe environmental
disruption have been inevitable byproducts of the development of the
timber and mining industries, and disposal of domestic wastes has become a serious problem for the growing cities and towns. Subdivisions
have spread from the urban areas to the shores of many lakes, destroying
their aesthetic qualities and damaging the fishery through sewage pollution and timber removal — to mention only two of the most obvious impacts. All these things are the result of a cause-and-effect relationship;
the problems are the effect, and the cause is people's attitudes.

Modern society has blessed its members with increased amounts of
leisure time, and growing affluence has given them many new ways to
spend it. Fleets of recreational vehicles now flood the Interior, forming
impromptu cities on the shores of lakes where their occupants unload
boats with overpowered outboard motors, trailbikes, portable generators
and all manner of noisy mechanical contrivances. For the most part,
these people are newcomers to the outdoors, lacking in knowledge of
natural values. Perhaps it is more a problem of ignorance than attitude,
or perhaps it is both, but the result is misuse and abuse of the resource
on a very broad scale. These weekend campers cut timber to fuel their
fires, leave oil slicks on the lakes from their outboard motors, strew
campsites with sewage and garbage and frighten away wildlife with their
machines. The effects are cumulative, and the damage to the aesthetic
qualities of the lakes is only the least of them.

All the users of the Kamloops trout lakes are not this way, of course;
but the sad truth is that most of them are. Their casual treatment of the

72

fragile environment is the single most serious threat to the survival of the resource.

Agriculture is another important industry in the Interior, and while it has been responsible for some problems — instances of overgrazing, pollution or occasional diversion of spawning watercourses — it also has had many beneficial impacts. Mostly these have occurred when dams were built to raise the level of existing lakes. The dams were meant to provide water for irrigation, but often they also created impoundments capable of supporting trout where before there were none. Many of the Interior's most famous lakes — Peterhope, Leighton, Tunkwa and Roche among them — owe their fishing at least in part to irrigation dams at their outlets. In dry years, the drawdown of these lakes often is rather severe, but the trout seem to have survived well in spite of it. There have been a few instances — Knouff Lake may have been one — where raising the water level harmed more than helped, but these are in the minority.

In its largely beneficial impact on the fishery, agriculture is the exception rather than the rule among man's activities in the Interior of British Columbia. The past decade has seen an enormous increase in pressure on the fishery and the environment that created it; already some of the best lakes have been lost for all practical purposes, and more will follow unless the trend is somehow reversed. Man is the problem, and the future of the fishery depends on whether there are a few wise and willing men who can convince the rest of what is necessary to preserve it.

Predators

The list of animals that prey upon the Kamloops trout is a long one. From the moment of conception, the trout is a target for the hungry appetites of birds, other fish, animals and man. Predation is responsible for most trout fry loss, and it has been estimated that as many as 90 to 95 percent of the fry of any single year class may fall victim to predators.

The figures sound high, but the fecundity of the trout is natural insurance that there will always be enough trout that a sufficient number will survive despite predation. And predation itself is an integral part of the natural scheme of things that provides a check on the population of trout and helps the cruel but efficient process of natural selection go forward.

Left alone, the predator-prey relationship works very well and helps to assure that the natural carrying capacity of the environment is not exceeded. But man's intervention in these relationships, sometimes unwitting, often upsets the careful natural balance. The extermination or dispersal of a predator species may result in an over-population of the prey, with a ripple effect that is soon felt throughout the whole food chain. Usually it takes time for these distortions to become apparent,

73

but by the time they do the system is so far out of balance that natural relationships may never be restored.

An example is that of the osprey, surely the most spectacular of all the predators of Kamloops trout. Osprey populations suffered a severe decline as a result of the application of persistent pesticides that had the unforeseen effect of causing the birds to lay eggs with shells that were abnormally thin or soft, so that few chicks were hatched. This problem was more serious in the United States than in British Columbia, but in the province − as elsewhere − timber removal has destroyed some of the osprey's nesting habitat, and the noisy activity of anglers and campers on some of the more popular lakes often has forced these shy birds to leave. A nesting pair of ospreys with young consumes an awful lot of small fish and helps to keep trout populations in balance. In the absence of these predators, trout survival is higher than it otherwise would be. This, in turn, puts a greater strain on the food stocks of the lake. Unless some other predator is able to step into the ecological niche vacated by the osprey, the problem grows worse with each succeeding generation of trout, due to the absence of the important population-control mechanism the osprey once provided. Food stocks are overgrazed and as the trout population increases the average size decreases.

Even greater distortion of predator-prey relationships occurs when non-native species are introduced into the environment. A classic case was the introduction of the redside shiner into Paul Lake, which completely upset the ecological balance of the lake with drastic consequences for the fishery. The results of that introduction will be examined in detail in a later chapter.

Birds and other fish are likely to be the first predators encountered by the Kamloops trout. Fortunately the Dolly Varden char (*Salvelinus malma*) has access to only a few of the streams in which Kamloops trout spawn, but where it is present it is an eager and efficient consumer of eggs and fry. Kingfishers and herons begin their attacks on fry migrating downstream toward the lakes and continue them when the young trout reach the shallows of the lakes themselves. There they are joined by mergansers and loons, and the ospreys and eagles join in when the trout reach yearling size or better.

Squawfish (*Ptychocheilus oregonensis*) are present in some of the larger Kamloops trout lakes, and these fish − which may grow to very large size − tend to feed in the shallows where fry congregate, taking a heavy toll. And although it is relatively rare, large Kamloops trout sometimes prey on smaller ones, though this usually occurs in lakes where competition among trout is especially keen and other food stocks have been depleted. The lake trout (*Salvelinus namaycush*), whitefish (*Prosopium williamsoni*) and fresh water ling (*Lota lota*) are other predators found in some of the larger Kamloops trout lakes.

These fish and others also compete for some of the same food sources utilized by Kamloops trout, which has an indirect but significant effect on trout survival and growth.

Animals do most of their predatory work along the spawning tributaries in the spring, taking both ripe unspawned adults and spawned-out kelts. Bear, lynx, mink, marten and raccoons all get into the act and the bloody evidence of their visits is often visible along the streambanks. Otters also take a heavy toll of trout, hunting efficiently in the lakes throughout the season.

But the greatest predator is man, usually the only one who takes more than he needs. He disguises his predation by calling it a sport, and as an individual he is usually not very efficient. But because of his large numbers, the cumulative effects of his activities are great. It is for that reason that regulations are necessary to limit the size and number of fish each angler may take, and often to limit the means he may use to take them. Of all the predators, man alone is capable of reducing trout populations to the point they no longer can sustain themselves.

Contiguous Species

In addition to predatory fish, there are a number of other species that are native or have been introduced within the natural range of the Kamloops trout. Some of these fish provide valuable forage for the Kamloops, some compete for the same food resources, and some do both. The predator-prey-competitor relationship sometimes varies from one lake to the next, for reasons that are not clearly understood; a species that provides valuable forage in one lake may be a more efficient competitor in another, and there is no certain way to forecast the impact of forage-species introduction.

It is clear, however, that Kamloops trout and other species cannot co-exist in a lake without one having some effect on the other. If the presence of another species is not beneficial to the trout, then almost certainly it will prove detrimental in some direct or indirect way. There is no middle ground; if trout share their environment with another species, it is either going to help them or hurt them. That statement carries obvious implications of risk for the introduction of foreign species.

The species that commonly prey on Kamloops trout already have been listed. The species that provide forage for the Kamloops — at least some of the time — include the kokanee and its anadromous counterpart, the sockeye salmon (*Oncorhynchus nerka*); the redside shiner (*Richardsonius balteatus*); various species of sculpin (*Cottus*); the fine-scaled sucker (*Catostomus catostomus*), and the coarse-scaled sucker (*Catostomus macrocheilus*). Some of the former also compete with Kamloops trout for food stocks in various waters, as do the Eastern brook trout (*Salvelinus fontinalis*), the carp (*Cyprinus carpio*) and the chub (*Mylocheilus caurinus*).

The kokanee is a landlocked version of the sockeye salmon that is native to most of the large, deep valley lakes and has been introduced to

75

a number of others. In some waters, such as Kootenay Lake, it has been extremely valuable as a forage fish. Introductions into smaller lakes have not been so successful, however, and it has been found that under some circumstances the Kamloops and the kokanee compete for food with the latter being more efficient.

In most of the Interior lakes in which it is found, the kokanee grows to a length of 12 to 15 inches, but in some instances — notably Kootenay Lake — it grows much larger. It is a game fish in its own right, but does not take the fly well and generally does not grow large enough to provide satisfactory sport. Sometimes it is called the silver trout or by any of half a dozen local names.

The anadromous sockeye salmon is important as a food source in the Adams and Little Rivers, where it spawns. The spring migration of sockeye fry brings Kamloops trout into the rivers to feed, providing angling of an unusual sort. The sockeye is important only in this isolated instance, but it has generated one of the most famous Kamloops trout fisheries.

The redside shiner is a small fish, usually not exceeding 4½ inches in length. It is native to the watersheds of the Columbia and Fraser Rivers and has been introduced either purposely or by accident in a number of Kamloops trout lakes. It is of some forage value, especially to larger trout, but its value is offset by its propensity to overpopulate and compete more effectively for available food.

The fine- and coarse-scaled suckers also are native to the Fraser and Columbia River drainages and are present in most of the large, low-lying lakes. Smaller individuals sometimes become prey for large Kamloops trout, but the opposite also is true. Suckers also compete with the trout for other food stocks. They spawn in the spring, often using the same tributaries as the trout, and the suckers feed heavily on trout eggs in these circumstances. Their minor value as a forage fish is far outweighed by their own predatory and competitive natures.

The carp is not native to British Columbia. It probably was introduced from Washington State, where it was stocked in the 1880's. It has been introduced to several British Columbia lakes, including Okanagan and tributary lakes, Osoyoos, Arrow and Shuswap Lakes and some others. In these cool-water environments, it is a sluggish, unattractive fish with very little sporting value. In small, enclosed lakes, the carp can be a very serious management problem because of its tendency to develop large populations that literally vacuum up the food stocks and make the lake useless for other species. And once established, carp are very difficult to eradicate. Fortunately, their distribution in British Columbia has been limited.

The Eastern brook trout is, of course, not a trout at all but a char. It is an extremely desirable game fish in its own right and was brought to British Columbia from its natural habitat in the East. It has been planted in a few lakes which, for one reason or another, were judged not suitable for Kamloops trout. It also has been introduced along with Kamloops trout to some lakes, where it has not been an altogether desirable companion fish. The feeding habits of the two species are somewhat similar and their coexistence seems detrimental to both. Larger brook trout also may feed on Kamloops trout fry where they are present.

A lake containing both species will produce a lesser weight of fish than a lake containing only one. And even in those waters where it has done well, the fight of a large brook trout on light tackle does not begin to compare with the spectacular struggle of the Kamloops.

The chub is an annoying little fish that inhabits the shallows of a number of lakes. It is distributed widely in the low-lying lakes of most major watercourses in the province. It multiplies rapidly and feeds heavily on the same food stocks utilized by younger trout; in large numbers, it is capable of depleting the food stocks of a smaller lake in a relatively short time. It also is an annoyance to fly fishermen because it takes small flies eagerly. It has been introduced to only a few of the higher-elevation lakes that provide most of the Kamloops trout fishery, and that is a good thing.

Altogether those species which share the Kamloops trout's environment contribute little to its well-being; more often, the opposite is the case. The single exception is that of the kokanee, which has established its usefulness as a forage fish in a few instances. Fortunately, the great majority of Interior lakes — which were free of any fish to begin with — remain free of any species other than the Kamloops, and that is how it must continue to be if the Kamloops trout fishery is to be preserved.

The fishery is a resource that consists of more than just the fish, or the lakes, or the streams flowing into the lakes. All these things are vital parts of it, but they are only the most visible components of a vastly complicated whole. The forests and fields, the soil and the shape of the land, the complexities of climate, the wildlife of the water, woods and air — all these things, and more, play subtle and interconnected roles that make the resource what it is. Some are understood and some are not; some can be measured and some cannot, and some still await discovery. Together, their ultimate yield to the angler is the miraculous, beautiful living thing that takes his fly with incredible strength and leaps wildly into the sunlight, its sides flashing brighter than all the world around it.

Chapter Four

Management of Kamloops Trout Lakes

O f British Columbia's nearly 22,000 lakes, 3,448 are located on the Southern Interior Plateau. A survey taken in 1963 showed that 191 of them, or 5.8 percent, were under management for sport fishing; another 308 contained sport fish but were not under management. Of the remainder, 1,864 were classified as unsuitable for sport fish; 10 were classified as suitable but did not contain fish, and the status of 1,075 others was unknown.

The number of lakes under formal management and the number containing sport fish are undoubtedly higher now. And surely both totals will continue to increase as new roads are punched into previously inaccessible lakes and growing numbers of anglers put more pressure on the fishery.

If they had been left to themselves, the Kamloops trout lakes long since would have ceased to produce the fishing that has made them famous. Of course there probably would have been exceptions — a few lakes with just the right combination of circumstances to maintain a natural balance between fish and food stocks over a period of decades. But there are not many of these, and the mission of management is to ensure the continued healthy production of as many lakes as possible. From humble origins, it has grown to be a complex and expensive task that involves much more than merely balancing food stocks and trout populations; it also entails setting regulations to govern the activities of fishermen who use the resources, enforcing those regulations, protecting and restoring the lakes and their surrounding environments, and many other diverse and complicated labors.

History

The original range of the Kamloops trout was somewhat limited, but was vastly increased by the stocking of previously barren lakes. As we have seen, these early stocking efforts often were haphazard. Sometimes they resulted in spectacular success; the planted trout took advantage of untouched food resources in the barren lakes and grew to very large size in the first few years after stocking. These trout retained all the splendid characteristics of the wild Kamloops trout because, in truth, they were

79

wild fish, taken from wild native runs. At first there were no hatcheries to provide an alternative source of trout for stocking. This was fortunate, for it preserved the unique character of the Kamloops trout at the same time its range was being increased.

Often the lakes planted with Kamloops trout produced their best fishing in their third, fourth or fifth years. But by the time trout had been in these lakes for six or seven years, the spectacular growth rates tapered off as surplus food stocks were depleted and a natural balance was struck between the trout population and the resources of the lakes. This was true at least for those lakes where trout reproduced in limited numbers. But in those waters where trout reproduced in large numbers, there was no balance; the increasing population drew heavily on the food stocks of the lakes and the average size of the trout continued to decline until, eventually, only large numbers of small trout remained. In some others, the average size of the trout varied widely from time to time because there was no spawning or no fry recruitment in dry years. And finally, there were many lakes were no spawning could take place at any time, and these were totally dependent upon continued periodic stocking.

At first the reasons for all this were not fully understood. Management, insofar as it existed at all, was unsophisticated and lacking a sound biological base. But that began to change with Mottley's study of the trout populations in Paul, Knouff and Hyas Lakes.

Paul Lake received its first trout in 1909; Knouff in 1917, and Hyas, which lies in the same watershed as Paul Lake, was planted in 1923 with eggs taken from the spawning run that had developed in Paul Lake. Mottley examined records of the average size of the trout in the 1926 spawning runs at all three lakes and found that the fish in Paul Lake, 17 years after the initial plant, averaged 2½ pounds; those in Knouff Lake, eight years after stocking, averaged 8 pounds, and those in Hyas, three years after introduction, averaged 12 pounds. From this, Mottley concluded that changes in the size of the trout populations and subsequent depletion of food stocks was responsible for the declining average size of the trout. He also found that in some lakes natural factors inhibited spawning or tended to reduce survival so that a natural balance was established between numbers and food stocks, and in these waters the trout remained at a good average size. He saw that it was necessary to establish and maintain such a balance in all waters in order to ensure good fishing in the future, and that in order to do so it would be necessary to treat each lake individually in terms of its capacity to produce trout and food for them to eat. Left alone, the resource functioned inefficiently; management was needed to assure optimum yield.

In order to establish a management program along these lines, it was first necessary to do a great deal of research. The life history and habits of the Kamloops trout had to be learned and documented, along with the characteristics of each lake targeted for management. This was the job Mottley set out to do at Paul Lake.

The fishery at Paul Lake was on the decline when he arrived and Mottley began a study of the lake and its trout to see what could be done to restore it. From his surveys he concluded that Paul Lake was capable of producing a yield of 8 to 10 pounds of fish per surface acre. He decided on a plant of 200,000 fry, figuring a survival rate of 5 percent or 10,000 fish. The surface area of Paul Lake is about 1,000 acres, so a survival rate of 5 percent should have yielded about 10 fish per acre weighing 1 pound each.

The plants were made and Mottley's calculations proved almost exactly correct. Paul Lake gave up catches that were very similar numerically and in weight to what Mottley had predicted; the fishery was stabilized, and for the first time a program based on sound scientific management had been applied to one of the Kamloops trout lakes.

But Mottley's work at Paul Lake was only a beginning. Little or nothing was known of the productivity of other lakes in the area, and they continued to be managed mostly by seat-of-the-pants guesswork. Funds were scarce and there was little public interest or support for a large-scale management program. Not until after World War II did such an effort begin to materialize. The Fisheries Research Group was then established and began a survey of more than 300 lakes in the province, gathering information about their productivity and the species of fish that inhabited them. The survey yielded data on water temperature, climate, drainage, chemical content and all the factors known to influence productivity. Using this information as a guide, the province was divided into separate "limnological areas," each with its own characteristics and management problems. The survey also led to a more sophisticated formula for stocking Kamloops trout lakes.

The formula was based on the dissolved mineral content (TDS) of each lake and its shoal area (littoral development, or percentage of bottom area lying at a depth of less than 10 meters). The acreage of shoal area multiplied by the TDS value yielded a figure for the productivity of the littoral zone. This information, combined with a determination of the average size and numbers of trout desired and a calculation of expected fry survival, produced a figure for the number of trout to be stocked per acre of shoal. The remainder of the lake − that portion with a bottom area lying more than 10 meters below the surface − was stocked at one-tenth the rate of the shoal area.

Establishing such a formula is the easiest part of the whole business. The problems really begin once the lake has been stocked. In order to ensure that it will continue to produce at maximum levels, there must be measurements of natural reproduction and angling harvest, and if there is some special problem of predation it must be measured too. It is, at the very least, extremely difficult to obtain accurate measurements

81

of all these things without the expenditure of a great deal of time, effort and money — and no publicly-supported management agency, least of all the B. C. Fish and Wildlife Branch, has the resources to do this adequately on every body of water under management. Instead, it is necessary to use estimates and averages based on the experience of a large number of waters and update them periodically by checks on individual waters. This usually works well enough for the fishery as a whole, but it may mean that individual lakes will be at least temporarily out of balance from time to time due to changes in the local environment that cannot be anticipated. But it is the best method that knowledge and available resources permit.

Despite the knowledge gained through the research begun by Mottley and the experience gained in all the years since, the stocking and management of lakes still is far from being an exact science. In fact, much the opposite is true; even with sophisticated formulas and surveys of the characteristics of individual lakes, so many variables enter into the equation that the outcome of a management program usually can be predicted only in the most general terms. Dr. Peter Larkin summed it up well when he wrote:

"The difficulty of categorizing types of established trout populations in lakes which contain only trout is abundantly reflected in the dilemma of the management biologist when he is asked to decide if a barren lake will be suitable for trout. Even at an expense out of proportion to the situation it is doubtful if he could predict, except in the most general terms, what type of trout population would eventually develop. In some recent situations in British Columbia it would have been difficult even to predict whether Kamloops trout would survive in a lake. Thus the fish culturist does not as yet have sufficient knowledge of the limnological and physiological requirements of Kamloops trout to make a rapid and inexpensive evaluation of the potentialities of a barren lake. Considering the complexity of the problem he is not likely to have such knowledge for some time to come.

"In consequence, the cheaper and more direct alternative of experimental introduction is most frequently employed, despite the possibilities of failure. The guiding principle has been and probably will continue to be for some time, that it is better to get something done and perhaps guess wrongly than to be overcautious and accomplish nothing."

Source of Stock

While some researchers were at work surveying the lakes, others were studying the best source of the trout that would go into them. There were a number of important questions to answer: Would it be more economical and efficient to use hatchery brood stock instead of wild fish? If so, could other strains of rainbow trout from alien habitats be used? Would they offer the superior game qualities anglers had come to

A large Kamloops trout leaps vainly in an attempt to escape a fish trap on the inlet stream at Knouff Lake. The trap is one of many built by the Fish and Wildlife Branch to hold ripe trout before they are stripped of eggs and milt.

expect of the Kamloops trout? And if trout from wild stocks proved to be more desirable, could they be raised in hatcheries before stocking?

The answers to all these questions now are pretty well settled. But they did not come easily, and the search for them sometimes produced serious damage to the fishery.

The traditional source of trout stocked in the Kamloops waters always had been existing runs of wild fish. This was a satisfactory source as long as introductions were carried out in a haphazard, informal way. But when the government began a formal program to stock barren lakes and maintain the populations of those where there was no natural spawning, the need for eggs and fry became much greater. Traps were erected in spawning tributaries and spawning trout were captured in them and stripped of their eggs and milt. Sometimes the eggs were held until the eyed stage and then stocked; more often they were hatched and the off-spring were held in hatchery ponds before stocking. But this method had shortcomings. For one thing, there never was enough money to build as many traps as were needed, or to pay personnel to operate them. For another, weather sometimes interfered with operation of the traps; in dry years, the spawning runs often lasted such a short time it was impossible to service all the traps, and in high-water years floods or freshets some-times swept away the traps or left them filled with debris.

In an effort to solve these problems, it was decided to import rainbow trout eggs from hatchery stocks in Washington, Oregon and California. The eggs were hatched in British Columbia hatcheries and the fry were planted in some Interior lakes. The result was near disaster. The eggs were from domesticated stocks that had been held in hatcheries for many generations where they were bred selectively for early maturation. This is a desirable trait for trout used in a "put-and-take" management scheme where longevity is not important and it is necessary to raise new "crops" of trout for harvest in the shortest possible time. The eventual result is a strain of trout that becomes sexually mature at an age of 1½ to 2 years, before the trout have had an opportunity to grow large enough to provide any real sport. "Put-and-take" management is based on the early harvest of large numbers of small trout, and many of the fisheries of Washington, Oregon and California are managed in that way. But the Kamloops trout fishery is based largely on the harvest of maiden 2- or 3-year-old fish weighing 1 to 2 pounds or more, and the imported trout simply could not live long enough to grow to that size. Anglers complained they did not provide sport comparable to the native Kamloops.

Stump Lake was an example. It was treated to remove coarse fish in 1957 and stocked in 1959 with fish from various hatchery strains in the United States. These included some "Donaldson trout," an extremely fast-growing strain of fish bred by Professor Lauren Donaldson of the University of Washington. The lake was opened to fishing in May, 1961, and it quickly became apparent that the foreign fish had not adapted well.

They did not produce firm flesh, they "fought like squawfish" and there was an extremely high mortality rate of 2-year-old Donaldson trout — almost resembling winter kill. Fortunately, Stump Lake lacks any tributaries where trout may spawn so that these fish were unable to reproduce and perpetuate their undesirable sporting characteristics. But some of these fish were planted in at least one other lake where spawning does occur, and they quickly cross-bred with the Kamloops trout already in the lake. The resultant offspring were a far cry from the fast-growing, spirited native Kamloops, and even now — nearly 20 years after the event — the trout population of the lake still suffers from this unfortunate genetic intrusion.

These highly unsatisfactory results put an end to the importing of eggs and made it clear that only the native Kamloops trout provided a satisfactory source of eggs for the stocking program, despite the difficulties inherent in gathering them from the spawning tributaries. It would simply be necessary to put up with those difficulties in order to preserve the quality of the fishery.

But there still remained the question of how fry from these eggs were affected by hatchery rearing before release. The fact that for many years fry had been held in hatchery ponds before stocking did not provide the answer; nothing was known about their survival and growth after release. How successful were they in competition with wild fish? Did they survive and grow as well? More research was needed to find the answers.

Stuart B. Smith, former head of the province's trout hatcheries and now head of the research secretariat for Alberta Environment, selected Corbett Lake near Merritt for an experiment designed to answer these questions. He took trout from the same stock and divided them into two lots; one lot was raised in hatchery ponds and the other in natural ponds under wild conditions. Then both lots were placed in Corbett Lake. Records were kept of their size as they were caught and a comparison of those records was made to see which group had fared better. Not surprisingly, the fish raised under natural conditions were found to be more efficient in competition with those raised in the hatchery, but the difference in growth rate was not exceptional. Furthermore, there was no evidence to indicate the hatchery fish had suffered any great mortality. Finally, it was found that the cost of raising fish in a natural environment and then transplanting them was considerably higher than the cost of raising fish in a hatchery and transferring them. From this, Smith concluded that in a lake where anglers made heavy demands upon a naturally-reproducing population of trout, supplemental stocking with fish reared in a hatchery environment would be practical, economical and acceptable to anglers (so long as a wild, native run of Kamloops trout was the source of the hatchery stock).

Present management policy follows the results of this research. In lakes where no spawning takes place, stocks are maintained by the periodic introduction of hatchery-reared fry taken from the eggs of wild fish. Hatchery-reared fry also are used to augment populations which are at least partly self-sustaining but are subject to unusual angling pressure. There is no lack of wild fish to provide the eggs for these fry, but it seems there never will be enough money or personnel to build and operate as many egg-taking stations as could be used.

There also have been attempts to transplant Kamloops trout to waters outside the province, and this seems a good time to consider them. As we have seen, the introduction of Gerrard strain Kamloops trout to Pend Oreille Lake, Idaho, was notably successful, but the story of other experiments is almost uniformly one of failure; if the trout survived in their new home, they did not grow or perform as well as the Kamloops trout in its native environment, and in some cases they did not survive at all.

One example was the planting of 250,000 yearling Kamloops trout by the Washington State Game Department in the pools behind Priest Rapids and Wanapum Dams on the Columbia River. Very few of these fish ever were caught by anglers; the great majority simply disappeared, either having migrated to sea or died.

In another experiment, Kamloops trout from Pennask Lake were obtained for stocking in Lenice Lake, an exceptionally fertile low-lying lake in the semi-desert environment of Central Washington. The experiment was prompted by members of the Washington Fly Fishing Club of Seattle, who were dissatisfied with the rainbow stock that had been planted in Lenice Lake. These fish displayed the early maturation typical of domesticated hatchery strains, with most reaching sexual maturity by the age of 2 years. Many died at that point, and many of the survivors were spawn-bound and did not grow much beyond the size they had attained when they reached sexual maturity. Since Lenice Lake was under restrictive regulations designed to produce trophy-sized trout, the hatchery strain seemed ill-suited to the management program.

The club, in cooperation with the Washington Game Department, other clubs and the Cooperative Fisheries Research Institute at the University of Washington, obtained the Pennask Lake stock in the hope that these fish would grow larger than the hatchery stock in Lenice Lake. Pennask Lake trout normally reach sexual maturity at 3 or 4 years of age, so it was possible they would have one or two years more growth than the hatchery fish before ripening the first time.

But it didn't work out that way. For reasons not completely understood, but possibly related to the higher water temperatures of Lenice Lake and its tributary, the Pennask fish matured at an earlier age in their new home and did not grow appreciably larger than the hatchery stock already in the lake. The experiment provided a lot of interesting work for club members and graduate students from the university, but in terms of its purpose it was largely unsuccessful.

The results of these and other experiments involving importing or exporting trout have made it abundantly clear that trout do best in the environment to which they have adapted through ages of evolution, and they cannot be transplanted into a radically different habitat with any reasonable expectation that they will survive, grow and perform as they did in their native waters. In the early years of North American fish culture, transplants and the introduction of exotic species were the rule rather than the exception, but modern biologists have learned to be a great deal more cautious.

Access and Management

In order to effectively manage the trout population in a lake, a biologist must have a good estimate of the harvest by anglers — in addition to some knowledge of the lake's productivity and the extent of natural reproduction. The size of the harvest depends on the intensity of angling effort, and that seems directly proportional to the accessibility of the lake.

Many of the population centers of the Southern Interior Plateau are built on the shores of major lakes, and most important highways also follow natural watercourses and provide access to some of the large, low-lying valley lakes. These lakes, because of their size, accessibility, physical characteristics and intermingled species of fish, almost defy any effective management. For example, it once was estimated that intensive trout management of Okanagan Lake would require stocking 3.5 million fry annually. A fry plant of such massive size could be made only at the expense of hundreds of smaller lakes which require annual stocking.

So it is in the smaller, higher-elevation lakes that fisheries managers exercise most control, and accessibility is an essential element to be considered in their management plans. Lakes that lie close to major population centers and are easily accessible by road usually receive the heaviest angling pressure and have the highest rates of angling harvest. They require the most intensive management, including frequent checks to gauge the degree of angling effort and success. Waters that lie somewhat farther from cities or towns, or that are reached over somewhat more difficult roads, receive somewhat less attention and therefore require somewhat less intensive management. And lakes that are nearly inaccessible — reached only by anglers on foot or horseback or in float planes — usually receive only light fishing pressure. The harvest in these lakes is minimal, and unless there is some specific problem that requires management attention, they may be left largely on their own.

A new road built to a previously inaccessible lake almost always sets off a predictable sequence of events. Fishing pressure increases rapidly as more and more anglers find their way to the lake, and the harvest rate goes up. The removal of part of the standing population of trout leaves more food for each of the survivors, and soon there is an increase in the average size of the trout. This may add to the lake's reputation among

87

anglers and cause even more of an increase in angling pressure. Angling methods and locations and the natural tendency of fishermen to keep the largest fish combine to favor the selective harvest of larger trout until most of them are gone. This leads to a decline in the number of spawning fish and repeat spawners and an increase in the number of young fish taken in the catch. After several years of this, the cream of the crop has been skimmed off, no large or older fish remain and the harvest cuts further and further into the population of younger, smaller fish. At this point, word begins to get around among anglers that the lake is "fished out" and the pressure begins to ease off as fishermen look elsewhere for their sport. If this happens, the lake eventually may return by itself to its former character. But if a competing species is present it may quickly fill the gap left by the depleted trout population and prevent its recovery. And if the lake happens to be one with a fishing camp or resort, the owner may suffer economic hardship from the decline of the fishery.

Ideally, a management program should anticipate such problems and move to solve them before they get out of hand. But this is much more easily said than done. Constant vigilance over all these lakes is an impossibility, and often problems do not become apparent until it is too late to reverse them easily. The recent increase in the popularity of winter ice fishing has made matters even more complicated than before, creating additional management headaches. The Fish and Wildlife Branch, with its limited resources, does all that could reasonably be expected to keep track of what is going on in the numerous waters under its stewardship, but the number of accessible lakes grows steadily larger and the task grows increasingly difficult.

The size of a lake has much to do with the impacts of accessibility. Smaller lakes are easily covered by anglers and are easier to manage. Angling exploitation of larger lakes is less efficient, but they also are more difficult to manage.

British Columbia's lakes are under public ownership, and this is both good and bad. It is good in the sense that angling opportunities are available to everyone, not just to those able to afford them, and presumably this means a larger reservoir of public support for fisheries conservation and management. It also allows the government to pursue a policy of uniform management and to establish and follow long-term programs for the development of fisheries, and these things would not be possible if some or all of the water was in private hands. But public ownership also creates the problems caused by unlimited access and intensive harvest. Pressure on the lakes also means pressure on their surroundings, which may indirectly damage the fishery. The unenviable task of fisheries managers is to somehow find the delicate middle ground between the privileges of public access and the problems it inevitably creates. And that is why they must manage people as well as fish.

Regulations

The purpose of regulations is to protect fish from people. This is ironic, because the purpose of management is to provide fish for people. But because man exists in such great numbers, and is such a wasteful creature, and is so often ignorant of the consequences of his acts, it has become necessary to adopt regulations to ensure that no individual takes a disproportionate share of fish or commits other acts that might damage the use and enjoyment of the fishery by others. No one much cares for regulations, but generally we have only our own bad habits to blame for them.

The Indians who were the original inhabitants of the British Columbia Interior were partly dependent upon fish for their subsistence, but their attention was focused more on salmon than on the native Kamloops trout. In each case, however, the fisheries survived and were healthy despite the Indian harvest, and much has been made of the fact that the Indians apparently treated the resource more wisely than white men. It is questionable whether that was a result of a conscious attitude on the part of the Indians or merely a reflection of the relatively small Indian population and the relatively primitive technology of the Indian fishery. But there is no doubt that the Indians held the salmon and other fish in reverence and treated them accordingly, so that both salmon and trout fisheries were at or near their natural levels of peak abundance when the first white settlers arrived in the country.

Those settlers lacked the reverence toward fish that the Indians had, and they caught and killed both salmon and trout in any way they could, without much thought of the future. In so doing they were no different from any other colonists of the time; the world still was a very large place with seemingly unlimited resources, and the prevailing philosophy was that it made little difference if all the trout in a lake were exterminated because there would always be another lake over the next ridge that would hold just as many. And in the case of the Kamloops trout, most of the lakes that provided its native range were so large that even the more intensive fishery of the white man was not able to do too much damage to their trout populations.

But growing population and access and individual catches of several hundred fish a day – like those of Lambert at Fish Lake – eventually made it obvious that some form of regulation would be needed to preserve the fishery, especially in the smaller, more vulnerable lakes that were then being stocked for the first time. At first these regulations were in the form of bag limits that were applied uniformly to all waters, without any consideration for the characteristics of individual lakes or the varying size of the trout populations in them. These regulations were intended only to prevent greedy fishermen from taking so many fish that others would be deprived of a share, or to prevent the

89

Anglers

Coarse fish were removed in 1962

This lake contains only trout. Please keep it that way.

The transport of live fish and the use of fish for bait is illegal and can result in spoiled trout fishing.

Province of British Columbia

Ministry of Recreation and Conservation

This sign above the boat dock on Roche Lake warns anglers what can happen if live minnows are used for bait. The Fish and Wildlife Branch has erected similar signs at many lakes.

collective angling effort from taking so many trout that none would be left to spawn. They worked well enough to start with because the angling pressure was extremely light by modern standards.

But as more and more fishermen found their way to the province and put more pressure on the fishery, it became necessary to make the bag limits more restrictive and to establish other regulations to prevent snagging, spearing or shooting fish and to ban the use of explosives or traps. And the explosive growth of population and transportation in recent years has forced the adoption of additional regulations designed not only to protect the fishery but its surrounding environment. Regulations were enacted banning the use of fish eggs, corn, meat or other substances as "chum" to attract fish, to control the use of baits in certain areas and to regulate canning of trout. Strict laws were written to prevent littering and to control the discharge of sewage from recreational vehicles. All these measures are designed to control people's behavior, and it seems that nowadays a fisheries biologist must have training in psychology, sociology and law enforcement as well as science.

Licenses were sold to pay for the management program and support the enforcement of the regulations. And, like anglers nearly everywhere else, British Columbia fishermen seem to have adopted the attitude that purchase of a license gives them an inherent right to criticize the management of the fishery and the activities of the Fish and Wildlife Branch. Indeed, many anglers seem to treat their licenses as if they were a doctoral degree in fisheries biology instead of a piece of paper that gives them the privilege to fish.

This does not mean that management people should not listen to their public critics. Their duty is to provide the kind of fishing the angling public desires, so they must be aware of those desires. Similarly, regulations cannot be established in a vacuum; the regulatory process is essentially a political one, and regulations are worthless without at least some public agreement on their necessity. Problems arise when vocal groups of fishermen insist upon having their way and pressure managers into actions that are against their better judgment, or when the management authorities forget who is paying the bill and go their own way. Good communications and a happy medium between these two extremes is necessary for effective management and public satisfaction.

British Columbia anglers have frequently been critical of the management of the Kamloops trout fishery, and sometimes with ample justification. It has been far from perfect. But most of the critics lack the perspective that comes from comparing the efforts and policies of the Fish and Wildlife Branch with those of the management authorities in other provinces or states. When such a comparison is made, the record of the Fish and Wildlife Branch stands among the best in many areas, most notably in its thorough and patient research into the life history of the Kamloops trout and the productivity and carrying capacities of various Kamloops trout lakes. This research has allowed the Kamloops trout management program to be based on solid biological data that is sorely lacking in the management programs of most other jurisdictions, and the fishery has profited greatly from it. At least in this one respect, British Columbia anglers are more fortunate than they think they are.

Perhaps one reason for the criticism of fisheries management is that the angling public usually is not all of the same mind in what it wants. There always are some who want to catch large numbers of fish regardless of size, and others who are willing to settle for a few trout if only they are large. There are some who do not understand why bait fishing or trolling gear should not be allowed in every lake, and others who do not understand why such methods are not banned from more waters. There are those who enjoy ice fishing and those who oppose it, those who claim they cannot fish without an outboard motor to push them around and those who say outboards ought to be banned from all but the largest lakes. Often the debate over such issues is acrimonious and more emotional than factual, and the managers are caught squarely in the middle. Whatever decisions they make will be unpopular with some.

The ironic thing is that all sides are correct. The resource still is large enough and varied enough to accommodate all these interests, and each license buyer, as a "stockholder" in the fishery, is entitled to the kind of fishing he desires. In essence, each point of view is that of a particular minority, and the trick that managers must master is how to accommodate all these conflicting minority views.

Until recently, regulations establishing seasons, angling methods and bag limits were applied uniformly to nearly all the waters of the province. There is a certain advantage in this; such uniform regulations are easily understood and remembered by anglers, and they are relatively easy to enforce. But there also are serious disadvantages; uniform regulations ignore the special desires of certain angling groups and the special needs of certain lakes or trout populations. The increasing pressure on the fishery and the growing expressions of support for certain kinds of fisheries have prompted a trend away from general regulations to specific rules for individual waters. These exceptions now are listed as "Restrictions Specific to Certain Waters" in the regulations published annually by the Fish and Wildlife Branch.

Among the most important of these new regulations are those establishing trophy fisheries or fisheries where only artificial flies may be used. Peterhope, Pennask and Salmon Lakes were the first to receive these special regulations. Dr. James Hatter, then director of the Fish and Wildlife Branch, announced in the summer of 1969 that in the following year those three lakes would be managed under rules that permitted the use of artificial flies only. The regulation is less restrictive than the "fly-fishing-only" regulations in force in many areas, permitting the use of any type of gear so long as there is an artificial fly at the end of the leader (the actual regulation requires a lure consisting of "a single hook that is dressed only with fur, feathers, textiles, tinsel or wire or any combination thereof and does not have a spinning device or any external weight").

The British Columbia Wildlife Federation, an organization of sportsmen's groups, had given a qualified endorsement to the idea of the restrictions, but there was some internal opposition within the Fish and Wildlife Branch. Eventually this was overcome and the restrictions were adopted in recognition of the desires of fly fishermen, but also — and perhaps even more important — as a means of protecting the fisheries of the three lakes involved. The success of similar regulations as conservation measures in other jurisdictions undoubtedly had much to do with the decision to go ahead.

In the decade since, seven other lakes have been added to the "artificial flies" list in the management area that includes much of the Kamloops trout fishery. These are Corbett, Doreen, Flyfish Lake No. 1, Hagsquith Lake, Rampart (also known as Hans Lake), Rock Island and Siglet Lakes. Many others have been established elsewhere in the province, and a separate, more restrictive fly-fishing-only classification has been established on other waters, including Spruce Lake in the Kamloops management region and Valentine near 100 Mile House (the regulation requires "angling with a rod to which is attached a reel, a fly line connected directly to the reel or attached to a backing line connected to the reel, a leader and not more than two artificial flies").

Even more important has been the establishment of seven "trophy" lakes in the Kamloops area during the past few years. At first, the "trophy" regulation banned bait and restricted anglers to lures with a single hook, and in most of these waters the limit is two fish a day. Beginning in 1979, the regulations were amended to require artificial flies only in these lakes — Badger, Spooney, Blue, Ernest, Island (in the Highland Valley), Janice (also known as Long Island Lake) and Pass. These are among the most productive waters in the area, and under trophy management they will receive only limited plants of trout and the harvest will be controlled so they always will have good numbers of older, larger trout available for anglers to catch. This type of management not only caters to the desires many anglers have to catch trophy-sized fish, but it also represents the highest and best use of these productive lakes.

The trophy regulations are a fine thing for the future. As long as they remain in effect they will assure the availability of at least some of the type of angling that made the Kamloops trout fishery famous in the beginning. If there is a flaw in the program, it is that most of the lakes designated for trophy management are only marginally accessible and so far the same protection has not been extended to rich waters that are easily reached. Some of these waters — Lundbom Lake near Merritt is an example — are among the most valuable and productive lakes of all, priceless resources that should be preserved at any cost. In the case of

Lundbom Lake, a proposal was made to place it under trophy management, but fishermen in Merritt who enjoy quick, easy access to the lake, quickly joined in vocal protest and caused the Fish and Wildlife Branch to drop the plan — a classic example of group pressure defeating a management plan that obviously was in the best interests of the lake and, over the long term, would have been in the best interests of those who selfishly opposed it. Without the protection of trophy regulations, Lundbom has been badly misued and abused, and under the present anything-goes management its days as a productive fishery surely are numbered — a senseless waste of an irreplaceable resource. It is to be hoped that other popular, productive waters will receive protection before they are ruined by overuse, wrongful use or ignorance.

To date there has been no catch-and-release requirement imposed on any of the Kamloops trout waters, although the serious decline of the province's steelhead runs has prompted such regulations on many rivers. Still, even in the absence of such regulations, growing numbers of Kamloops trout anglers have begun to release most or all of their catch. This is a sign of growing public acknowledgement that fishing ought to be considered primarily a form of recreation and only secondarily — if at all — a source of food. It is a healthy attitude, one that permits anglers to use the resource without taking anything from it. The Fish and Wildlife Branch has encouraged this trend, even going so far as to publish instructions on the proper way to release trout — which is far more than most management agencies have done. The voluntary acceptance of this philosophy may mean that catch-and-release regulations eventually will be used to protect outstanding but threatened fisheries, such as the one in Lundbom Lake.

But regardless of whatever form they may take, the wave of the future almost certainly will be one of increased regulations. As long as there continues to be more fishermen, and more users of the resource, there will be a need for more regulations to protect the latter from the collective impacts of the former.

Habitat Improvement

There is another side to management that usually does not receive much attention from the public. It involves the restoration of damaged habitat or the improvement of marginal waters. Usually it is very costly work, both in terms of manpower and materials, and it is undertaken only when the potential benefits seem relatively certain and substantial. In its most common form, this type of management involves the chemical treatment of lakes to remove coarse fish and improve the habitat for trout. But it also sometimes involves structural improvements of one kind or another.

There are many examples of this kind of work and we will mention here just two that are typical. One was the construction of a diversion ditch by the Fish and Wildlife Branch which connected the Salmon River

A fly caster at work on Corbett Lake. To his right is a floating pondmill and on the hill at upper right is a windmill, both used to help aerate the lake in winter.

with Salmon Lake. The flow of water through the ditch aided circulation in the lake and solved a chronic problem of summer and winter kill. A concrete flow-control structure later was added to allow better control of streamflow through the diversion ditch, reducing erosion, improving fish passage and increasing survival and recruitment of trout to Salmon Lake.

Another project — small but nevertheless important — involved the inlet to Heffley Lake. Trout ran up the stream to spawn during the spring runoff, but the lower reaches of the stream usually had dried up by the time their offspring were ready to migrate downstream to the lake, and as a result there was no fry recruitment to the trout population in the lake. The Fish and Wildlife Branch installed an 8-inch pipe in the streambed with a catchment box at the upper end, providing a safe passage through the normally dry section of the stream so that the fry could reach the lake.

A more unusual type of structural work has involved the construction of pondmills on lakes with marginal oxygen levels. These devices are small windmills that drive a piston or compressor, forcing air through a perforated pipe below the surface where it is dissolved into the water of the lake. This raises the oxygen content of the lake during periods of the winter when it otherwise might ebb to the point that trout could not survive. Two of these devices have been installed on Corbett Lake in an effort to prevent recurrence of recent winter kills.

Pondmill construction also has provided an opportunity for citizens to participate in habitat improvement. Members of the Kamloops Flyfishers Club, with permission from the Fish and Wildlife Branch, have built and installed a number of their own pondmills on small barren lakes lacking sufficient oxygen to support trout throughout the year. The results of this work probably have fallen somewhat short of expectations, but enough progress has been made to warrant continued interest and experiment. Perhaps one day the developing technology of pondmills will prove useful for expanding the range of Kamloops trout to many waters that are now incapable of supporting them.

Recently the Fish and Wildlife Branch has begun another program, one that probably is best described as a sort of preventive maintenance. This involves erecting large signs at popular lake access areas warning anglers not to use live minnows for bait because of the danger that some might escape and become established in the lake, eventually damaging or destroying the trout fishery. Scrap fish have been introduced in a number of lakes in this way, and it is much less expensive to post signs warning against the use of minnows than it is to chemically destroy large populations of scrap fish and restock with trout. The signs emphasize the importance of keeping a pure environment for trout.

All the activities described in this chapter — and others not described here — go together to make up the complex, costly business of fisheries management. At its best, management can never make all anglers happy all of the time; because it must balance a variety of competing interests and conflicting uses and somehow deal with the vagaries of natural systems, it must be content to settle for making some of the fishermen happy some of the time. Considering the resources it has had available, the Fish and Wildlife Branch has done that about as well as anyone could do. Whatever it has not been able to do, or has done imperfectly, is likely the result of the provincial government's unwillingness to give it more funds.

The attitude of the provincial government has become a serious threat to the continued management of British Columbia's fish and wildlife resources. While management needs have increased steadily and inflation has driven costs to enormous heights, the government has failed to provide the support or budgetary assistance needed to keep pace with either of these needs. Not only have the programs of the Fish and Wildlife Branch suffered from these attitudes, but so, inevitably, has the morale of its personnel. Fisheries managers have been forced to adopt what is essentially a defensive posture, trying — mostly by regulation — to save the best of what is left in the hope that future governments will act more responsibly toward the fish and wildlife resources of the province.

Fishing has become a big industry in British Columbia, bringing in millions of dollars annually. This alone is sufficient reason for any government concerned about the economic welfare of its people to see to it that the fishery is well cared for. But the value of the Kamloops trout transcends economic considerations; it is now a part of the heritage of British Columbians and of all the world's anglers, a fish of legend and a priceless legacy to future generations. It deserves the very best management, the most vigorous research, the most careful regulation. If the Kamloops trout could win from bureaucrats just a small measure of the respect it has won in the hearts of anglers, its future would be assured.

This remarkable photograph shows a sedge at the moment of emergence as the adult fly heaves itself out of the pupal shuck at the surface. The photo was taken by the author in a portable aquarium used for capturing and observing aquatic insects.

Chapter Five

The Food
of Kamloops Trout

The diet of the Kamloops trout is as rich and varied as the country it lives in. Its rapid growth and surprising strength are due to the assortment of mature and immature aquatic insects, crustacea, terrestrial insects, leeches and sometimes forage fish that are available to it. With so many possibilities to choose from, it seems the angler would face a difficult choice of what imitation to use; but each of these items has its own habits, time and place, and a little knowledge of these things will serve the angler well.

One may spend as much or as little time as he chooses in the study of entomology, but the time invested is well spent. It is hardly necessary to memorize a long list of Latin names, although some anglers seem to regard such knowledge as a sort of status symbol, and the names are provided here for those who wish them. But it is essential to be able to recognize the basic types of insects, to know something of their habits, their times of peak abundance and the places they are most likely to be found. Armed with such basic knowledge and with sufficient skill to properly present his fly, even an angler new to the Kamloops trout lakes is assured of some success. That success will grow with experience if time spent fishing also is spent in careful observation of all the subtle events that constantly go on around the fisherman. Slowly their nuances will begin to have meaning, and the meaning will grow to recognition of the many little clues that nature offers to the angler.

But at least some knowledge of basic entomology is required to begin with. Conventional fly fishing entomology has emphasized the mayfly, and in the long history of the sport more imitations of mayflies have been constructed than for any other insect. Mayflies are important in some of the Kamloops waters, but in general their role is much less than that of the caddis, or sedge, or of the scuds, midges, damselflies and dragonflies. This is the reverse of what many anglers have been taught, and the entomology of the Kamloops trout lakes therefore is likely to be at least somewhat new to them. Anglers from other parts of the world also often are surprised by the size of the insects they find in the Kamloops lakes, some of which are very much larger than anything they have seen elsewhere. This is particularly true of the sedge. And because the insects of still water have somewhat different habits from those of rivers, fishermen who have served their apprenticeships on trout streams must learn some new insect habits in order to fish their imitations properly.

The feeding habits of Kamloops trout also vary from those of trout in streams. And that seems a good place to begin.

Feeding Habits

When a Kamloops trout alevin has absorbed its yolk sac and emerges from the gravel into the open stream, it must quickly learn to pursue and capture its own food in order to survive. Rarely is there sufficient food in the stream to support all the emerging alevins, and the competition is fierce; the survivors are those which learn quickly and well.

To begin with they wait for the current to bring them food, taking in their mouths the myriad small items carried by the flow, sampling them and deciding quickly to reject them as inedible or to accept them as legitimate food. In this way they soon learn to recognize what is edible and what is not, and once recognition is established they no longer wait passively on the stream to serve them, but begin to pursue whatever food is available. In this way they acquire the habits of foraging beneath the surface for small nymphs or larvae and rising to sip in tiny flies trapped in the surface film.

These habits are carried with them as they migrate downstream to the lake where they will spend most of their lives. And once they reach the lake, their schools fan out into the shallows and begin feeding on the more abundant food resources they find there: Water fleas and copepods, small midges or little terrestrial insects that fly or are blown onto the water. They feed eagerly and well, and the mark of their passage is a succession of tiny dimples in the surface near the shore.

As yearlings, they begin feeding on smaller scuds found in shallow weedbeds and turn to the pursuit of the larger nymphs and pupae of aquatic insects. Most of their feeding still is close to shore, and they continue to feed on terrestrials caught in the surface film. While feeding in the shallows they are extremely vulnerable to predation from herons, ospreys, kingfishers and eagles, and the survivors of these aerial assaults soon learn the value of cover. Somehow they sense they are less visible from above when they are over weedbeds or dark boulders on the bottom, and they concentrate more and more in such areas.

As adults they feed heavily on scuds and these are the mainstay of their diet. The nymphs and larvae of aquatic insects also play an important role, and because of the abundance of subsurface fauna the trout are content to forage in the depths for much of the year. Only a hatch of considerable size and duration will induce adult Kamloops trout to rise freely and feed upon the surface. The spectacular sedge hatches of late spring and early summer produce the best rises, and the appearance of flying ants in late spring or early fall also sometimes triggers a good rise of fish. Some lakes also have mayfly hatches that prompt a fair rise in late

May or early June, and the trout feed eagerly just beneath the surface film during the spring midge hatches and damselfly nymph migrations.

Food is most abundant in weedbeds and over shoals, but adult Kamloops trout have learned the value of caution and enter shallow water reluctantly. On bright, calm days, they may not enter the shallows at all until the light is off the water in the early evening. On dark or windy days the larger trout enter the shallows more willingly, but they are wary and alert and a disturbance — such as that caused by an outboard motor in operation — may cause them all to leave for hours at a time.

When feeding, larger trout tend to follow the edges of the shoals or cruise in a regular pattern. If the shoals offer abundant cover, such as dark gravel or thick weedbeds, the trout may remain over them for long periods and browse for food within a relatively small area. But if good cover is lacking, the trout usually will not stray far from the protection of deep water, making only occasional short forays onto the shoals, then returning to their outer edges. By studying rise patterns carefully, or observing the movements of trout if the water is clear enough, an angler can deduce with fair accuracy the usual course of feeding trout and take station at an appropriate place to intercept them. The characteristics of cover and shoal conformation often channel different trout along the same feeding lanes, and when a hatch is in progress the trout will tend to rise often at points along these lanes. Once such a spot is discovered an angler may go back to it with confidence that it will reward him again and again, but keen and careful observation is necessary to locate such places.

The feeding patterns of Kamloops trout generally follow an established order throughout the year. Small midges usually are the first insects to hatch when the ice goes off the lakes in May, and trout take the rising pupae and sometimes the adults resting on the surface. The small midges are followed quickly by larger ones, and some lakes have enormous emergences in the last few days of May. The incredible abundance of these insects on waters such as Tunkwa Lake is difficult to describe; they are so numerous they fly into the mouths, eyes and ears of anglers, driving them near the point of distraction. The pupae are so abundant that it is a simple matter for trout to cruise under the surface with open mouths and intercept dozens at a time with little effort. Fishing frequently is poor at such times because there is so much natural food available to satisfy the trout.

As the midge hatches taper off, the mayflies begin to come on. There are mayfly hatches in virtually all the Kamloops trout lakes, but only a few waters have hatches large enough to stimulate a consistent rise of trout. The best rises occur on windy days when the breeze concentrates the adult flies in one particular corner or area of a lake.

A few warm days in late May or early June may be enough to bring on the flying ants, and great numbers of these may end up trapped in the surface film of a lake. Their futile struggles attract the attention of trout and may set off a rise.

The same warm weather sets the damselfly nymphs in motion, and under normal conditions their hatching migrations will peak during the first two weeks of June. Trout take them avidly just beneath the surface, sometimes with splashy rises that mislead anglers into thinking that some surface fare is being taken. The dragonfly nymphs also are active at this time, but their movements are seldom visible to the casual observer and they are most often taken by trout in submerged weed thickets or along the bottom.

The middle of June usually brings the first great sedge hatches and the trout feed wildly on emerging pupae and adults. The awkward, fluttering motions of the big traveling sedges set off spectacular rises and this is the time when the dry-fly fisherman comes into his element on the Kamloops trout lakes.

The hatches taper off quickly after the first week in July; the summer sun begins to warm the surface waters of the lakes, circulation ebbs and in the depths the temperature zones begin to form their invisible layers. Discouraged by the heat and light of the summer sun and the lack of surface food, the trout seek deeper water. The scuds, taken in lesser numbers during the spring hatches, now become the most important food, along with snails and leeches. It is a hard time for the fly fisherman on most waters, a time when he must fish his fly slowly and deep in order to tempt the trout, or plan his fishing very early in the morning or late in the evening in hopes of finding a few fish that will rise when the light is off the water. The problem is not so acute in the cooler, high-elevation lakes, but even in those waters there is a summer lull to the fishing.

Early in September the flying ants come again, although usually not in such large numbers as in the spring. But they are much more eagerly received; having gone two months without substantial surface fare, the trout rise to them willingly and still will take a floating imitation days after the flight has ended and the last natural has disappeared. These flights offer the dry-fly angler his last good chance of the year, though their timing is very uncertain.

Warm Indian-summer days often bring on a hatch of backswimmers, but the trout usually are reluctant to take them and will not do so with consistency until the hatch has been under way for several days. From early September on through ice-up, the scud remains the principal source of food for the Kamloops trout. On balance, over a year's time, it is the most important food of all. Sedges, in those lakes with good hatches, are next, followed by the midges, which continue to hatch at a steady rate throughout the season following the peak emergence in the spring. The nymphs of damselflies and dragonflies are next most important in the season-long diet, followed by leeches, water boatmen and backswimmers, mayflies and other organisms.

The time sequence of insect activity and emergence may be acclerated or delayed by the vagaries of weather, but the order generally is unchanging. But the same is not true for the preference of trout for certain organisms. Not only does it vary from season to season, but it may vary from one generation of trout to the next, depending upon changes in the lake. When trout are stocked in a lake for the first time, they begin to prey on the most vulnerable organisms in it — usually the scuds and the sedges. In time, the numbers of these organisms may be reduced to the point that succeeding generations of trout are forced to turn to other foods. If the lake becomes seriously overpopulated, the stocks of all aquatic insects and scuds may be depleted, leaving plankton as the main source of food — a situation in which the top of the food chain must prey upon the bottom, since the intervening links will be absent. The presence of forage fish also complicates matters, and we will see later what complex relationships may develop when forage fish are part of the equation.

Fortunately, angling harvest, natural factors and/or management policies act to keep trout populations within safe limits in the majority of lakes, so the angler can feel confident that the feeding patterns and sequences described here generally will hold true for most of the waters he fishes.

Plankton

The plankton consists of a multitude of tiny plants and animals, most too small to be seen individually by the unaided eye. But the plankton is of critical importance; it is the foodstuff of many larger organisms that provide food for trout, and it may be an important fish food itself.

The planktonic organisms are the link in the food chain through which nutrients in the water are converted to proteins. The plankton is a teeming population of plants and animals, producers and consumers, living in open water near the surface, a complex community within itself.

The plant life of the plankton consists of diatoms, blue-green and true-green algae, flagellates and the pollen or spores of terrestrial or shore-based plants. These, plus bacteria and parasitic fungi, are the instruments for converting nutrients to organic proteins. In turn, they provide food for the animal life of the plankton.

The diatoms are most numerous, and they are found in many shapes and sizes, offering a fascinating study beneath a microscope. Blue-green algae is very common in the Kamloops trout lakes and often is apparent as the extremely thick and heavy bloom that occurs in many lakes during the warm summer months. The blooms come in pulses, followed by dieoffs which leave the stench of rotting algae hanging heavily in the air.

103

Decaying blue-green algae also draws heavily upon the oxygen in the water and is a primary factor in summer kill.

True-green algae also is common, as are the chlorophyl-bearing flagellates, and one of the latter, called *Ceratium,* may cause heavy yellowish blooms in the late summer.

The animal life of the plankton includes crustacea and rotifers. The crustacea are the more important of the two. They are the largest organisms found in the plankton, the greatest consumers of plant material, and they provide the largest source of trout food. They include the Branchipods, Ostracods and Copepods.

The Brachiopods include the Cladocerans, which numbers among its species *Daphnia,* the water flea, so named because they move around in a series of "hops" through the water. Barely visible as individuals, they are an extremely important source of food for younger trout in the Kamloops lakes.

Daphnia feeds on algae, protozoa, bacteria and most any other form of organic material it can find. Relatively few individuals survive through the winter, but eggs deposited before winter begin to hatch as the water warms in the spring. The population grows rapidly as hatching continues, but then just as quickly declines as trout and other creatures begin to consume the little organisms in large numbers. In lakes with long growing seasons, or during especially warm summers, a second population pulse may occur early in the fall. One survey found that *Daphnia* comprised 58 percent of the food of Kamloops trout fry in lakes.

The Copepods include *Cyclops, Diaptomus* and *Epischura,* among other species. These tiny creatures feed upon algae, especially diatoms, and other animal plankters. They also make up part of the diet of young trout, but do not rank near the importance of *Daphnia.* The Ostracods are minute crustaceans of lesser significance.

All the tiny animals and plants of the plankton follow a fairly regular cycle. Some rise to dominance at one time and some at another. There never is a time when the water is entirely free of these organisms. In the winter some remain dormant and there is little growth or reproduction among those which remain active. Diatoms are the most common forms during winter and there are one or two maverick species which reach their maximum populations during the coldest months.

The amount of plankton is least as winter draws to a close. But gradual warming of the water after ice-out restores the activity of the dormant creatures and speeds the hatching of eggs deposited before the snows. Then, like a garden bursting with the freshness of spring, the tiny organisms begin to grow and breed until they explode in a climax of energy and movement until the environment no longer can sustain them, and other organisms move in to feast upon them. Their tiny societies grow and collapse beneath the unseeing eyes of anglers, and both in

104

life and death they provide the basic fodder for all the other living creatures of the lake.

Throughout this cycle, the sun gives and sustains life. The plant colonies must remain near the surface where they can receive maximum light, and the animal plankters must stay close by in order to be near their source of food, which is the plants and one another. The greatest concentrations of plankton usually are within three to five feet of the surface. Where all this food is present, the trout also must be somewhere near. Unless driven down by oppressive heat and light, trout will be found where they are able to feed on the creatures that consume the plankton, or where they are able to get at the plankton themselves. To know and understand the cycles of the plankton is to know and understand the key to life in a lake, and such knowledge is pleasing in itself as well as being useful to an angler who will take advantage of it.

Scuds

 Among the larger forms of crustacea, there are two members of the order Amphipoda that are common in the Kamloops trout waters. One of these, *Gammarus limnaeus,* is the single most important source of food for adult Kamloops trout and is a creature readily imitated by anglers.

Gammarus is present to some extent in nearly all the Kamloops trout waters and is taken as food by trout from spring through late fall, usually constituting the bulk of the trout diet during the summer and fall months. It ranges in length up to an inch or a little more and in color from a dull khaki to a brilliant turquoise, with light olive the most common. Scuds and the fly patterns tied to imitate them invariably are called "shrimps" by anglers; undoubtedly this is because while they are at rest, scuds hold themselves in a crescent-like posture that superficially resembles the shape of a true shrimp. This has prompted many fly tiers to construct imitations on bait hooks or other curved-shank hooks, and although these patterns look deadly, they really are not very good imitations. The reason is that the scud's body becomes elongate when it is in motion, and trout rarely take scuds that are not in motion. Scuds are very mobile little animals, using their seven pairs of legs for swimming or to grasp and climb submerged plantstocks. Their normal swimming motion is in a forward direction, but they are also capable of swimming upside down and/or backwards, which they do frequently under stress.

The segmented exoskeleton (literally a skeleton on the outside of the body) is formed of relatively hard material that is manufactured from calcium absorbed from the water. In order to grow, the scud must periodically shed its exoskeleton and grow a new and larger one. The abandoned exoskeletons often may be found floating on the surface of lakes.

Gammarus is an omnivorous scavenger, feeding on both decaying plant and animal matter. It ranges to depths of 50 feet, but is most at home from the surface to a depth of about 10 feet. It is sensitive to light and in shallow water it tends to hide in weedbeds or under rocks during the day, but its presence usually may be established by turning over a few rocks in the shallows near the shore — which will send the scuds scurrying in search for a new hiding place.

Gammarus is an extremely fertile creature and under favorable circumstances will breed several times during a single growing season. It is common to see mating pairs locked in embrace while swimming through the weedbeds. Females carry their young in brood pouches and these so-called "pregnant" scuds are easily recognizable by the bright orange spot of the brood pouch, which actually is the color of the tiny scuds inside it.

Hyalella is the other Amphipod genus common to the Kamloops trout waters, and two species — *Hyalella azteca* and *Hyalella knickerbockeri* — are represented. In general appearance and habits they closely resemble *Gammarus,* but there are several important differences. Most significant is the difference in size; *Hyalella* seldom exceeds a third of an inch in length. It also appears in a wider range of colors, from blue to bright red, although light brown, yellow and green specimens predominate. *Hyalella* also prefers shallower water than *Gammarus,* and is found in greatest numbers in aquatic vegetation very close to shore. Its preference for extremely shallow water makes it an especially important food source for juvenile Kamloops trout, and that fact — plus its diminutive size and enormous numbers — usually discourages anglers from attempting to imitate it. *Hyalella* also is sometimes taken by larger trout, but their primary interest is in the larger, deeper-ranging *Gammarus.*

A good gammarid imitation is absolutely essential for a Kamloops trout fly fisherman. Patterns recommended for the purpose include the Golden Shrimp, Werner Shrimp and "Baggie" Shrimp (these and other fly patterns will be discussed in detail in a following chapter).

Snails

 The snails (*Gastropoda*) are extremely important as food for trout in some lakes, particularly during the months of July and August when the trout tend to feed in deeper water. Snails are most abundant at depths of 15 to 30 feet, although they occur in good numbers at lesser depths. They are at home in beds of *Chara* weed or other submerged aquatic plants, and the trout browse for them there.

In most of the Kamloops trout lakes, snails are a supplement to some main item in the trout diet — albeit an important one. In some lakes, however, they are the primary summer food source, and the trout in such lakes almost invariably are thick and fat and well-conditioned from feeding on them. Snails are extremely abundant in Stump Lake, for instance, and they account for much of the bulk and weight of the trout in that lake. A layer of snail shells several feet wide may be found at various points around the shoreline of the lake and it is impossible to walk along the shore without having shells crunch underfoot like so much broken glass.

Lymnaea and *Physa* probably are the two most common genera found in the Kamloops trout waters. Both are snails that build distinctive spiral shells and the primary means of identification is the direction of the spiral — *Lymnaea* spiraling to the right and *Physa* to the left. Despite their importance as food for trout, snails are of only minor direct concern to anglers because of the difficulty involved in imitating them; there is simply no way to match the appearance and habits of a nearly stationary organism that spends most of its life clinging to the stems or leaves of submerged plants.

Yet there are occasional circumstances in which snails may become temporarily susceptible to imitation. This is the phenomenon known as the "snail rise" in which the snails abandon their usual haunts and rise to the surface, attaching their "foot" to the bottom of the surface film and hanging there. In this posture, they are extremely vulnerable to trout. The reasons why they do this are not clearly identified, but are thought to be related to oxygen depletion in the water associated with the warm temperatures and poor circulation of some lakes in late summer. The theory is that the snails rise to the surface in an effort to obtain more oxygen. Anglers in the British Isles have developed imitations to fish in the surface film during such occasions, but it hardly seems worthwhile for Kamloops trout fishermen to follow suit; the phenomenon apparently occurs only rarely in North American waters, and the temperature and oxygen conditions associated with it surely would make the trout themselves slow to feed and so sluggish they could scarcely give a good account of themselves. Those who fish the Kamloops waters should be content to give thanks that the snails are there to help grow trout that are fat and strong and should be satisfied to use other imitations in their fishing.

For the angler-naturalist interested in pursuing such matters, this partial listing of species common to the Interior lakes is provided:

Gastropoda

Gyraulus arcticus	*Lymnaea modicella rustica*	*Physa politissima*
Gyraulus parvus		*Physa propinqua*
Helisoma hornii	*Lymnaea stagnalis wasatchensis*	*Stagnicola vahlii elongata*
Lymnaea caperata	*Menetus exacuus*	*Valvata lewisi*

KAMLOOPS

Annelida

The annelids include the leeches (*Hirudinea*), aquatic earthworms (*Oligochaeta*), flatworms (*Turbellaria*) and roundworms (*Nematoda*). Of these, the leeches are most useful to both fish and fishermen.

Aquatic leeches are flat, ribbon-like creatures found in a wide variety of lengths, although those between one and two inches long are most often found in trout stomachs. They swim with a distinctive motion similar to that employed by the sidewinder rattlesnake in its perambulations across the desert sand. The most common colors are black, muddy brown, dark gray and gray with mottled dark green spots. Their mouths are in a small sucker at the anterior end; another, larger sucker is at the posterior end. They feed on small worms, snails and insect larvae, but they also have a well-known prediliction for blood, and anyone who makes a regular practice of swimming in the Kamloops trout lakes should be prepared for the ugly sight of a leech clinging to his body.

Leeches are hermaphroditic, with each individual having both male and female reproductive organs. However, they do mate, exchanging packets of sperm cells, and are incapable of self-fertilization. Eggs are laid in cocoons in the water and development and growth are direct without a larval stage. They are nocturnal in their habits and during daylight they remain hidden under rocks or vegetation. Like many other types of fauna in the Kamloops trout lakes, they may be found easily by turning over rocks in shallow water. Leeches are most abundant at depths of 10 to 50 feet, but also are commonly found in shallow water. Despite their nocturnal preferences, solitary individuals frequently emerge from hiding during the day and swim within two or three feet of the surface, and these are taken readily by trout. They are most important to trout during the summer months when they may constitute a substantial portion of the trout's diet, along with scuds and snails.

The other annelids — aquatic earthworms, flatworms and roundworms — are of lesser significance. The first two are relatively abundant but are seldom taken by trout (except for the earthworms used as bait by trollers).

The following leech species are common in the Interior lakes:
Hirudinea

Erpobdella punctata	*Nephelopsis obscura*
Glossiphonia complanata	*Piscicola punctata*
Haemopis marmoratis	*Placobdella montifera*
Helobdella stagnalis	*Theromyzon occidentalis*

Fly patterns often used to imitate the leech include the Black Matuka Leech and the black-bodied Carey Special tied on a large, long-shank hook.

Insecta

The insects, both aquatic and terrestrial, provide much of the food for Kamloops trout and offer a wealth of subjects for imitation by the angler.

The study of aquatic insects is a captivating one. For most anglers it begins casually when they catch a trout and note, when they clean it, the wonderful and diverse contents of its stomach. If they think about it at all, it soon occurs to them that it makes good sense to imitate these things, and in just this way has many a fly fisherman been born. From such beginnings it often is just a short step to the assembly of a collecting kit, killing bottle, preservative formula, microscope, books and a growing knowledge of the insects that spend all or most of their lives in or on the water.

A fly fisherman never can learn too much about the insects he tries to imitate, and knowledge — particularly for the Kamloops trout fisherman — is not always easy to obtain. The past decade has seen the publication of a literal flood of new angling books, many concerned with entomology, but even so the literature still lacks a comprehensive survey of the entomology of Western waters. The series of magazine articles by Jim Kilburn remains the best entomological work for the Kamloops fly fisherman, but those articles never have been combined in a single publication and are not readily available. And even Kilburn's work was not all-encompassing, although it covered the most important aquatic insects of the Interior lakes.

So the angler who wishes to learn more about the entomology of the Kamloops trout waters must rely primarily on his own resources, although there are many published works that will provide useful background information and teach him to recognize the types of insects he encounters. Some anglers have set up small freshwater aquariums in their homes and stocked them with plants and insects taken from the Interior lakes and have learned much by watching the behavior of their captives. Others have taken samples and preserved them for study under microscopes, using entomological keys to identify them by individual species. But such elaborate study is the exception rather than the rule, and most anglers are content to take a few samples and use them as models for imitative fly patterns. It is important, however, that the imitation be constructed while the sample still is fresh because the subtle colors of the natural will fade even in the best preservative.

Collecting insects need not be a complicated business and it requires only a little equipment. A small-mesh net or a common kitchen strainer with an extension added to the handle will work as a collecting tool — and something of the sort is necessary because it is amazingly difficult to capture an insect on the surface with bare hands, and the insect may end up getting crushed in the process. A few small bottles will serve as containers, but they must be airtight to prevent evaporation of the liquid preservative. For the casual collector, a satisfactory preservative may be made by mixing a solution of one part white vinegar to 10 parts of rubbing alcohol.

One should not take more samples than he needs; the insect populations of the Kamloops trout waters already are under pressure enough from predation by trout in the lakes and the birds that live around the lakes.

Obtaining specimens of the natural insect may only provide half the information necessary to construct an effective imitation. Some effort also should be made to study the behavior of the natural in the water, whether in its natural environment or in a home aquarium. The reason is that many insects have distinctive forms of locomotion which must be considered in designing a fly pattern. A fly that is close in color, shape and size to a natural still may appear lifeless in the water if it is not tied with the proper design and materials to imitate the movements of the insect it is intended to represent. Observing the motion of the natural will also provide the angler information that will be useful in fishing the imitation.

The insects of greatest importance to the Kamloops trout fly fisherman include the damselflies and dragonflies (*Odonata*), the sedges (*Trichoptera*), midges (*Diptera*), mayflies (*Ephemeroptera*), water bugs (*Hemiptera*), beetles (*Coleoptera*), stoneflies (*Plecoptera*), and the terrestrial ants, bees and wasps (*Hymenoptera*).

Dragonflies and Damselflies

The order *Odonata* is divided into two suborders, *Zygoptera*, the damselflies, and *Anisoptera*, the dragonflies.

Damselfly nymphs are characterized by long, slim, segmented abdomens culminating in two or three distinctive leaf-like gills that are positioned vertically in relation to the body. They have three pairs of legs attached to the thorax and large eyes set widely apart at the front of the head. They are predaceous animals equipped with an extensible labium which they use to capture prey. The nymphs range in color from dark olive to light reddish-brown, always lighter on the ventral surface. Color is not a determinant of species because it may vary among individuals of a single species. The most reliable method of identification is to examine the vein structure of the gills.

Adult damselflies usually deposit their eggs in weeds or rushes near the shoreline just under the surface, or on the surface itself. Once the eggs hatch, the nymphs go through a series of instars, or molts, before reaching maturity. Mature nymphs may be as long as 1½ inches.

Nymphs usually are found clambering over submerged vegetation in shallow water or waiting there in concealment, hoping some form of prey will pass within striking distance.

 In most years, the annual damselfly migration – or hatch – occurs during the first two weeks of June in Kamloops trout lakes at about the 3,500-foot elevation level, although the emergence may begin a little earlier or later if the spring season is warmer or cooler than usual. At this time the mature nymphs swim to the surface and then strike out in a horizontal direction until they encounter rushes, weeds, logs or other structures upon which they can climb out of the water. They swim with a sculling motion created by rapid flexing of the abdomen, with the posterior gills acting as a sort of oar. During their migration they are silhouetted by the light from above and become easy targets for feeding trout. During a heavy emergence trout may become extremely selective and it is necessary for anglers to have an imitation that is not only close in appearance to the natural, but also one which is somehow capable of closely resembling its swimming motion. An entirely satisfactory solution to this problem in fly design has yet to be found. However, during the early or late stages of a hatch, the trout do not seem to be so particular and an imitation that is close in color, shape and size to the natural usually is adequate.

If the nymph succeeds in safely reaching a plantstock or log or some object which extends from below to above the surface, it climbs out of the water and rests until the nymphal shuck begins to open and the adult fly crawls out. Then it must wait until its wings unfold and dry before it is able to take flight. As an adult, it continues its predatory habits, feeding on terrestrial insects or the adults of other aquatic types.

Adult damselflies are a common sight around any lake or pond during the summer months. Members of the genus *Enallagma* are practically ubiquitous on North American waters; they are bright blue and black damselflies familiar to nearly every fisherman. Like all damselfly adults, they are strong fliers with two pairs of clear, heavily-veined wings that are held vertically over the abdomen while the flies are at rest. The males are more vividly colored than the females. Members of the genus *Ischnura* also are common in Kamloops trout lakes; their adults are black with greenish markings on the thorax and blue markings on the tips of the abdomens in males and some females, while other females are brownish or dull orange.

Mating may take place in flight or while the insects are at rest, depending upon the species. The adults usually are not available to trout, but spent flies sometimes are taken in the surface film and occasionally trout will rise to adults blown momentarily to the surface on windy days.

Common species include:

Zygoptera

Enallagma boreale *Ischnura cervula*

Enallagma cyathigerum *Ischnura perparva*

Virtually every experienced angler/fly tier has developed his own imitation of the damselfly nymph and some of these will be discussed in detail in a later chapter. Two patterns often used as damselfly nymph imitations are the Self-Bodied Carey and the Six Pack, a variation on the Self-Bodied Carey. Nation's Blue is a pattern designed to imitate adult damselflies, although oddly enough it was intended to be fished under the surface, as we shall see later.

The nymphs of some dragonfly species are short, stocky and powerfully built; others are long, thick and bulbous in the abdomen. In all species, the gills are inside the abdomen and water is drawn in through an anal opening for respiration. This water may be expelled quickly by muscular action, resulting in a crude form of jet propulsion that drives the nymph forward in quick spurts. But the nymphs also have three strong pairs of legs attached to the thorax which allow them to crawl over bottom debris.

The dragonfly nymph is a fierce predator with a very powerful extensible labium that reaches out with incredible speed to capture prey. The nymphs range in color from olive gray to muddy brown, which provides appropriate camouflage in their preferred habitat of mud or decaying vegetation. Nymphs of smaller species may scarcely exceed an inch in length when they reach maturity; those of some larger species may range up to 2½ inches long.

Adults of different species use different means to deposit their eggs; some are laid in weed or plant stems, some are left in silt or mud on the lakefloor, and some are merely dropped into the water. The nymphs go through 10 to 14 molts during a span ranging from several months to a year or more, depending upon the species and the water temperature. When the mature nymphs are ready to hatch, they crawl toward shore until they find an object on which they can crawl out of the water, after which their hatching is similar to that of the damselfly. During their shoreward movement they become more vulnerable to trout than at other times, but still are far less susceptible to capture than damselfly nymphs swimming near the surface. Their emergence period in the Kamloops trout lakes is not as clearly defined as that of the damselfly; it may be-

112

gin as early as late May and continue through June or even longer.

Some adult damselflies have wingspans measuring up to five inches. They are strong fliers with clear, heavily-veined wings that are held horizontally at a 90-degree angle to the body when the insects are at rest. Like the damselfly adult, they have two pairs of wings, and again like the damselfly they continue their predatory habits during the adult stage.

Species of *Aeschna, Gomphus* and *Sympetrum* are common in the Kamloops trout lakes. *Aeschna* adults are large with blue markings; *Gomphus* adults also are large with black and yellow markings, and *Sympetrum* adults are smaller with shorter abdomens and a distinctive — and rather pretty — wine-red color.

These species are common to the Kamloops trout lakes:

Anisoptera

Aeschna eremita	*Gomphus graslinellus*
Aeschna palmata	*Sympetrum costiferum*
Aeschna umbrosa	*Sympetrum danae*
Cordulia shurtleffi	

Fly patterns used to imitate dragonfly nymphs include Nation's Gray and Green Nymphs; the Doctor Spratley in shades of black, brown, green and yellow, and the Black O' Lindsay. Nation's Red was tied as an imitation of the *Sympetrum* adult.

Sedges

The *Trichoptera*, caddisfly, or sedge, as it is customarily called in British Columbia, is as important to the Kamloops trout fly fisherman as the mayfly is to anglers who fish the British chalk streams or the limestone streams and spring creeks of the United States. Usually it is the only aquatic insect whose hatches are sufficient to set off a really good, consistent rise of Kamloops trout, and these rises occur periodically throughout the duration of the hatch, which may last several weeks. The annual sedge hatch unquestionably provides the dry-fly fisherman his best opportunity on the Kamloops trout lakes.

There are many species native to the Kamloops trout waters. The adults of some are quite small and take off quickly from the water after emergence; others are extremely large and are slow to take off. Frequently, the latter will rest on the surface for a time, stretching and drying their wings; then they spin or flutter for long distances across the surface, leaving little V-shaped wakes behind them, before finally taking flight for the first time. This behavior stimulates even the very largest trout to rise, and it is this phenomenon — the "traveling sedge" — that gives the Kamloops trout lakes an extraordinarily exciting type of dry-fly fishing that is unknown elsewhere in the world.

The sedges of the Interior lakes are case-builders. The larvae begin construction of a case soon after hatching, using whatever materials may be at hand. These may include sand or tiny bits of gravel, small empty snail shells, bark, twigs, bits of stems or leaves, even the needles from coniferous trees.

Characteristics of case construction vary between species and sometimes among individuals of the same species, so the cases are not a reliable guide to speciation. But regardless of species, the sedge larvae are remarkable architects; some of them construct intricate spiral cases from bits of plant fiber, or cylindrical tubes of sand and gravel, or miniature "log cabins" of bark and plant stems. Glands within the larva secrete a sticky silk that is used to bind together the materials of the case.

The cases seem to provide little protection to the larvae, at least as far as trout are concerned; they will willingly eat the larva, case and all. But the cases do offer camouflage; since they are made from material found in the natural habitat of the larvae, they blend well with their surroundings. But once a larva that has built its case from plant fibers at the bottom of a weedbed crawls away to an area of clear marl bottom, it becomes fair game for marauding trout.

The larva is a soft, segmented creature, usually light-colored over the portion that remains inside the larval case. The head and thorax, which may be extended beyond the opening of the case, usually are black or dark brown with a hard, chitinous surface. Legs attached to the thorax allow the larva to crawl slowly and awkwardly over the bottom debris, dragging the case behind it. The posterior end of the larva has small hooks to clutch the inside edges of the case to prevent the larva from being forcibly withdrawn through the anterior end. The head may be withdrawn inside the case when danger threatens, much as a turtle retreats into its shell. Sometimes there is a small opening in the posterior end of the case, sometimes not; in either case, water is drawn into the case by a gentle writhing motion of the larva and respiration is by means of gills on the abdomen.

The larvae go through several instars, either adding length to their cases or abandoning them to construct new ones. They are omnivorous feeders. Most species in the Interior lakes go through a single generation a year, entering the pupal stage in the early spring. During this stage the insect seals itself inside its case by constructing a porous membrane across the open end, which allows water to pass so that respiration can continue.

The transformation of the caddis pupa is as remarkable as that of the metamorphosis of the butterfly. The larva still is a humble, awkward, worm-like creature when it seals its case; when the pupa emerges two or three weeks later, it is a remarkably different creature. The color of the abdomen is darker and the abdomen itself is much larger; two pair of large, hairy wings have sprouted from its thorax and it has grown a pair of very long antennae, and its legs have grown longer, especially the middle pair, which have hairs along the trailing edge to help in swimming. It emerges from its case enclosed in a membrane, but the legs are free to allow it to swim to the surface. During its slow ascent it is extremely vulnerable to feeding trout, and the beginning of a large emergence may start the trout on an orgy of subsurface feeding. Once at the surface it may swim around for awhile, using its powerful middle legs like a pair of oars, but usually it begins to hatch as soon as it reaches the surface. The membrane splits slowly lengthwise down the back and the adult insect pushes and heaves to get itself out. Again at this point it is literally a sitting duck for feeding trout, and if the air and water temperature are cool it may take five minutes or longer for a large sedge to free itself from the pupal membrane. The hatching time for smaller species is much less.

The large sedges, which are of most interest to both trout and anglers, then begin the "traveling sedge" routine: They stretch and dry their wings, then flutter across the surface as if propelled by a tiny outboard motor, then take tentative, awkward flight, lifting off for short distances to fly like clumsy moths. They may return to the surface to repeat the performance a second or even a third time before they finally take wing again and fly to shore. While fluttering across the surface they are plainly visible to trout, which pursue and attempt to capture them with splashy, explosive rises. An angler can almost feel the mounting excitement of the trout as they chase the large, fat-bodied sedges; big Kamloops trout attack with a frenzy like that of housewives at a five-minute supersale. It is apparent there is a sort of competitive psychology at work among the trout at such times, and their normal instinct for caution is swiftly forgotten in their wild excitement.

At least, that is how it often is at the very beginning of the hatch. When it has been on for several days, and the trout have fed well, the excitement soon ebbs and the trout return to their normally cautious and selective ways. Then, even when the hatch is very heavy, an angler may have to work hard to fool just a few trout.

115

The surviving sedge adults fly to resting places in shoreside brush or trees, where they may remain for several weeks before mating. Most species mate in flight, but some return to the surface to do so. The adults are easily recognized by their long, tent-like wings, which they fold parallel to their bodies while at rest, and by their long, graceful antennae. The wings exceed the length of the body; usually they are mottled black and brown and are covered with tiny hairs. While the flies are on the water, the colors of their abdomens are visible to trout, and this is a key to proper imitation of the naturals. The colors range from black to orange, but the most common colors among the larger sedges are shades of green, ranging from dark olive to bright emerald; brown and gray occur with less frequency. The best advice is to capture one of the naturals and attempt to match the colors of its body as closely as possible. Adult sedges sometimes are confused with alder flies or the spongilla fly, but both of these are much smaller than the larger sedges found on the Interior lakes and both lack the mottled, hairy wings of the sedge.

Sedge adults do not undergo additional molts, as do mayfly adults, and after mating they deposit their eggs in various ways. In most cases, the female goes under water and deposits her eggs in gelatinous strings on the bottom, but some species deposit their eggs on the surface and others drop them in flight. Female adults returning to the water to lay eggs sometimes set off another rise of trout.

A full-blown traveling sedge emergence is an awesome sight, especially when one is seeing it for the first time. Anglers accustomed to fishing in other parts of the world usually are astounded both by the size of the flies and the size of the fish feeding on them. Few anglers come prepared with imitations large enough to match the size of the sedge adults, which may exceed 1½ inches in length. Often a No. 8 hook with a 2X long shank is needed for an adequate imitation, and the flies must be constructed to float well during a long retrieve across the surface to match the motion of the natural — a difficult problem in fly design when dealing with such a large imitation.

In the first edition of this book, I identified the traveling sedge as a member of the genus *Limnephilus*. Kilburn, in his later study of British Columbia entomology, identified it as a member of the genus *Phryganea.* His identification prompted me to collect additional samples and make further microscopic studies. As a result of that work, I now believe we both were correct and that "traveling" behavior is exhibited by both genera, and by more than one species of each. It may, in fact, be a behavior pattern that is related to the environment and the size of the insects, without any genetic origin. This is a rather esoteric question which probably has little interest for the average angler, who is probably content just to know that there are traveling sedges, but it illustrates how much work remains to be done on the entomology of the Interior lakes.

Hatches of the traveling sedge are not as widespread in the Kamloops trout lakes as they once were. The example of Knouff Lake already has been mentioned. When it was overstocked, the vulnerable traveling sedges were quickly eliminated by the large trout population. The same thing has happened on other lakes where the trout population grew too large either through natural reproduction or mistakes in management. The hatches never have become re-established under natural circumstances, and although there has been talk from time to time of attempting to transplant sedges from one lake to another, it seems unlikely this ever will — or could — be done. For one thing, it probably would require removal of trout from the lake into which the transplant was being made, and it would then be necessary to let the lake lie fallow for a good many years until the transplanted stocks had built themselves to the point that trout could safely be reintroduced. It seems very unlikely that either fisheries managers or the non-fly-fishing public could ever be persuaded that the traveling sedge is valuable enough to take a lake out of production for so long a time.

But there still are some lakes where the traveling sedges hatch in good numbers, and large trout still rise to them as they once did during the golden days on Knouff Lake. In a normal season, the first meaningful hatches may be expected around June 15 in a lake at about 3,500 feet elevation. For about two weeks the hatch will be heavy, but around the first of July it will begin to taper off. Fairly good hatches will continue sporadically through the first week of July, but usually by July 10 the numbers will begin to tail off rapidly and by mid-July the hatch will be completely over. On most lakes, the best hatches occur between 11 a.m. and mid-afternoon, convenient hours for the angler, but many lakes also have large nocturnal hatches which may stimulate the trout to feed even more aggressively than by day. Usually the latter half of June provides the best two weeks of dry-fly fishing for Kamloops trout — something the angler should keep in mind when planning a trip.

At least 10 genera have been identified in the Kamloops trout lakes and probably there are more. Very little work has yet been done to identify individual species of these genera, and the task of identification is formidable — the genus *Limnephilus* alone has about 250 separate species; *Phryganea* alone has about 30. So the following list includes only those genera which have been identified from the Kamloops trout lakes:

Trichoptera

Glyphopsyche   Molanna
Hesperophylax   Mystacides
Hydroptila   Oecetis
Ithytrichia   Phryganea
Limnephilus   Polycentrophus

Few efforts have been made to specifically imitate the larval stages of the sedges in the British Columbia lakes and there are no familiar patterns. But at least two old, familiar fly patterns — the original Carey Special and the Knouff Special — have a long history of use as pupal imitations, and recently a host of anglers have developed personal patterns, incorporating such modern materials as latex. The importance of the traveling sedge adults prompted the first efforts at dry-fly design in British Columbia, resulting in Bryan Williams' Sedge and several patterns attributed to Colonel Carey. Nation's Green Sedge, Nation's Silhouette Sedge and Nation's Silvertip Sedge, all wet flies, were impressionistic imitations of sedge adults. In recent years, the Tom Thumb and several variations of it have gained widespread acceptance as dry-fly imitations, mainly because the deerhair used in construction of these patterns gives them excellent floating qualities. Still more recently, the Vincent Sedge has won a growing number of followers as a particularly deadly floating imitation. Other patterns have enjoyed a brief place in the sun over the years, and the increasing popularity of fly tying in the past decade has spawned an ever-growing number of personal favorites.

Midges

The *Diptera,* or true flies, include a very large number of insects. The most important of these in the Interior lakes are the midges of the family *Chironomidae* and the so-called "phantom midge," *Chaoborus.*

Identification of individual genera and species of *Chironomidae* is difficult; it has been estimated there are more than 2,500 North American species, and the work of classifying all of them is far from complete. The problem is further complicated by the relatively small differences between some species.

 Chironomid larvae are found over a very wide range of depths, but are most common in shallow water, particularly in areas where the bottom consists of soft mud or silt. Many species construct soft, fragile tubes, which may be attached permanently to the bottom or carried around by free-moving larvae.

The free-moving larvae are taken most often by trout. The long, cylindrical, worm-like, segmented larvae respire by undulating inside their tubes; many feed on diatoms or algae, although some are predaceous.

There are four instars in the larval stage, which may last from two weeks to as long as four years for some species. In warm, eutrophic lakes, some species go through a number of generations in the space of a single summer. The larvae range in color from almost total transparency to deep red, with shades of green and bronze also common. The red larvae, known as "bloodworms," contain haemoglobin and are especially common in shallow, eutrophic lakes. Bloodworms are important trout

118

food in a number of Kamloops trout lakes, and the larvae are most active in late summer and early fall before they enter the pupal stage.

The pupal stage is brief. It begins when the outer larval covering, or integument, separates from the inner pupal integument, and the pupa then generally hides in bottom debris until pupation is complete. The pupae themselves are easily identified by white, tuft-like gills at the head, a thin, plainly-segmented body and a developing wingcase over the thorax. They swim with a rapid flexing motion of their bodies, but all this hard work propels them at a very slow rate. During their slow ascent to the surface, they are taken in very large numbers by trout, and they are most important to anglers at this point. Most are colored black over the body and most of the thorax, with plainly visible white rings around their bodies where the segments are joined. Other common colors are bronze with golden or yellowish rings where the segments join, or various shades of green with brownish rings. The presence of haemoglobin gives a distinctive reddish-bronze hue to the bloodworm pupae.

Once having reached the surface film, the pupae assume a horizontal attitude and continue swimming until the moment for hatching has arrived; then they become motionless while the pupal shuck splits open and the adult fly heaves itself onto the surface. On warm days the hatching flies may take flight immediately; on cool, damp days they may buzz rapidly across the surface for some distance before lifting off the water, and this rapid movement sometimes stimulates slashing rises from trout. Trout also sometimes rise selectively to flies sitting motionless on the surface in the brief moment between hatching and take-off.

The adults are rather like a mosquito in shape, although many are much larger than any mosquito. The pupae and adults of some species range up to an inch in length. The adults have thin, tapered bodies and clear, transparent wings, which may appear white in reflected light. The wings are held flat over the back of the fly while it is at rest, and in larger species the length of the body considerably exceeds the length of the folded wings. Adult males have prominent feather-like setae protruding forward from their heads, and all adult chironomids normally rest on the surface with their forelegs held forward and off the water.

Black is the most common body color in adults, especially in smaller species (the "black gnats"). Kelly green or emerald-colored adults also are not unusual, and tan, gold, bronze and red colors are found in the larger species, usually with black rings where body segments join. The adults join in mating flights over the water or around shoreside brush; after fertilization, the females deposit eggs in horizontal flight over the water or on the surface, or on emergent vegetation, depending upon the species.

Chironomids are available to trout throughout the season, from ice-out to ice-up. They may begin hatching as soon as a patch of open water appears on an otherwise still-frozen lake, and normally the first hatches are of very small insects, many too small for any practical imitation. Hatches grow steadily in volume until the last week or so in May when they peak on many lakes, and by then many larger species are hatching, including the "golden chironomid," which ranges up to an inch in length. In some lakes — Tunkwa already has been mentioned, and Minnie is another — the insect swarms are phenomenal and constitute a real annoyance. Thankfully, they do not bite.

The hatches taper off after late May or early June, but continue steadily throughout the season, usually heaviest in early evening. By late summer the first adults from the bloodworm larvae make their appearance and these also are large flies, comparable in size to the golden chironomid. These insects may hatch over a period of several weeks, from late August to early October, and all stages of their life cycle provide anglers with imitative opportunities during this time. The adults of all species survive from a few days to as long as two weeks, and die after mating and egg-laying.

In the wake of a heavy chironomid hatch, the surface of the lake is left littered with the vacated pupal shucks. The long, tapering, segmented cases, which appear black-and-white in the water, are familiar sights to anglers on the Interior lakes — and a possible clue that the trout will respond enthusiastically to a pupal imitation.

The woefully short list of genera identified in the Kamloops trout waters is good evidence of the large amount of work that remains to be done in this field:

Chironomidae

Allochironomus	*Endochironomus*
Chironomus	*Limnochironomus*
Cryptochironomus	*Prochironomus*

Despite its season-long importance as a food source for Kamloops trout, the chironomid has not attracted very much attention from fly tiers. The Carey Special, which, it seems, has been used at one time or another to imitate almost everything, sometimes is tied with a red body and is fished as a bloodworm imitation. Several tiers have experimented with personal patterns to imitate the larval stage of the chironomid, but none of these has caught on widely. The pupal stage is the most important to anglers and one of the first patterns designed to imitate it was Nation's Black. By modern standards, it is a relatively crude imitation and seldom is used any longer. Two fairly recent patterns which have received widespread acceptance are the TDC and the PKCK. There are no standard patterns for the adult, although again a number of anglers have experimented with different designs.

Chaoborus is a member of the family *Culicidae,* which includes the mosquitoes, but fortunately for anglers *Chaoborus* does not share the biting habits of its kin. Eight species are known, but it has not been determined how many of these are present in the Kamloops trout lakes. Its common name of "phantom midge" apparently is derived from its sensitivity to light; the free-swimming larvae remain out of sight in deeper water during the day, rising to the surface at night. Consequently, they are rarely seen by anglers, except when they are found in the stomachs of trout.

During its evening ascent or morning descent, the *Chaoborus* larva becomes a likely target for feeding trout, and Kamloops trout often feed on the larvae with a high degree of selectivity. A study by members of the Washington Fly Fishing Club of the stomach contents of Kamloops trout in Hihium Lake showed that *Chaoborus* larvae were an important item in the trout diet during the summer months.

Chaoborus is a small insect, seldom exceeding a third of an inch in length. The larvae are very difficult to imitate, not only because of their small size, but also because — for all practical purposes — they are transparent. If they have any color at all, it is likely to be a pale yellowish-orange. The adults bear a superficial resemblance to the chironomid, but may be identified by their distinctive, blunt proboscis.

A few anglers have experimented with larval imitations, usually sparsely tied with floss or dubbing, but there are no standard patterns.

Water Bugs

The order *Hemiptera* includes the backswimmers, *Notonectidae,* and water boatmen, *Corixidae,* both of which are of some importance in the diet of Kamloops trout. The *Corixidae* include 121 known species, the *Notonectidae,* 30; it is not known how many of each are present in the Kamloops trout lakes.

The water boatmen feed on the tiny plants and animals of the plankton and play an important role in converting this material into a form that is more readily available to trout. Water boatmen are short, stocky insects, the adults usually measuring little more than half an inch long. They prefer shallow, weedy water. Water boatmen overwinter as adults and lay eggs in the spring; the eggs hatch after a week or two and the nymphs go through five instars, each one lasting about a week. The only noticeable difference is a gradual development of the wings.

Water boatmen have three pairs of legs. The hind pair is most strongly developed, with a fringe of long hair on the trailing edges. These legs are used like oars to propel the insect at a very rapid rate through the water, and this distinctive swimming motion is the basis for the insect's common name. They rely on surface air for respiration, swimming periodically to the surface, quickly piercing it with their heads and gathering a "bubble" of air which is held against the ventral surface as they return to the bottom. With this small supply of air they are able to remain submerged for considerable periods.

The wings of water boatmen are finely-mottled black and brown, their abdomens creamy-yellow and segmented. However, the colors of the abdomen usually are obscured by the silvery bubble of air the insects carry with them under water. Adults are capable of flight, but only the nymphs are important to trout — and to trout fishermen. Although they are readily available to trout throughout the season, they seldom are taken in quantity, and then only when other food is lacking.

Backswimmers, in contrast with the water boatmen, are extremely fierce predators and will unhesitatingly attack creatures larger than themselves, including fish fry. They are somewhat longer, thinner insects than the water boatmen and adults may exceed three-quarters of an inch in length. Their name is derived from their unusual habit of swimming on their backs, using the rear set of their three pairs of legs which, like those of the water boatmen, are powerfully developed and equipped with a fringe of swimming hairs. Using these paddle-like appendages, they are able to swim at an astonishing rate of speed.

The swimming habits of the backswimmer have led to color adaptations which are the opposite of most aquatic creatures. Its wings, which are held over the back in beetle fashion, are mostly light yellow with mottled patches of black or dark brown; its abdomen, which faces up when the insect is swimming, is flat black and segmented. The backswimmer also is dependent upon surface air for respiration, but unlike the water boatman it pierces the surface film with the tip of its abdomen and hangs there, suspended, with its swimming legs outstretched, taking a much longer time to gather its air supply. Its sudden departure from the surface normally leaves a tiny dimple in the surface during flat-calm conditions and these may be observed by anglers from time to time. The backswimmer stores its air supply in abdominal grooves so that it, too, appears to be sheltered by a silver bubble while it is under water. Their life cycle is very similar to that of the water boatman, except that the backswimmer may go through more than one generation a summer, with adults emerging both in late spring and early fall.

Trout occasionally feed on backswimmers in the nymphal stage, but their greatest interest seems to be during large-scale emergences. Even then, it usually is two or three days before Kamloops trout begin to take notice of the hatch and start to respond to it. It would seem that the backswimmer is not one of the favorite foods of Kamloops trout, but they will take it when it is present and available in such numbers it cannot be ignored.

The order *Hemiptera* also includes the giant water bugs of the family *Belostomatidae,* and although these apparently are not widely distributed in the Kamloops trout lakes, they may be important in individual waters. Trout from a small lake in the Thuya chain were found to be feeding heavily and selectively on these bugs, which may exceed 1½ inches in length. These obloid bugs have a yellowish, segmented abdomen, three pairs of legs and faintly iridescent black or brown wings which curve over their backs in beetle fashion. Respiration is similar to that of the backswimmer.

Few fly patterns have been developed to imitate these insects. Jack Shaw, in his book *Fly Fish the Trout Lakes,* suggests using a standard Brown Hackle Peacock pattern with the hackle trimmed off on the top and bottom as an imitation of the water boatman, and it probably is as good an imitation as any. I have enjoyed some success with an experimental pattern designed to imitate a backswimmer and it will be described later. There are no standard imitations for the giant water bug, but an experienced fly tier who carries his equipment with him should have little difficulty constructing an on-the-spot imitation if it should prove necessary.

Beetles

The *Coleoptera* — aquatic beetles — are abundant in only a few of the Kamloops trout lakes. Those which are present are predaceous members of the family *Dytiscidae.* There are more than 400 species and they vary widely both in appearance and habits, particularly in the larval stage — which is when they are most available to trout. Roche Lake has a large population of these beetles — species unidentified — and the larvae are common in the weedy margins of the lake. With their free-swimming habits, slim silhouette and pale olive color, these larvae easily may be mistaken for damselfly nymphs by a casual observer. A survey of Okanagan Lake turned up members of the genus *Hydroporus.*

Kamloops trout apparently feed on these larvae only rarely, when other food sources are not readily available. For this reason, and because the larvae vary so widely in appearance, there are no standard fly patterns to imitate them.

Mayflies

Ephemeroptera, the mayflies, have received far more attention, in the literature of fly-fishing entomology than any other insect. Dry-fly fishing was invented because of mayflies, specifically the delicate duns and spinners that hatch in quantity on the British chalk streams. To tie and carefully present an imitation of the mayfly on a flowing stream is the very epitome of fly fishing, and the beauty and grace of these fragile flies exceeds that of the trout that rise for them so willingly.

Mayflies are much more abundant and important in streams than they are in the stillwater environment of the Kamloops trout lakes. Still, they are present to some degree in nearly every lake, and some waters have significant hatches that may provoke a good rise. It is a treat to see the hatching duns, fleeing before the wind like a fleet of tiny sailboats, and an even greater treat to see large Kamloops trout knifing through the waves to take them.

 At least five genera have been identified in the Kamloops trout lakes. Of these, the most important undoubtedly are the members of the genus *Callibaetis,* which includes 23 species (the number of species present in the Kamloops trout waters has not been determined). *Callibaetis,* in fact, probably is the most important stillwater genus on the Pacific Coast and is common in lakes from Northern British Columbia to Northern California.

From their earliest development, the nymphs of this genus are available to trout. They swim or crawl through weedbeds in shallow water. The nymphs have three tails and their fairly long, tapering abdomens have 10 segments, typical of all mayfly nymphs. There are three pairs of legs, each attached to a different thoracic segment. Depending upon the species and the water, mature nymphs range from a quarter to a half inch in length and typically are a dark gray color. Possibly because of the abundance of other subsurface food usually available, Kamloops trout do not seem to take the nymphs very often, except during prolific hatches when the ascending nymphs are most vulnerable.

Kamloops trout do feed willingly on newly-hatched duns, however. The duns, or subimagoes, usually are dull or dusky gray in color, with two tails. After hatching, they may rest for a time on the surface before taking flight, especially on cool days, and it is then that they are taken eagerly by trout. Those which escape the rising trout fly to shore and find resting places in the timber or brush where they quickly undergo a final molt. The resulting fly is called a spinner, or imago, and has a glossy look, with shiny, nearly transparent wings. Typical *Callibaetis* spinners have mottled reddish-brown markings along the leading edges of their otherwise transparent, graceful wings; they are dark blue or black along the upper surface of the abdomen and reddish-brown underneath, and their two long tails are smoky blue.

The spinners are so named because of their appearance in the mating flight, which takes place over the water; the flies bob up and down in a vertical posture which makes them look like tiny spinners, their shiny wings flashing like sparks in the sunlight. The female *Callibaetis* spinners may live for several weeks, mating and laying their eggs before finally falling spent to the water where again they are vulnerable to rising trout. In

124

many Western waters, the spinner fall interests the trout even more than the hatching duns, but this does not seem to be the case on the Kamloops trout waters.

Depending upon the elevation of the lake and the progress of the season, mayflies may begin to appear on the Kamloops trout lakes in the last week of May or the first few days of June. Prolific hatches may continue through June and even later on some waters, and the *Callibaetis* spinner fall may continue sporadically throughout most of July on lakes with heavy hatches. Occasional hatches of other genera may be noted through August, but usually these are not sufficient to set off a rise of trout.

In addition to *Callibaetis,* these other genera have been recorded in the Kamloops trout lakes:

Choroterpes	*Siphlonurus*
Hexagenia	*Tricorythodes*

The number of mayfly imitations is legion, and whole books have been devoted to various imitative theories and designs. However, the overriding importance of *Callibaetis* on the Kamloops trout lakes simplifies the problem for the angler; only a few basic patterns are needed to prepare for this hatch. Probably the best standard dry-fly pattern for the purpose is the familiar Adams, tied upright to imitate the dun and with spent wings to match the spinner. The Adams usually will work well enough on windy days, but on calm, bright days when the trout are feeding cautiously and selectively, a closer imitation usually is necessary. A slightly altered version of the Hatchmatcher series often works well at such times, tied with a dark gray goose flank feather for the body and wing and a very dark blue dun feather for the hackle. Various Dark Blue Upright patterns in size 14 work well as spinner imitations, and these also may be tied spent-wing fashion to match the fallen spinners. A selection of other standard mayfly patterns usually will be sufficient for the infrequent occasions when flies of another genus appear in numbers large enough to set off a rise.

Stoneflies

The *Plecoptera* — stoneflies — are fast-water dwellers never seen on lakes unless carried there by the wind from a nearby stream. Usually there are never enough of them to matter. But stoneflies are of seasonal importance on the Adams and Little Rivers where Kamloops trout from Adams Lake or the Shuswap Lakes often go to feed.

Stonefly nymphs cling to rocks in fast water. They are easily recognized by their two long, distinct tails and a pair of long antennae, a heavy wingcase and large, plainly segmented abdomens. The presence of two claws on each foot is another distinguishing feature. Mature nymphs may exceed 1½ inches in length and usually are yellow-brown or light tan in color. They go through a series of molts until they are ready to hatch into adult flies, at which time the nymphs climb out of the river onto rocks or boulders, their thoraxes split and the adult flies emerge.

Adults fly awkwardly with their four coarse wings. The heavily-veined wings are held flat over the back when the flies are at rest. The abdominal colors of the adults range from deep red or reddish-brown to yellow. The Adams and Little River hatches usually occur about the middle of April and provide good fishing in the week or two before the trout begin to turn their attention to the migrating swarms of sockeye salmon fry.

Most fishing is done with a nymphal imitation, and there are many standard patterns.

Terrestrials

Terrestrials are insects whose origins are of the earth rather than the water, but they include many forms whose mating flights or foraging may carry them over water where they become available to feeding trout. They include the ants, bees and wasps of the order *Hymenoptera*.

Of these, the ants are by far the most important to the Kamloops trout fly fisher. There are more than 700 North American species, so the task of identification is extremely formidable. For the trout fisherman's purposes, it probably isn't worth worrying about; it's enough to know that ants are on the water, and to be able to present an imitation of the appropriate size and color.

It is the winged, sexual stage of the male ant that appears on the water after the mating flight. Many times I have seen the surfaces of Kamloops trout lakes littered with the wreckage of these mating flights, with a density of more than a dozen insects per square foot of surface area. An ant fall of this magnitude presents a tremendous food resource for the trout and may set off an enormous rise. Many ant species may be present simultaneously, ranging from tiny black or cinnamon ants (the equivalent of a size 18 to 20 imitation), to medium-sized brown or golden ants (sizes 8 or 10). Sometimes the trout feed avidly on all of these, and sometimes they feed selectively on only one. And occasionally, on frustrating bright, still days, they may feed rarely, if at all, even though the surface is literally covered with struggling, dying ants. Usually the latter circumstance is not only a result of the weather conditions, but also is at least partly due to the abundance of subsurface food.

A string of warm days in late May or early June will start the ants flying. The spring flights usually consist of the large, black carpenter ants or smaller black ants. The response of the trout to these flights is not always consistent because they may occur simultaneously with prolific midge and mayfly hatches and damselfly emergences, and the trout may focus their feeding on one of the latter. But the season's second flights, which usually occur on warm days during the first two weeks of September, seldom fail to stir an enthusiastic response from the Kamloops trout.

126

These flights usually are dominated by medium-sized brown or golden ants, and their appearance almost always triggers a tremendous rise of trout that may continue for days.

The September flights usually involve smaller numbers of insects than the spring flights, but still there are more than enough to interest the trout. The eager response of the trout to these insects probably is at least partly due to the absence of surface food from their diets throughout most of July and August, and the fish rise as if they had been saving up all their energy for the occasion.

When trout are feeding wildly on ants, almost any fly that suggests the size and color of the natural will take fish. I have even caught them on a well-greased Leadwing Coachman under such circumstances. But there are a number of standard ant patterns, and many fly tiers have devised imitations of their own. The key is to design a fly that is not only a good match for the color and size of the natural, but also one that floats in the surface film. During the September flight of golden ants, I have enjoyed success with a pattern fashioned from cream-colored polypropylene yarn with a sparse deehair wing that floats in the surface film. No hackle is necessary.

Bees, yellow jackets and wasps, which are familiar enough they should need no description, seldom occur on the water in large numbers. Yellow jackets probably are the most common on the Kamloops trout lakes, but even these usually aren't present in sufficient numbers to tempt more than the occasional trout. There are no standard floating imitations, unless one considers the Steelhead Bee in small sizes.

Forage Fish

In a lake which contains only trout, the food chain is relatively simple and direct. Salts and nutrients in the water are converted to organic material by the plants and animals of the plankton. These, in turn, become food for the larger crustacea and aquatic insects in the lake which, in their own turn, become food for the Kamloops trout. The final yield is measured by the angler in the numbers, length, weight and strength of the trout he catches. Many variables may affect the efficiency of the system, but the progression itself is fairly direct.

The situation becomes much more complex, however, when a second species of fish is introduced to the environment. Regardless of what kind of fish it is, its presence complicates the existing relationship between the trout and the food stocks in the lake. The biomass — the total accumulation of all the plant and animal life of the lake — does not change, but now it is called upon to support two species at the top of the food chain. Directly or indirectly, some competition between the different species must develop for the available food stocks. Some interdependence also may be established between the two species, with adults of both preying on the young of the other. The two species may even develop an interrelationship that is partly competitive, partly interdependent. Any number of things could happen, but the point is that it is impossible for trout to share their environment with another species without being affected in some way, either subtle or radical, and the presence or introduction of a second species complicates the progression of the food chain and nearly always makes it function less efficiently.

The result need not always be totally unfavorable to the trout. It may establish a satisfactory predatory relationship with the second species and benefit in growth, if not always in numbers. This is what has occurred in Kootenay and Pend Oreille Lakes, and examples like these have led to experimentation elsewhere with forage fish. But these experiments have not always gone well, and in some cases the results have been extremely harmful to the trout. It now appears that a successful predator-prey relationship between trout and another species depends upon environmental factors that have not all been identified, and not enough is yet known to predict with any certainty the outcome of forage-fish introduction.

Of the forage fish utilized by Kamloops trout, the kokanee and the redside shiner are the most important and the most frequently encountered. The kokanee has been the more successful of the two, but the shiner has been more thoroughly studied, particularly in Paul Lake.

 The redside shiner (*Richardsonius balteatus*) is a small, silvery fish marked by a dark lateral band from its nose to its tail. Its lower sides and belly are silvery, its back dark olive or brown. Its name comes from the spawning coloration of the male, which develops crimson markings along its sides. Its natural distribution in British Columbia is within the Columbia and Fraser River watersheds, but it also has been deliberately introduced as a forage species in some lakes and accidentally introduced in others. It may grow to a length of five inches or more, but in most lakes with large populations adult fish seldom exceed three inches.

The redside shiner spawns in May or June, depositing its eggs over aquatic plants in lakes. The life span of an individual may exceed four years. Shiner fry feed on diatoms, copepods and other planktonic organisms. Adults feed on aquatic insects, crustacea and plankton. Shiners tend to move about and feed in schools. They spend the winters in deep water and move onto the shoals or into shallow water to begin feeding in the spring. Smaller fish have a particular preference for shallow water, and in lakes with abundant populations the schools along the shorelines sometimes are so dense that it is possible for anglers to scoop up fish in their hands. With warmer water temperatures in midsummer, larger shiners move off the shoals into deeper water, returning to the shallows again by the end of August. The winter offshore migration to deep water begins in October.

Shiners also tend to move into the deeper water during hours of darkness or on heavily overcast days. This movement is accompanied by a change in their feeding pattern. Observations in Pinantan Lake indicated that shiners fed primarily on algae during the day, then moved offshore and began feeding primarily on *Daphnia* during hours of darkness.

Shiners originally were absent from the watershed that includes Paul and Pinantan Lakes. The first shiners were observed in Paul Lake in 1945 and it is believed they were introduced via a stream flowing into the lake. Before the advent of the shiners, the diet of Kamloops trout in Paul Lake always had consisted chiefly of scuds, aquatic and terrestrial insects and plankton. At first, no change was noted in the feeding habits of the trout, and from 1946 to 1949 not a single shiner was found in trout stomachs, although it was obvious that the shiner population was increasing gradually. Then, after 1950, some drastic changes occurred.

These changes were of great interest to biologists and, because of the large amount of research that already had been done at Paul Lake, the situation offered a unique opportunity to study the results of the introduction of shiners on a Kamloops trout population whose prior history was well known and well documented. Peter Larkin, Stuart B. Smith, D. J. Crossman and R. E. Johannes carried out a series of studies aimed at determining the impact of the shiners on the trout population.

The first of these studies revealed that significant changes had taken place in the diet of trout by 1952. *Gammarus* and *Hyalella,* which had been important food for trout in earlier years, were found only rarely in trout stomachs, but shiners suddenly had become the main source of food for trout more than 12 inches long from July to September. Shiners also were becoming a significant part of the diet of smaller trout.

Later studies showed an increase in the consumption of shiners by trout of all sizes, along with a proportional decrease in the amount of plankton consumed by the trout. Terrestrial insects also declined in importance and the incidence of scuds in trout stomachs remained negligible.

A major decline in the growth rate of younger trout soon was observed. The sport fishery in Paul Lake always had been based primarily on two- or three-year-old trout, but by 1952 the growth rate of young trout had declined to the point that two-year-old fish no longer were reaching legal size. The average length of three-year-old fish had declined from nearly 14 inches in 1948 to less than 10 inches in 1952, although growth began to accelerate in the third year as trout began to feed more heavily on shiners.

These changes soon began to show up in the angling harvest from the lake. In past years, four- and five-year-old trout never had accounted for more than 10 percent of the annual harvest; in 1952, they rose to nearly

20 percent of the catch. The numerical size of the harvest also was affected. It averaged about 10,000 fish a year through the 1940s, but fell to 2,349 in 1954. It also was obvious that anglers were selecting heavily in favor of faster-growing trout, removing them from the population as soon as they reached legal size.

All these things were evidence of some sort of competition between the trout and the shiners. Apparently it had taken the trout several years to learn to prey on the shiners, or to develop a need to do so because the shiners had consumed the food stocks historically available to the trout. The biologists deduced that several things had happened. Competition between trout and shiners for scuds had reduced the scud population to negligible numbers, forcing the trout to turn more and more to the shiners as an alternative source of food. Smaller trout were handicapped in this competition because they were less able to capture or consume shiners than their larger brethren; without an easily available alternative food source to turn to, their growth rate declined. Larger shiners also preyed on small trout fry, with the result that the whole trout population declined.

Additional research revealed that the shiners were somewhat more efficient in their feeding habits than the trout. Not only were they much more numerous, but the shiners also were more methodical in their search for prey and consistently captured items that were smaller than those taken by trout — thus consuming many small, immature organisms before they had reached a size and age to reproduce or to become food for trout. The shiners ranged deeper into the *Chara* beds to search for scuds in places where they had been relatively safe from foraging trout. These safe havens in the weedbeds always before had protected a breeding population of scuds, even in the face of heavy predation by trout, but they were no defense against the shiners. The numerical advantage enjoyed by the shiners also was enormous (one estimate placed the shiner population of Paul Lake at between 5 million and 10 million), so that it was impossible for the trout to compete on an equal basis.

A similar situation was found in Pinantan Lake, where *Daphnia* appeared to be the primary casualty of competition between shiners and trout (scuds already being rare in the lake at the time shiners were introduced). In August, 1958, sampling showed that adult shiners were consuming about 2,200 *Daphnia* a day, leaving few available for young trout. The growth rate of young trout in Pinantan Lake fell even below that of their counterparts in Paul Lake.

The factors at work in interspecific competition do not remain stable. Changes in temperature, oxygen content of the water, precipitation, rate of food production, accessibility of food and the influence of outside predators, parasites and disease on the densities of the competing species may affect the degree of competition from one season to the next. Because of these changes, the population of shiners in Paul and Pinantan

Lakes was greater in some years than in others, and the size of the trout populations was similarly affected. At all times, however, the fast-breeding shiners greatly outnumbered the trout in both lakes.

In 1954, biologists began planting Paul Lake with yearling trout that had been raised in hatcheries. The theory behind this decision was that the yearling trout would be too large to become prey for shiners and their growth in the hatchery would relieve them of the disadvantages faced by young trout in the lake. These introductions raised the 1955 angling harvest to about 10,000 trout, the same it had been in the 1940s. It also restored reliance of the fishery on two- and three-year-old fish. The recovery of the fishery was aided somewhat by natural circumstances. The trout in Paul Lake were showing an ever-growing tendency to prey on shiners, and increased consumption of shiners by two-year-old trout boosted growth rates so that more two-year-old fish were able to reach legal size and enter the catch.

Collectively, all these studies produced a sort of biological model for what is likely to happen when shiners are introduced to a small lake which formerly held only Kamloops trout. The shiners multiply rapidly and begin to exhaust the food stocks formerly utilized by trout; they also begin to prey upon trout fry. The trout, however, are not so quick to regard the shiners as a source of food; only after their traditional sources have been consumed by the shiners do the trout gradually begin to prey upon the shiners. During this period of change and adjustment, the trout population is likely to suffer serious damage, both in numbers and rate of growth. Eventually the trout learn to rely more and more on the shiners for food and some of the damage is reversed.

But this reversal cannot take place without some outside help, and management of the lake becomes much more complicated and expensive. Supplementary plantings of hatchery-reared fish may be necessary, and it costs a lot of money to rear fish to yearling size. Environmental factors also may interrupt or delay the recovery of the trout fishery. Research also has indicated that the character of the fishery changes, with artificial lure and fly fishing becoming less effective. Finally, because both trout and shiners are part of the relatively fixed biomass of the lake, it is obvious that the total weight of trout will be less from a lake containing both trout and shiners than it will be from a lake containing trout alone.

Considering all these things, it is obvious both from an angling and management standpoint that it is undesirable to allow shiners to become established in lakes containing trout, and it is necessary to remove them if they do. Paul Lake and its adjoining waters were poisoned and restocked with trout, and the fishing eventually returned to much the way it was before shiners entered the lake. Other lakes also have been chemically treated to remove shiners, but these operations have not always been completely successful. In some cases, shiners in a pothole or upstream beaver pond have remained beyond the reach of the poison, and from these sheltered stocks the population slowly rebuilt itself. And some lakes have a character that simply defies any hope of effective chemical treatment; they have boggy, swampy shorelines, or are connected by a maze of small waterways to other potholes, swamps or beaver ponds, so that it literally is impossible to apply the poison so that it will reach every bit of water where shiners are likely to be. The most that may be done in such lakes is to treat them periodically to keep the shiner population at a manageable level, but the expense of such treatment and its inevitable damage to the fishery and the food stocks of the lake make it impractical. In the long run, the shiners are bound to win and the lake's value as a trout producer is sharply reduced or altogether lost.

Fortunately, most lakes where shiners have been introduced have been susceptible to effective chemical treatment that has restored them as producers of trout. But the problem remains a serious concern, as is evident from the Fish and Wildlife Branch program to post signs warning anglers of the damage that may be done by introducing shiners or other foreign species to trout lakes.

It seems likely that managers of the Kamloops trout lakes always will have to cope with shiners, and one hopes the problem will be no worse in the future than it has been in the past. The value of the shiner as a forage fish for Kamloops trout obviously is outweighed by the damage it does.

The kokanee (*Oncorhynchus nerka*), a landlocked version of the sockeye salmon, has been the most successful forage species for Kamloops trout. However, it has not been successful in every case, and there is much about the relationship between kokanee and trout that remains to be learned.

The kokanee is native to some lakes in the Columbia and Fraser watersheds and has been introduced to others. It is a small silvery fish, a miniature model of its seagoing counterpart, and in most fresh waters it seldom grows to a length of more than 12 inches. There are notable exceptions to this; kokanee as large as 9 pounds have been caught in Kootenay Lake, and fish of several pounds have been taken from other unusually rich waters.

The kokanee matures and spawns for the first time at an age of three to five years. Spawning takes place in tributary streams, and the ripe fish take on the same brilliant green and red colors of seagoing sockeye salmon that return to their native rivers to spawn. The primary food of the kokanee in most lakes consists of cladocerans, copepods, diatoms and midge larvae. The opossum shrimp, *Mysis relicta,* is extremely important in the diet of kokanee in Kootenay Lake and is a major reason why the fish reach unusually large size in that lake. Kokanee are native in Kootenay and Okanagan Lakes and contribute substantially to the diet of trout in both waters. They have been introduced in other lakes with the hope that they would provide useful forage for the trout, but these experiments sometimes have led to totally unexpected results that ended up making the managers' job more complicated and difficult.

One example is that of Jones Lake, near Hope. Jones Lake is outside the natural range and environment of the Kamloops trout and the trout involved were ordinary rainbows, but the case history is a useful illustration of the unpredictable results of stocking kokanee as forage fish. The average size of the rainbow trout in Jones Lake had been declining, and in 1938 a decision was made to introduce kokanee to the lake in the hope that they would provide sufficient forage to check the decline. But it didn't turn out that way; the growth rate of the kokanee in the first few years after stocking was much faster than anyone had anticipated; they grew rapidly to weights of two or three pounds, at which size they were far too large to be useful as forage fish. Trout ate only a few of the smaller kokanee and the hoped-for increase in the size of the trout did not occur. Ultimately, the kokanee became an important part of the Jones Lake fishery in their own right and eventually contributed more to the sport catch than to the benefit of the trout.

A different pattern was observed when kokanee were introduced in Premier Lake. At one time Premier Lake had produced Kamloops trout of enormous size, but eventually the average size of the trout went into sharp decline. Again kokanee were stocked in hopes that the trout would feed on them and the decline in the trout's growth rate might be reversed. The eventual result was that the lake held large numbers of small kokanee and small numbers of large trout – a case of partial success.

Kokanee also were planted in Borgeson Lake near Princeton, which held trout and seven other species. The lake later was poisoned. Several hundred kokanee were counted among the poisoned fish, but only two Kamloops trout were found. The conclusion was that of all the other species of fish in the lake, the kokanee had turned out to be the chief competitor with the Kamloops and in this instance had turned out to be more efficient than the trout in utilizing the food sources available to both species.

The relationship between Kamloops trout and kokanee in small lakes has not been studied nearly as thoroughly as that between Kamloops trout and shiners, but experience has indicated that kokanee are much more useful as a forage species in large lakes than in small ones. Where it has been successful, it sometimes has been very successful indeed, as in Pend Oreille Lake. Why the kokanee is successful as a forage fish in some lakes but not in others is a question that awaits further study.

There are other species of fish, such as the coarse- and fine-scaled suckers, that occasionally provide forage for Kamloops trout. However, this occurs only sporadically under natural circumstances and, because of their undesirable characteristics, no attempts have been made to use suckers or other species as forage fish in management.

If there is a lesson to be learned from all this, it seems to be that the introduction of forage species in Kamloops trout lakes is something that should be approached with a good deal of caution. So far the negative results of such introductions have been far in excess of the positive, and until more is known about the complicated relationships that develop between trout and forage fish it seems a needless risk to introduce them in lakes that already are producing well. If forage fish are to be used at all, it would appear best to try them in waters that are lacking one or more of the food stocks traditionally available to trout, or in waters where those stocks have been depleted. Conceivably, this might improve some fisheries which presently contribute little, and if that does not prove to be the case, then at least little will be lost.

For the present, the angler is likely to encounter forage fish in only a few of the Kamloops trout waters. But where they do exist, they are likely to play a very important role so that it is necessary to be able to recognize them and know something of their habits. The attitude of the fly fisherman toward forage fish perhaps is expressed by the fact that no fly patterns have been developed to imitate them. However, some of the established Eastern streamer patterns or the minnow imitations devised by stillwater anglers in the British Isles might be expected to do the job, and the availability of modern materials such as mylar should make it easy to develop specific imitations of the shiner or the kokanee — if anyone wishes to do so. But I suspect that if fly fishermen have their way, the Kamloops trout lakes will continue to be largely free of forage fish, and fly tiers will continue to concentrate their efforts on improving imitations of the nymphs, larvae, pupae and adults of the aquatic insects that are abundant in so many of these waters and have made them so appealing to anglers for so long.

INCIDENCE TABLE FOR SCUDS, LEECHES AND SHINERS IN KAMLOOPS TROUT WATERS

	May 15-30	June 1-15	June 15-30	July 1-15	July 15-31	August 1-15	August 15-31	September 1-15	September 15-30
Scuds	**	*	*	*	***	***	***	**	***
Leeches	*	*	*	*	**	**	**	**	*
Shiners	*	*	*	**	***	***	***	**	*

Frequency of occurrence in trout stomachs:
*** – Abundant; main item in trout diet.
** – Frequent; secondary item in diet.
* – Occasional.

INSECT EMERGENCE TABLE FOR KAMLOOPS TROUT WATERS

	May 15-30	June 1-15	June 15-30	July 1-15	July 15-31	August 1-15	August 15-31	September 1-15	September 15-30
Chironomids	***	**	*	*	*	*	*	*	*
Dragonfly Nymphs	*	**	**						
Damselfly Nymphs	*	**	**						
Mayflies	**	**	*	*					
Flying Ants	*	***				***			
Sedges			***	*					

Calculated for a lake at 3,500 feet elevation; local conditions may change emergence dates.

*** – Prolific hatches, daily occurrences.
** – Fair hatches, usually every day.
* – Sporadic hatches, inconsistent.

135

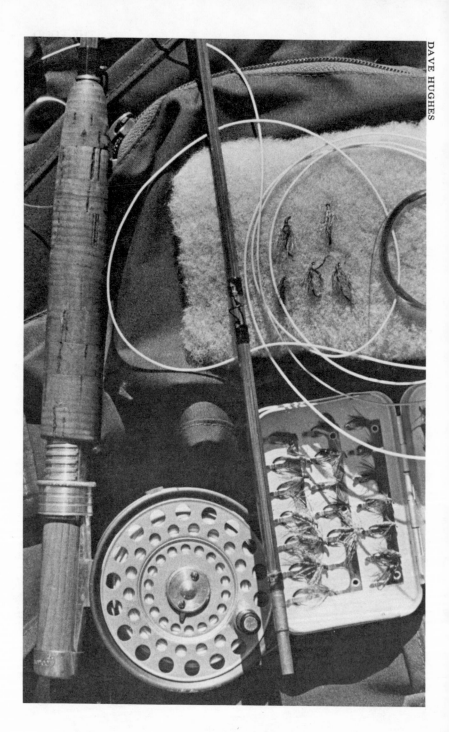

Chapter Six

Fly Patterns

L ike prospectors searching after gold, men have followed trout to the most distant and isolated lands of the earth, there to fish for them with artificial flies. In each time and each place, new fly patterns have been devised to try to capture the fancy of feeding trout, or meet the requirements of local waters, or simply to satisfy the prejudice and whims of the men who tied them. If fly tying had a family tree, it would have many tangled branches; but even the work of tiers at the tips of the newest and remotest limbs would reflect the roots established by Berners, Cotton, Halford, Gordon, Skues and so many others, with each new generation adding its own layer of thought and theory.

And so it has been in British Columbia. The earliest tiers carried on traditions they had learned in other lands, slowly adapting their patterns and approach as they learned more about the preferences of the Kamloops trout and the characteristics of the lakes in which it lives. The influence of the salmon and sea-trout flies of the British Isles is plainly evident in their work, and indeed such old established patterns as the Jock Scott, Alexander, Claret and Mallard and Teal and Red were among the first flies ever cast into waters of the Kamloops trout. Even when British Columbia fly tiers began to produce their own patterns for Kamloops trout, the influence of the British style remained evident, especially in the work of Bill Nation. But there also were some departures from this style in some of the early Kamloops trout patterns; the Carey Special was a radically different fly for its time, and some of the earliest floating sedge patterns showed adaptations that were incorporated to suit the hatches and conditions of the Kamloops waters.

Still, for a good many years the emphasis on wet-fly patterns for the Interior lakes showed a clear preference for the "attractor" fly, and there was little effort made to imitate the larvae, nymphs, pupae or scuds so common in the Kamloops trout waters. Nymphs were almost unknown, and most of the patterns created from the 1920s to the 1950s were wet flies with long, sweeping hackles and bright colors. But the growth and development of nymph fishing in other areas since has been felt in British Columbia, as shown by the rise of the scientific approach to fly tying in recent years. Today's tiers carefully study the habits and appearance of aquatic insects and experiment with new imitative patterns and methods for fishing them. The result has been a number of popular new patterns that are close imitations of the naturals, mainly nymph or larva patterns,

137

but also some fine new dry-fly designs.

In the first edition of this book I wrote that "it seems reasonable to assume that as both fishermen and fish become more sophisticated, this (the use of attractor patterns instead of imitations) will change. There are signs that the change already is beginning, as anglers put away old patterns and turn to new, untested designs. In 20 years I would expect the list of Kamloops trout patterns to be quite different. . ." Half of those 20 years now are past, and there are significant changes to the list. Some of the historic old patterns still are in use, but others have been all but forgotten and new ones have emerged to take their place. Hence this chapter will omit some of the older patterns described in the first edition of this book and list in their place some newer ones that have found favor among contemporary Kamloops trout anglers.

The business of tracing fly patterns often is a difficult one. The difficulty begins the moment an original pattern is copied by another tier. No two fly tiers do everything exactly alike and a trout fly is as individual as a set of fingerprints. Once a pattern has passed through the hands of half a dozen tiers — with each one adding his own individual touch — the design and intent of the originator may be drastically altered or altogether lost, unless he had the foresight to make written notes. Few tiers have been prescient enough to do that, and frequently the history of fly patterns has become tangled and confused. Sometimes several tiers have come forth to lay claim to the original idea for a popular pattern.

The task becomes easier if the pattern bears the name of the original tier. But in the case of most of the historic Kamloops trout patterns, the tiers have been dead for many years so the names are not of much help. The effort to establish the originator's design and intent then becomes a search for old flies, old records or the memories of old-timers who may have known the original tier. Sometimes the researcher is lucky and sometimes not.

It has been 45 to 50 years since many of the most important Kamloops trout patterns were devised, but every effort has been made to track down the history of those still in use. In addition to these and the newer patterns born on the Kamloops trout waters, a number of patterns from outside the province have become popular on British Columbia's Interior lakes. Some are relatively new; others are old, traditional patterns from the British Isles. The most important of them also are listed in this chapter.

The Carey Special

Any discussion of Kamloops trout fly patterns must begin with the Carey Special. It is by far the most widely-known Kamloops pattern and its fame and use have spread far beyond the borders of British Columbia. It is tied now in countless different versions and has been used effectively for rainbow, cutthroat and brook trout along the length of the Pacific

Coast and inland to Montana. It is the staple fly of the Northwest angler, the single pattern most likely to be found in every fly book. In its many variations it is used as an imitation for many things its originator probably never intended, and often it is fished by anglers who have no idea it ever was meant to imitate anything at all.

Although it bears the name of Colonel Carey, once an officer in the British Army (some say his first name was Tom, but he was known almost universally as "the Colonel"), there is some evidence that the original idea may not have been his. Tommy Brayshaw spoke of a fly called the Pazooka that was in use on Knouff Lake early in the 1930s and referred to it as a "forerunner of Carey's Dredges" (as the Carey Special was known early in its history). So it is possible that Carey borrowed at least some features of the pattern from one that was in use even earlier.

Some accounts (including the one given in the first edition of this book) say the Carey Special was devised by Colonel Carey and Dr. Lloyd Day in the Beaver Lake chain near Kelowna to imitate emerging sedge pupae. But Brayshaw, a contemporary of the Colonel, disputes this and gives a rather precise account of the origin of the fly: "He (Colonel Carey) started the fly when he was camped at Arthur Lake and I think dressed it for a dragonfly nymph," Brayshaw wrote. "At any rate, we did the same thing at Knouff with the 'Pazooka' and fished it the same way: Throw it out, lay the rod down, fill a pipe, light same, half smoke it and then, wallop! You had him!

"The old boy used to use ground-hog hair (or do you call it fur?) quite a lot and I am not sure that his tail and body may be that . . . The body is made by winding the hair around the body and ribbed for protection with waxed black linen thread in the reverse direction . . ." But the most striking feature of the pattern was its hackle, which consisted of several turns each of at least two Chinese pheasant rooster rump feathers. This produced a very full hackle of long, sweeping flexible fibers that gathered around the body of the fly as it was being retrieved and gave a fine illusion of movement in the water. The Carey Special undoubtedly was one of the first – if not the very first – patterns employing the pheasant rump feathers for hackle, and the hackle unquestionably accounts for much of the fly's success. It is about the only feature of the original that survives in the many modern versions of the pattern, although now it usually is tied sparsely.

The original pattern also incorporated a short tail – a feature that has been dropped from many of the modern versions. The tail consisted of ground-hog hair fibers, the same material used for the body. So the full pattern of the original, as nearly as it can be traced, appears to have been as follows:

Hook: No. 6.
Tail: *Thick bunch of ground hog hair fibers.*
Body: *Ground hog hair wrapped around the hook shank, with*

139

> *heavy black tying silk (or "linen," as Brayshaw called it)*
> *wrapped in the opposite direction to bind the hair in*
> *place.*

Hackle: *Two brownish-gray Chinese pheasant rooster rump*
feathers, tied very full with several turns each.

Depending upon how it was fished, the original pattern seems to have worked equally well as an imitation of a dragonfly nymph or an emerging sedge pupa. Many anglers also were quick to see that a more sparsely-tied version made an excellent damselfly nymph imitation, and many of the modern Carey Special designs were constructed with that intent.

Perhaps the most popular and effective of the modern versions is the one known as the "Self-bodied" Carey, which employs the pheasant rump feather for both the body and the hackle. The pattern:

Hook: *No. 6 or 8, regular or 2X-long shank.*

Tail and *A pheasant rump feather is tied in at the bend of the*
Body: *hook with the tip fibers extending rearward as the tail.*
The remainder of the feather is twisted forward around
the hook shank to form the body and is tied off behind
the eye.

Hackle: *One or two turns of a rump feather to form a sparse*
hackle.

An excellent variation on this pattern is known — perhaps somewhat irreverently — as the "Six-Pack." It is tied the same way except that the rump feathers are dyed olive. Both the Self-bodied Carey and the Six-Pack are good imitations of the damselfly nymph.

The most common variation on the original pattern involves substitution of the body material. Modern designs incorporate floss, chenille, moose mane, peacock herl and wool in various colors. Occasionally the fly is tied with a tail of golden pheasant tippet feathers. Patterns tied with stout bodies of olive-colored chenille sometimes make effective dragonfly nymph or sedge pupa imitations, and some anglers use a black chenille body tied on a long-shank hook as a leech imitation.

But regardless of how it is tied, the basic Carey Special pattern seems to have a certain look about it that fish find appealing, and that undoubtedly accounts for its long and widespread use.

Several other fly patterns have been attributed to Colonel Carey, but none survive in common use.

The Doctor Spratley

Next to the Carey Special, the Doctor Spratley probably is the best-known pattern to come from the Kamloops trout waters. Like the Carey, it is a wet-fly pattern, and was first tied by a Mount Vernon, Washington,

140

fly tier who named it after Dr. Donald A. Spratley, a local dentist. Dr. Spratley used the fly in the Interior lakes where it became popular long before his death in 1968. It also has enjoyed some use by steelhead fly fishermen. The original pattern was as follows:

Hook:	No. 6.
Tail:	*Guinea hackle fibers.*
Body:	*Black wool, cigar-shaped.*
Rib:	*Silver tinsel.*
Hackle:	*Guinea, tied down as beard.*
Wing:	*Red-brown fibers from Chinese pheasant rooster tail feather.*
Head:	*Peacock herl, several turns.*

The fly now is most often tied with barred rock (grizzly) hackle fibers for the tail and the hackle, and the peacock-herl head usually is omitted in modern versions. Within the past few years, several variations have appeared incorporating green, yellow or red floss or wool for the body in place of the black wool used in the original.

The Doctor Spratley does not bear a close resemblance to any of the insects that are common to the Kamloops trout lakes, so its effectiveness is difficult to explain. Perhaps, like the Carey Special, it simply is one of those flies with a certain quality that appeals to the fish. However, some anglers trim the pheasant-tail wing to about a third of its normal length to produce what they claim is an effective dragonfly nymph imitation. Others sometimes trim both the tail and hackle so that virtually only the body of the fly is left, and this makes an acceptable chironomid pupa imitation.

The Black O'Lindsay

This fly is virtually unknown outside British Columbia and even within the province it is not nearly as popular as it once was. But it is one of the oldest and certainly one of the most beautiful Kamloops trout patterns. Its history dates back to the days before World War I when it was developed as a grasshopper imitation for trout fishing on the Thompson River. Judge Spencer Black of Lindsay, California, is credited with devising the pattern, which he fished in the Walhachin reach of the Thompson during the late summer months when warm breezes carried the hoppers from the dry, grassy hillsides onto the river. The judge's name and hometown gave the fly its colorful name.

Later the fly was adopted by other anglers for use in the Interior lakes, where it was fished primarily as an attractor pattern. With its colors and its large, bulky silhouette, it turned out to be a very effective stillwater fly. Some anglers also have used it as a dragonfly nymph imitation, and

141

its silhouette certainly bears a resemblance to the natural even if its colors do not.

The original pattern, as well as can be traced, apparently was as follows:

Hook:	*No. 6.*
Tail:	*Dyed blue saddle hackle fibers.*
Body:	*Yellow wool, thick.*
Rib:	*Embossed gold tinsel.*
Throat:	*Dyed blue saddle hackle fibers.*
Hackle:	*Light brown, tied down as beard over throat.*
Wing:	*Barred mallard breast, parallel to hook, laid over 6 to 8 strands of peacock sword.*

As with most popular patterns, the Black O'Lindsay has spawned its share of variations. Most common is the use of brown hackle rather than blue for the tail and elimination of the blue throat altogether. Some tiers have substituted black hackle for the brown, and occasionally one sees the fly tied with full hackle rather than a beard. Some modern tiers also use a dubbed body of seal's fur dyed yellow, and a few who used it strictly as an attractor pattern added jungle cock cheeks.

Until the last decade, the Black O'Lindsay still was a common weapon in the arsenal of Kamloops trout fly fishermen, and it probably still resides in the fly boxes of many anglers. But with the advent and success of many new imitative patterns, it is not often used anymore — which seems a pity for such a handsome fly with such a long history.

The Patterns of Bill Nation

In addition to being the foremost Kamloops trout guide of the 1930s, Bill Nation also was an innovative and prolific fly tier. Some of his patterns became standards for Kamloops trout fly fishermen, remaining in widespread use for several decades.

His approach to fly tying reflected his own background and the times. His patterns show the influence of English sea-trout and salmon flies in their shapes and silhouettes, but the colors and combinations of materials were clearly the result of his own vivid imagination. For the most part, his patterns were not attempts at exact imitation; he seemed to believe that a fly should be tied to suggest something or create an impression of it rather than depicting it exactly. There are some exceptions: One could argue that his dragonfly nymphs (Nation's Gray Nymph and Nation's Green Nymph) are more than fair imitations of the natural, and that his chironomid pupa imitation (Nation's Black) is at least somewhat close to the appearance of the actual insect. But his most successful flies were bright and colorful and bore only an abstract resemblance to the insects of the Kamloops trout waters.

Sophisticated modern fly tiers sometimes chuckle when shown some of Nation's flies. The flies are not what one would call classic patterns;

many are bulky to the point of seeming awkward, and few have the precise, trim, carefully-balanced and proportioned appearance that is the pride of most contemporary tiers. Part of this was by design; Nation tied the flies that way because he intended them to look that way; part of it also probably was due to the relative lack of materials available to Nation. After all, Paul Lake in the 1930s was not the most easily accessible place, and it seems likely that Nation often had to make the most of whatever materials happened to be on hand, since it would have taken considerable time and effort to obtain others. But whatever else one may say of Nation's flies, they caught fish for many decades — and that, after all, is the ultimate test of any fly.

Nation sold flies to some of the anglers he guided (his advertisements said the flies were "guaranteed to kill") and a number of his originals survive in various collections. With the generous assistance of the late Letcher Lambuth, I was able to examine the Nation flies in his collection and those in the collection of his friend, the late Dr. Thomas Mesdag. Dwane Scott, operator of Echo Lodge at Paul Lake (which, alas, has since been razed), also was helpful in allowing me to inspect and photograph some of Nation's originals in a display kept at the lodge. From these and other sources, it was possible to prepare the following list of Nation's original patterns:

Nation's Black

Hook:	*No. 8.*
Body:	*Black floss, thin.*
Wing:	*Several strands of dark brown or black bucktail, very sparse.*

This was Nation's version of a chironomid pupa. It still is used occasionally on the Kamloops trout lakes, but has largely been replaced by more realistic modern patterns such as the PKCK, TDC and others.

Nation's Blue

Hook:	*No. 8.*
Tail:	*Long, thin strands of barred mallard breast.*
Body:	*Rear two-thirds: Flat silver tinsel. Front third: Blue floss.*
Rib:	*Oval silver tinsel over both body sections.*
Wing:	*Barred mallard breast, tied parallel to hook, with topping of blue chatterer wing.*
Hackle:	*Badger, tied wet and full.*

This fly was a fanciful attempt to suggest the appearance of damselflies locked in mating flight. The fact that it was a wet fly did not deter Nation; he reasoned that if it were fished close to the surface, trout would not be able to discern the difference between the water and the air and would assume the fly was a pair of damselflies flying near the surface.

Certainly there have been few theories more radical than this in the history of fly tying! This fly has been effective at times, although it seems likely that trout take it as a drowned spent damselfly — or perhaps merely as a curious item worth investigating.

Nation's Fancy

Hook:	No. 6.
Tail:	Thick clump of long golden pheasant tippet fibers.
Body:	Rear half: Silver tinsel. Front half: Black floss.
Rib:	Oval silver tinsel over both sections of body.
Wing:	Barred mallard breast with several strands of golden pheasant tippet enclosed.
Hackle:	Guinea.

This fly is well named. It appears to have been a flight of fancy on the tier's part, not meant to imitate or suggest anything in particular. But over the years it has proven very effective as an attractor pattern or exploratory fly.

Nation's Gray Nymph

Hook:	No. 6.
Tying Silk:	Olive green.
Tail:	Very short clump of golden pheasant tippet with only the ends showing.
Body:	Gray wool, very thick, with barred mallard breast wound over and around it.
Rib:	Gold wire.
Wing:	Ground hog hair, thick.
Beard:	Ground hog hair, shorter than above.

This pattern was Nation's imitation of a small dragonfly nymph. It is broad and bulky, like the natural, and the use of mallard breast wound over the body gives it a very realistic appearance in the water.

Nation's Green Nymph

Hook:	No. 2.
Tying Silk:	Gold.
Tail:	Very short clump of golden pheasant tippet fibers.
Body:	Light green wool or chenille, built up very thick, with barred mallard breast wound over it.
Rib:	Gold tying silk wound in one direction, gold wire in the other.
Wing:	Ground hog hair, thick.
Beard:	Ground hog hair, shorter than above.

This fly was Nation's version of a mature dragonfly nymph, on the verge of hatching. The barred mallard breast wound over the green body gives the fly an especially effective appearance when both are soaked. The fly's size and bulk make it difficult to cast on a light line and Nation

The dragonfly (above) and damselfly (below) are found in abundance during the summer months in the Kamloops lake country.

FAVORITE PATTERNS FOR
KAMLOOPS LAKES

Carey Special
(original version)
    "Self-bodied" Carey Special
    Dr. Spratley
(original version)

Black O'Lindsay
(modern version)
    Nation's Black
    Nation's Blue

Nation's Fancy
    Nation's Gray Nymph
    Nation's Green Nymph

Nation's Green Sedge
    Nation's Red
    Nation's Silver & Mallard

Nation's Silvertip   Nation's Silvertip Sedge
    Nation's Special

ALL PATTERNS TIED BY
STEVE RAYMOND

Knouff Special

Bryan Williams'
Gray-bodied Sedge

Werner Shrimp

"Baggie" Shrimp

Golden Shrimp

Halfback

TDC

PKCK

Tom Thumb
(original version)

Tom Thumb
(variation)

Vincent Sedge

Hatchmatcher

Anderson's Stone Nymph

Backswimmer

Black Matuka Leech

The road to Minnie Lake.

sometimes let it trail behind the boat, which was rowed at a very slow rate of speed.

Nation's Green Sedge

Hook:	No. 6.
Tail:	Dyed red swan.
Body:	Spun seal's fur dyed dark green.
Rib:	Gold tinsel.
Wing:	Barred mallard breast, parallel to hook shank.
Hackle:	Badger.

This was Nation's impression of the green-bodied sedge that hatches on Paul Lake and so many other waters. Again, it was a wet pattern even though the adult sedge rides on the surface. Legend has it that Nation carried a bottle of peroxide and bleached the body of the fly to match the color of the sedges that were hatching at the time. The pattern bears a close resemblance to the traditional Grizzly King, but Nation's own version of the Grizzly King was quite different, as the following pattern indicates.

Nation's Grizzly King

Hook:	No. 6.
Tail:	None.
Body:	Natural gray seal's fur, tapered larger forward.
Rib:	Embossed silver tinsel.
Wing:	Barred mallard breast, parallel to hook shank.
Hackle:	Yellow, possibly golden pheasant crest, tied as beard.

This fly was one of Nation's least-known patterns, one that never caught on. Its description in the first edition of this book was the first time the pattern appeared in print. Now it is little more than a historical curiosity.

Nation's Red

Hook:	No. 2.
Tail:	Thin strands of barred mallard breast.
Body:	Rear two-thirds: Flat silver tinsel. Front third: Red wool or spun fur.
Wing:	Barred brown mallard flank, parallel to hook shank.
Sides:	Strips of dyed red swan.
Hackle:	Badger, tied full and wet.

This is the counterpart to Nation's Blue. Sometimes known as Nation's Red Dragon, it was intended to represent adult red dragonflies (Sympetrum) in their mating flight. It was a somewhat more popular fly than Nation's Blue and tiers who copied it sometimes tied it on hooks as small as No. 8.

Nation's Silver and Mallard

Hook: No. 6.
Tail: Thin clump of long golden pheasant tippet fibers.
Body: Rear two thirds: Flat silver tinsel, thin. Front third:
           Black wool, thin.
Rib: Flat silver tinsel wound over both body sections.
Wing: Barred mallard breast, parallel to hook.
Hackle: Badger, tied full and wet.

This pattern also has been called the Silhouette Sedge. It was sometimes used to imitate a female sedge laying eggs under the surface, with
the tinsel representing the silvery air bubble clinging to the body of the
sedge. It also was fished as a fry pattern at Adams and Little Rivers with
some success.

Nation's Silvertip

Hook: No. 6.
Tail: Small clump of golden pheasant tippet fibers, about half
           the body length.
Body: Rear one-fourth: Flat silver tinsel. Front three-fourths:
           Black floss.
Rib: Oval silver tinsel over both body sections.
Wing: Brown mottled turkey feather, tied parallel to hook with a
           few strands of golden pheasant tippet enclosed.
Hackle: Guinea, tied down as beard.

This may have been Nation's most popular fly. It was widely used during the 1930s and remained popular until a few years ago. In one survey
of 80 "record" fish taken from Paul Lake over a 10-year period, the
Silvertip accounted for exactly half. Though not suggestive of any insect,
the Silvertip was an excellent attractor pattern or exploratory fly.

Nation's Silvertip Sedge

Hook: No. 6.
Tail: Dyed red swan.
Body: Two or three turns of flat silver tinsel at the end; remainder
           dyed green spun seal's fur.
Rib: Gold tinsel.
Wing: Brown mottled turkey, tied parallel to hook shank.
Hackle: Badger.

Another wet sedge pattern with the added bit of flash that Nation
seemed to feel was a necessary part of any good Kamloops trout fly.

Nation's Special

Hook: No. 6.
Tail: Small clump of golden pheasant tippet fibers, about half
           body length.

Body:	Rear one-third: Flat silver tinsel. Front two-thirds: Black floss.
Rib:	Oval silver tinsel.
Wing:	Brown mottled turkey, parallel to hook shank, with a few strands of golden pheasant tippet enclosed.
Sides:	Jungle cock.
Hackle:	Guinea.

This was another popular pattern, not suggestive of any particular insect but useful as an exploratory fly. It bears a close resemblance to the Silvertip, but Nation regarded the two flies as separate patterns.

Nation was meticulous in his directions for tying and fishing his flies and he experimented with many variations before arriving at the patterns listed here. His flies are distinctive not only for the style of tying, but also for the materials used. His method for dividing the bodies into radically different sections and ribbing both with tinsel; his frequent use of mallard breast and turkey for wing materials and badger feathers for hackle, and his use of golden pheasant tippets to add a dash of color or decoration — all these were trademarks of Nation's flies.

For more than 30 years, Nation's patterns were the popular choices of anglers on the Interior lakes. But along with other historic patterns, their use has declined in the past decade as anglers have turned more and more to closely imitative flies. But if the future of Nation's patterns is uncertain, their place in the past is assured. Both the flies and the man who tied them occupy a place of honor in the history and traditions of Kamloops trout fly fishing that is unlikely ever to be eclipsed.

Knouff Special

Hook:	No. 6.
Tail:	Thick clump of long golden pheasant tippet fibers.
Body:	Green wool, thick.
Rib:	Orange wool, wound so that segments of green and orange are of equal width.
Wing:	Golden pheasant tippet feather.
Hackle:	Brown-gray Chinese pheasant rooster rump feather, tied very full.

As the name indicates, this fly was developed on Knouff Lake where it was fished as an imitation — albeit a highly impressionistic one — of the emerging sedge pupa. The date of origin of this pattern is unknown, though it goes back many years. The use of the Chinese pheasant rooster rump feather for hackle prompts one to speculate that this fly may once have been known as the Pazooka, which Tommy Brayshaw described as the forerunner of the Carey Special, but there is no direct evidence to support this. Whatever its origins, the Knouff Special is a very colorful and handsome fly that has been used for several decades and remains in occasional use by Kamloops trout anglers.

Bryan Williams' Sedges

Bryan Williams (see Chapter I) developed a number of fly patterns for use on the Interior lakes, including two floating sedge patterns that surely were among the first dry flies ever tied specifically for Kamloops trout. These patterns, graceful and realistic in design, were widely imitated and their influence still is evident in the designs of some modern tiers.

There were two patterns, the Gray-bodied Sedge and the Green-bodied Sedge. In a letter to Lee Richardson, quoted in *Lee Richardson's B. C.,* Williams told a little about the origin of these flies: ". . . June fishing brings back memories of Knouff, where I first originated the grey sedge fly, and later at Hyas where I found the green-bodied sedge. It was in Hyas Long Lake (as it usually was called then) I killed a fifteen-and-a-quarter pound fish on the dry fly. Certainly they are great fighters, and not only make terrific runs but tremendous jumps. I have never seen any other fish clear such heights."

Not many originals of these patterns have survived. I had high hopes of seeing some when Williams' daughter invited me to her Vancouver home and presented her father's fly box for inspection. But the box contained no sedges, only wet patterns which had suffered from the depredations of moths. But Letcher Lambuth provided an impeccably preserved original of the Gray-bodied Sedge from his collection. The pattern:

Hook:	*No. 8.*
Body:	*Gray goose primary feathers, wound on the hook shank and trimmed to form an even, slim body.*
Rib:	*Black wool, single thin strand.*
Hackle:	*Two light brown hackles tied dry and very full.*
Wing:	*Mottled gray sections from tail of Chinese pheasant rooster, paired and tied parallel to hook shank.*

I have been unable to obtain an original of the Green-bodied Sedge, but from published photographs the construction appears to have been as follows:

Hook:	*No. 8.*
Body:	*Seal's fur, dyed light green.*
Hackle:	*Two badger hackles, tied dry and very full.*
Wing:	*Barred mallard breast sections, paired and tied parallel to hook shank.*

Both these patterns are excellent imitations of the naturals in size, color and silhouette. Until the advent of high-floating deerhair patterns, fly tiers were able to do little to improve upon their appearance — although many tried. It seems likely these flies were fished with a dead float, since the materials used in their construction — and the unavailability of fine-wire hooks in those days — would have made it extremely difficult to skate them across the surface without sinking them. But

148

fished without movement, they undoubtedly were extremely effective imitations of newly-emerged sedges that had yet to begin "traveling" across the surface.

Other Patterns

A number of other wet-fly patterns enjoyed considerable following on the Kamloops trout lakes at various times in the decades from 1930 to 1970. These included the Cummings Fancy, a bright attractor fly; the Lioness, once a favorite on Peterhope Lake, and the Rhodes Favorite, another bright pattern often used as an exploratory fly. The Egg 'n' I was an emergent sockeye alevin imitation often used on the Adams and Little Rivers, and the Big Bertha was an elaborate and colorful pattern used on the same waters.

The dressings for all these patterns are given in the first edition of this book. They are omitted here because time has caught up with them and they are rarely used any longer. They are now mostly of interest to fly-tying historians.

As noted earlier, the preoccupation of the early Kamloops-trout fly tiers with bright attractor patterns was a result of their familiarity with traditional salmon and sea-trout flies. Even so, it seems strange that apparently no attempts were made to design flies to imitate — or at least suggest — the scuds that are so common in the Interior lakes and so important in the diet of Kamloops trout. Perhaps there were some; if so, the flies have not survived and apparently were not recorded. Whatever the case may have been, modern tiers have moved to fill the void and in the past two decades many scud imitations have appeared. A description of some of these seems an appropriate place to begin our discussion of modern Kamloops trout patterns.

Scud Patterns

The first commercially-tied scud patterns to appear on the shelves of British Columbia tackle shops were almost uniformly awful. They were nearly always too large or too brightly colored, or both. Bright orange patterns were particularly common, possibly because the tiers copied them from naturals that had been kept in preservatives too long (gamma-rids quickly loose their natural color and take on an orange hue when stored in preservatives).

More careful observation of the naturals soon changed all that. Fly-tying anglers studied the scuds in their natural environment or in aquari-ums and began to experiment with new, more realistic patterns, some of which became popular. The new patterns shared little in common with their predecessors, except for their names: Scud imitations invariably always have been called "shrimp" flies.

For all the attention they have received from contemporary tiers, the gammarids have proven surprisingly difficult to imitate successfully. The problems of capturing the color, shape and movement of the naturals are formidable, and of all the patterns created by modern tiers only a few are consistently effective. The following three may be safely said to fall within that category:

Werner Shrimp

Hook:	*No. 10.*
Tail and Overlay:	*Deerhair.*
Body:	*Olive-dyed seal's fur or chenille.*
Hackle:	*Brown palmered.*

Tying instructions: The deerhair is tied in at the bend of the hook with the tips pointing to the rear. Then the hackle and body material are tied in and the body is wound forward and the hackle palmered over it. The remaining deerhair then is brought forward and laid over the top of the body to form a "shellback" and is tied off behind the eye and trimmed.

Mary Stewart, a Vancouver tier, is credited with this pattern, but it bears the name of Werner Schmid, whose use of the fly on the Interior lakes led to its widespread popularity. While it is a relatively effective imitation, its acceptance undoubtedly is at least partly due to the fact that it is a very easy pattern to tie.

Some tiers have experimented with variations on the original pattern. One successful variation, which probably is more effective than the original, involves substituting olive-dyed mallard breast for the deerhair. This results in a fly that is more durable and has more uniform coloration than the original pattern.

'Baggie' Shrimp

Hook:	*No. 10 or 12.*
Body:	*Olive wool (other colors may be substituted).*
Rib:	*Olive tying silk.*
Overlay:	*Thin strip cut from clear polyethylene sandwich bag.*

Tying instructions: Cut polyethylene strip and taper to point at both ends. Tie in one end at bend of hook. Then tie in wool. Sufficient tying silk should be left at the bend of the hook to use for ribbing. Wrap the wool forward, building up thick body. Lay polyethylene strip on top of body and tie off behind eye, forming overlay. Then wind ribbing over body and overlay, binding the latter in place. Use dubbing needle to draw out wool fibers from the lower body; these constitute the legs of the fly.

The rather inelegant name of this fly stems from the use of a sandwich bag as one of the components of the dressing. It is a relatively new pattern, also very easy to tie, and makes a good imitation. It is new enough so that its popularity is not yet widespread, but it promises to become a staple pattern in years to come.

Golden Shrimp

Hook: No. 10 or 12.
Tying Silk: Olive or tan monocord.
Body: Golden olive rayon floss (manufacturer's number 163).
Tail, Legs &
Antennae: Ginger hackle.
Rib: Fine gold wire.

Tying instructions: Select a small ginger hackle feather and strip the
fibers from one side, being careful to leave the tip of the feather intact
and some fibers at the butt. The hackle tip is tied in at the bend of the
hook so that the tip extends rearward and downward, forming the tail of
the fly. Then the fine gold wire is tied in, followed by four to six strands
of floss. The floss is wound forward to form a thick, cigar-shaped body.
The hackle feather then is laid along the underside of the body and tied
off below and behind the eye of the hook; do not trim the remaining
feather. The gold wire then is wound on as a rib, binding the feather to
the body of the fly and giving the body a segmented appearance. A dubbing needle should be used to separate the hackle fibers so they are not
bound under the wire; they should remain free to hang down and form
the legs of the fly. When the ribbing is complete, the excess hackle is
doubled back over the eye of the hook so that the long fibers of the butt
extend forward to form the antennae. A whip finish then is applied to
the head of the fly and any remaining excess hackle is trimmed away.

As the instructions indicate, this is a complex fly to tie. Using a dubbing needle to separate the individual hackle fibers to make way for the
ribbing is a painstaking and time-consuming process. But the finished
fly, if tied correctly, makes a deadly imitation; the floss darkens slightly
in the water and provides a very close match for the color of the natural.

Although it may seem a bit immodest for an author to offer his own
fly pattern, that is what I have done in this case. The pattern was the result of nearly five years of experimentation on the Interior lakes involving many different materials and designs. This work led up to a morning
on Hihium Lake when the pattern listed above accounted for 43 trout
caught and released, and it has not been varied since. It has been used
successfully in many other Kamloops trout waters and other anglers have
reported similar success. The difficulty involved in tying the fly has perhaps kept it from being more widely accepted than it is.

A variation of the pattern, called the Suntan Shrimp, involves the use
of light tan or beige floss in place of the olive. This pattern is used in the
relatively infrequent situations where the majority of scuds are lighter-
colored. In all other respects, the tying instructions are the same.

Halfback

Hook: No. 6, 2X long.
Body: Bronze peacock herl, thick.

Wingcase: Gray-brown mallard secondary feathers.

This pattern made its first appearance in British Columbia about 15 years ago. Its origin is in doubt, though various accounts say it was first developed in Alberta or Montana. It is not imitative of any particular insect, but its bronze color may induce trout to take it for some types of chironomid pupae which display a similar color. A variation on this pattern, called the Fullback, usually is tied on a No. 8 4X long-shank hook. The body also is of peacock herl but the wingcase is of brown saddle hackle extending over the full length of the body, bound by a single rib of tying silk in the center. A brown hackle beard also is added.

TDC

Hook:	*No. 8 or 10 1X long.*
Body:	*Black wool or chenille, tapered larger toward the head.*
Rib:	*Silver tinsel.*
Hackle	
(gills):	*White ostrich herl, several turns.*

This fly is the creation of Dr. Richard B. Thompson of the (U.S.) National Marine Fisheries Service in Seattle and is the prototype for a number of new chironomid pupae imitations that have appeared in recent years. Fished on a sinking line with a very slow retrieve, or fished nearly motionless just beneath the surface film on a floating line, it is a fine imitation of a pupa on its way to hatch. This pattern has taken fish during the incredible late-May chironomid hatch at Tunkwa Lake when nothing else would.

PKCK

Hook:	*No. 8 or smaller low-water Atlantic salmon hook with long shank and turned-up eye.*
Tag:	*Silver.*
Body:	*Single strand of dark green or olive wool.*
Rib:	*Single strand of stripped eyed peacock herl.*
Wingcase:	*Brown turkey primary section.*
Gills:	*Two short (about 3/16-inch) strands of white emu, one on either side of head.*

Tying instructions: After tag is wound on near bend of hook, the stripped peacock herl and wool are tied in ahead of it. The wool then is wound forward about two-thirds of the length of the hook shank and is tied off. Then the stripped herl is added as the rib. The brown turkey section is tied in and the wool then is wound forward and built up to form a thorax, without ribbing. The turkey section is brought forward over the top of the thorax and tied off behind the eye to form a wingcase, the emu strands are added and the fly is finished.

This pattern was developed by Jim Kilburn and Dave Powell to imitate chironomid pupae during the heavy spring emergence at Minnie Lake near Merritt. The color matches the naturals that emerge from time to time in Minnie Lake, Pass Lake and many other waters. The PKCK caught on quickly with other anglers and its popularity still is growing throughout the Interior.

Another promising chironomid pupa pattern is Yoshida's Pupa, also known as the YDC, tied by Wayne Yoshida of Kamloops. It bears a fairly close resemblance to the TDC, although different materials are incorporated.

The recognition by fly fishermen that chironomid pupae form a substantial part of the diet of Kamloops trout and that they are more or less available throughout the season has stimulated the development of other new imitations in addition to those given here. Mostly these still fall into the category of personal patterns, although some show signs of wider acceptance and more probably will.

Tom Thumb

Hook: No. 8 or 10, 3X fine.
Tail, Body
& Hackle: Deerhair.

Tying instructions: A thick bunch of gray-brown deer body hair is held to the hook shank with the tips pointing toward the rear and bound tightly with tying silk so that the free ends of the hair flare outward in a rough circle. The tying silk then is carried forward and tied off behind the eye. The flared tips of the deerhair are gathered up, pulled forward and tied off behind the eye, and if this is done properly a neat, barrel-shaped body will be formed, completely enclosing the hook. A few hairs are allowed to continue to extend to the rear of the fly and these are trimmed to a uniform length to form the tail. Once the rest of the deerhair is tied in behind the eye it is cinched tight so that the tips again flare out into a circle. The head of the fly is built up in front of this circle and pressure from the tying silk causes the circle of hair to flare out at right angles to the hook, and this becomes the hackle of the fly.

It takes considerable practice to tie this fly properly, but the result is a pattern that is almost impossible to sink and one that may be fished very effectively as a traveling sedge imitation. The hollow deerhair fibers are filled with air so that the fly can be skated rapidly across the surface for long distances without fear of drowning it. But in addition to the difficulty involved in tying it, the fly has another disadvantage: Deerhair is extremely brittle, and a single fish may rip the body apart and make the fly useless.

The pattern given here is the "original" Tom Thumb. Apparently no one is certain of its origin, but some claim to have traced it back to Algonquin Indian fishermen.

Many modern anglers use a variation of the original pattern. Recognizing that the color of natural deerhair is a poor imitation for the bodies of most hatching sedges, they have added a body of wool — usually olive or green. Then, instead of building a barrel-shaped body of deerhair around the hook, they merely lay the hair over the top of the body, forming a sort of shellback that permits the color of the wool body to be seen from below. The deerhair hackle also is often disregarded in favor of a semi-upright wing, and the fly is hackled with a feather in the conventional manner.

These variations now are more popular than the original pattern, but they are not really "Tom Thumbs." In truth, they are little or no different from the Humpy fly, sometimes also called the Goofus Bug, that has been popular for many years on Montana and Wyoming waters. But regardless of the name it goes by, the pattern is effective and has become the standard traveling-sedge imitation on the Kamloops trout waters.

Vincent Sedge

Hook: *No. 10 or 12.*
Tail: *Brown-tipped deer body hair, "not too long, but fairly heavy."*
Rib: *Narrow light green floss.*
Body: *Light olive green seal's fur or wool.*
Underwing: *Same as tail.*
Outer-
  wing: *Mottled gray-brown turkey primary, sprayed with lacquer.*
Hackle: *One or two brown hackle feathers, tied dry.*

Tying instructions: Tie in the ribbing material first. Then tie in a short but fairly substantial clump of deerhair after evening it in a "stacker." The butts of the hair should extend two-thirds of the way up the hook shank toward the eye. In binding down the hair, ease pressure on the tying silk near the rear of the hook to keep the hair from flaring. Then add the body material and wind it two-thirds of the way up the hook shank and add the ribbing. A second clump of deerhair then is evened in a "stacker" and tied in on top of the front of the body material (do not tie it directly to the hook shank or it will flare badly). Next take the lacquered turkey feather and cut out a strip about half an inch wide, depending on the size of the fly. Double it over and cut a "V" in the rear end. Place the strip over the deerhair underwing, gathering in any stray hairs. Try to keep the lower edge of the wing close to, and even with, the side of the body. The wing should be tied in when it has been positioned correctly. Then add the hackle and the fly is complete. Green or olive tying silk usually is used.

Jack Vincent, the author of this pattern, is one of British Columbia's outstanding fly tiers, and this fly certainly is one of the most deadly sedge patterns ever devised for the Interior lakes. Jack gives this account of its origin:

"It was in mid-June, 1975, at Roche Lake, that my sedge first saw the light of day. Like countless other patterns, it was born out of frustration. The sedges were up but my luck was out, so I decided to head back to the trailer for a beer. When back at the trailer I just began experimenting with the new fly-tying materials I had with me." The result was the pattern listed above, "one reasonably good sedge pattern," as its originator says in a masterpiece of understatement.

"This fly seems to fish quite well, even when the water surface is flat," Vincent adds. "It appears to have a good silhouette when on the water (at least from the fisherman's viewpoint), so while it may not outfish other sedge patterns, it inspires me with a certain amount of confidence.

"A fly constructed in this manner (lacquered wings) eventually seems to split, usually in the top center fold. However, this is compensated for by the deer body hair underwing which fills in the space. At times this pattern reminds me of a newly-hatched sedge spreading and drying its wings when this splitting occurs. Fish do accept it like that."

Although it takes a sophisticated tier to construct this pattern, it has received a good deal of attention and admiration and many anglers believe it is the best pattern yet designed to imitate the prolific sedge hatches on the Kamloops trout lakes.

Because the adult sedge is of paramount importance to dry-fly fishermen on the Interior lakes, a good deal of thought and effort have been given to floating sedge patterns. The superb floating qualities of deer and elk hair have led to the wide use of these materials by modern tiers, in preference to the feather wings frequently used by the pioneers of British Columbia fly tying. The result of all this experimentation is a host of local patterns and some that have become known widely enough to be mentioned in print here and there. The latter include Peter McVey's Cinnamon Sedge, Mitch's Sedge, the Turner Sedge and two patterns from the United Kingdom, the Goddard Sedge and the Edwards Sedge. A few anglers also use Lloyd Frese's Salmon Candy sedge patterns created for the landlocked Atlantic salmon of Hosmer Lake, Oregon.

Now it seems that each angler has his own personal favorite pattern or assortment, and today's hot fly may be tomorrow's loser. But that is one of the fascinating things about fly fishing, and as long as the sedges continue to hatch on the Interior lakes and anglers continue to try to imitate them, the experiments will go on and the fame of certain patterns will rise and fall.

Hatchmatcher

    Hook: *No. 12 to No. 16, 3X fine.*
    Tail, Body
    & Wing: *Gray goose flank.*
    Hackle: *Dark blue dun.*

Tying instructions: A small gray goose flank feather is selected and the center quill is cut about two-thirds of the way up from the butt so that a "V"-shaped section remains. The last two fibers remaining at the tip end are left undisturbed — one on each side — to form the twin tails of a mayfly. The other fibers are pulled tightly forward to form the slim body of a mayfly and are tied down tightly to a bed of tying silk built up on the hook shank about a third of its length behind the eye. This will leave a thick clump of flank feathers extending forward over the eye. These are bent upward and secured in an upright position by a figure-8 weave of tying silk and are trimmed to form the wing. The hackle is then added, with at least two turns behind the wing and the remainder in front.

There are literally thousands of mayfly patterns, but this pattern is given here because it is extremely effective and not yet too widely known. Also often called the Hatchmaster, it frequently is tied with barred mallard breast and badger or grizzly hackle rather than the materials listed here. But I have chosen this pattern because it is an especially good imitation of the *Callibaetis* dun that hatches on so many Kamloops trout waters (the mallard breast-grizzly pattern is too light to imitate the color of the hatching duns). A very effective imitation of the *Callibaetis* spinner may be made by substituting the iridescent blue-green feather from the neck of a Chinese pheasant rooster for the goose flank and black hackle for the dark blue dun. Other materials also may be substituted to match mayflies of other hues.

This pattern has yet to receive much usage on the Kamloops trout lakes, but those who have used it are unanimous in their praise. Because mayfly hatches usually are only of secondary importance on these waters, there is no need to carry a wide assortment of patterns; a few Hatchmatchers in various sizes and colors should prove sufficient for most purposes. The hundreds of other standard mayfly imitations are so widely known and oft-published that it seems unnecessary to list any of them here.

Anderson's Stone Nymph

Hook:	No. 4 or 6, 2X long.
Body:	Yellow wool.
Overlay:	Brown wool.
Rib:	Tying silk.
Hackle:	Brown, palmered and trimmed.

Tying instructions: Tie in the hackle at the bend of the hook, followed by strands of yellow and brown wool. Build up a cigar-shaped body of yellow wool and tie off a short distance behind the eye of the hook. Lay the brown wool over the top of the body and tie it off. Then take tying silk and wind a spiral rib back to the bend of the hook; reverse direction at that point and spiral the silk back to the eye, creating a series of cross-hatched ribs that bind the overlay to the body. Then palmer the hackle forward and tie it off. Trim the hackle so that it is shorter in the rear, longer in the front.

A stonefly nymph has no business in still water, since stoneflies are river-dwellers exclusively. But this pattern, developed by Earl Anderson, has become established as a very good stillwater pattern, for reasons best known to the fish. It is especially popular on Dragon Lake, near Quesnel, famous for its large rainbows, but also has been used for Kamloops trout with good results. Its popularity is enhanced by the fact that it is a very easy pattern to tie.

Black Matuka Leech

Hook: No. 4 or 6, 2X long.
Body: Black chenille.
Wing: Two long black saddle hackles, tied Matuka style.
Rib: Black tying silk.
Hackle: Black, tied wet and full.

Tying instructions: Tie in chenille at the bend of the hook, leaving free a length of tying silk to serve as ribbing. Wind chenille forward to create body, then tie off. Place two long black saddle hackles back-to-back, with tips curving outward, and tie in the butts behind the eye of the hook. Then use the tying silk remaining at the bend of the hook as ribbing, spiralling it forward to bind the hackles in place on top of the body. A dubbing needle should be used to separate the hackle fibers so they are not bound flat by the ribbing. The free ends of the hackles should extend well beyond the hook. Add several turns of full black hackle behind the eye of the fly and whip finish.

The Matuka style of tying originated in New Zealand. Its name derives from that of a bird whose feathers were used to tie an extremely popular fly used on Lake Taupo. The fly became so popular, in fact, that the bird was hunted almost to extinction for its feathers and finally the fly was banned by authorities in an effort to save the bird. But the name of the bird − and the fly − was carried over and applied to the style of tying, which involves binding the wing feathers to the body. The great advantage of this over conventional streamer patterns with saddle hackle wings is that the wings are much less apt to wrap themselves around the hook in casting, which spoils the effectiveness of the pattern.

In recent years, the Matuka style has caught on widely in the United States and, to a lesser extent, in Western Canada. The Black Matuka Leech is one result. It has been used by some anglers as a replacement for a traditional pattern, known simply as the Black Leech, which incorporates exactly the same materials and is tied exactly the same way − except that the wings are not bound to the body.

Backswimmer

Hook: No. 8 or 10.
Body: Yellow wool, thick.
Rib: Embossed silver tinsel.

| Wing: | Eight or ten strands of black rayon floss, trimmed to equal length. |
| Hackle: | Brown Chinese pheasant rump feather. |

In the previous chapter I mentioned there are no standard imitations of the backswimmer, but promised to mention a pattern that has produced good results from time to time. The foregoing is that pattern; it is by no means considered "set," and I think the problems of imitating this insect deserve a good deal more attention from fly tiers.

The silver tinsel is meant to suggest the silvery film of air the insect carries with it beneath the surface. The black floss wing straightens out realistically as the fly is being retrieved rapidly through the water, and the full hackle suggests the appearance of the natural's strong swimming legs in motion. Because both the backswimmer and water boatmen bear a superficial resemblance in the water, in smaller sizes this pattern also may be used as an imitation of the latter.

There are a great many more fly patterns in use on the Kamloops trout lakes than we have listed here. Dozens of damselfly and dragonfly nymph patterns have been created by local tiers and more are added every year. Indeed, it seems as if each fly-tying angler has created his own version of these insects and there are no standard patterns in widespread use, except for the Carey Special variations designed to imitate damselfly or dragonfly nymphs – and these are probably as good as any of the other patterns.

A large number of other patterns have been adapted for use in the Kamloops waters from origins far beyond the borders of British Columbia. A partial list of these flies would include the Alder, Alexander, Black Gnat, Butcher, Claret and Mallard, Leadwing Coachman, Gray Hackle, Grizzly King, March Brown, Montreal, Muddler Minnow, Professor, Queen of the Waters, Royal Coachman, Teal and Green, Teal and Red and Teal and Silver. As with the early patterns developed within the province itself, most of these have fallen into disuse in the past couple of decades and are seldom seen anymore.

The next decade undoubtedly will see many more changes to the list of popular fly patterns used for Kamloops trout. Even now new patterns are being tried which may go on to capture the imagination of anglers throughout the province and beyond – perhaps another Carey Special or some other fly that will catch the fancy of trout wherever it is tried. It is likely too that new techniques and materials now being tried elsewhere will be transferred and applied to British Columbia waters, and these may play an important role in the years to come. Anglers and tiers are growing ever more sophisticated and educated, and as they continue to study the habits and appearance of the insects of Interior lakes, it seems certain that they will create ever more careful and realistic imitations.

Tradition will remain important, as it always has, but the ideas and experiments of modern tiers will continue to add to it and change it. Few aspects of the art of fly fishing change as rapidly as the flies themselves, and if there is ever another edition of this book I suspect it again will contain a list of patterns far different from the one presented here.

RITCH PHILLIPS

Chapter Seven

Tackle and Technique

F ly fishing is the only method guaranteed to bring the Kamloops
trout angler a full measure of satisfaction. To begin with, it is the
most effective method, allowing the angler to fish the weedy, food-rich
shallows that are the most productive part of any lake. It also is the only
means through which a wide range of lures or imitations may be offered
in a short time.

Fly fishing is more fun than any other method. The connection between the angler and the fish is direct, with no weight to intervene, and
the trout is free to run or jump with only the restraint of the line to
check him. And fly fishing also is the angling method most consistent
with the aims of conservation; it permits the angler to release under-
sized or unwanted fish with every chance they will survive — a most important consideration in these days when fishermen so greatly outnum-
ber fish and the pressure on the fishery grows more intense with each
passing season.

Many anglers have accepted the validity of these arguments in recent
years and the number of fly fishermen has grown explosively. While still
in the minority — as they are likely always to be — fly fishermen are well
organized, and they have done much to protect and conserve the fishery.
Undoubtedly they will do even more in the future.

It is assumed that the reader is himself a fly fisherman, with at least
some knowledge of the basic mechanics and nomenclature of the sport.
If that assumption should prove invalid, then it is hoped that this discussion — and this book as a whole — will lead the reader to consider fly fishing as a desirable alternative to his present method. Despite popular no-
tions to the contrary, the basics of the sport are learned easily and the
satisfactions derived from it often lead the newcomer into the science,
craft, literature and philosophy that are integral parts of fly fishing.
(There are numerous fine introductory texts to fly fishing; three of the
very best are *A Primer of Fly-Fishing,* by Roderick Haig-Brown; *Trout
Fishing,* by Joe Brooks, and *Modern Fresh and Salt Water Fly Fishing,*
by Charles F. Waterman.)

While the following discussion considers a wide range of equipment
and accessories for use in fly fishing for Kamloops trout, most anglers
accumulate these items a few at a time over a period of many years. All
that is really necessary to begin fishing effectively for Kamloops trout is
a basic outfit consisting of a rod, a selection of two or three lines and a
reel with extra spools to match, a leader and some appropriate flies — all

of which may be obtained at relatively reasonable cost. Indeed, most
fly fishermen start out with just such an outfit, adding to it later according to their degree of interest and the size of their pocketbooks.

Rods

The selection of a fly rod is a highly personal thing. Although there
are a number of tests that may be performed to determine precisely the
dynamic characteristics of a rod, most anglers prefer more or less subjec-
tive judgments on such matters as the length and weight of the rod; the
color of the shaft and its windings and the quality of finish; the shape of
the grip, and — most important — the rod's action, or "feel." A rod that
"feels" right in the hand — one that is not too fast or too slow, one that
seems well-balanced and never top-heavy or awkward — is a thing to be
treasured.

But even though these are matters best left to individual taste, there
are some general statements about fly rods that may be made safely —
beginning with the materials from which they are made.

From the late 19th Century until the years immediately after World
War II, all the best fly rods were built of Tonkin bamboo grown in
Southeast China. The bamboo culms, cured and heat-treated to remove
moisture, were split into separate sections that were planed or milled to
match and then glued together with their hard enameled sides facing outward to form the rod shafts or "blanks." Most rods were — and are — of
six-strip construction, and the very best were built by hand — a process
demanding a high degree of personal craftsmanship. Bamboo rods have
a number of advantages, and most anglers agree that "feel" is the most
important: There is something special about a bamboo rod; the long,
gleaming supple shafts of cane come vibrant and alive in the hand, and
the cool, varnished smoothness of them is a delight to touch. And there
is more to this than mere aesthetics; a well-crafted bamboo rod stops still
after a cast is made, and there is never any after-vibration from the tip.

But there are disadvantages, too. Bamboo is heavier for its length
than rods made of more modern materials, and bamboo fly rods are
somewhat less durable than glass or graphite shafts. Cost is another disadvantage; the disruption of trade between China and other nations shut
off the flow of cane, driving up the price of stocks already on hand in
North America. That, plus the cost of the large amount of personal labor
involved in crafting a fine cane rod, has driven the price of a finished rod
beyond the means of many anglers. A generation of master bamboo rod
builders has passed from the scene, and few have come along to take its
place. In the British Columbia Interior, the bamboo tradition is kept
alive in the workshop of Peter McVey at Corbett Lake, but the relative
scarcity of modern craftsmen has been another factor in the spiraling
cost of cane rods.

Still another factor was the advent of the fiberglass rod. The first

162

models, which appeared around 1950, were relatively crude, but the technology developed rapidly and the popularity of the new material grew along with it. Fiberglass rods are made of glass cloth wrapped around mandrels, impregnated with resin and baked to a hard finish in an oven. The taper and thickness of the cloth is varied to produce the desired action so that a wide variety of lengths, weights and actions is possible. The material weighs less than bamboo to begin with, and the completed shafts are hollow so that the overall weight of the rod is signficantly less than that of a cane rod of similar length.

The savings in weight was only one of the qualities that made fiberglass rods immediately popular with anglers. Because they could be mass-produced using advanced industrial techniques, their price was much less than that of bamboo rods, and fiberglass rods are more durable than their cane counterparts.

But fiberglass rods have disadvantages, too. They are aesthetically much less pleasing than bamboo rods, and they suffer badly from after-vibration — a problem no rod designer has been able to completely solve. Nevertheless, as a low-cost, mass produced alternative to scarce, expensive bamboo rods, they quickly took over most of the market.

Now graphite rods have come along to challenge the supremacy of fiberglass. Made from resin-impregnated graphite fibers, these rods represent a tremendous leap forward in rod-building technology. Most impressive is their savings in weight; the weight of a graphite rod may be less than half of a cane rod of similar length and significantly less than a fiberglass model. Using extremely strong and extremely light graphite fibers, engineers have been able to design 10½-foot rods weighing less than 8-foot bamboo rods, offering the promise of a whole new generation of extra-long, light rods for special angling purposes. Graphite rods also are largely free from the problems of after-vibration that have plagued fiberglass models, and their vibration characteristics have been compared favorably with bamboo.

But even these space-age fly rods are not completely free of problems. Aesthetically, their appearance is no match for a bamboo rod, and the extreme stiffness of graphite fibers often results in rods with actions that are too "fast" to suit the tastes of some fishermen. In addition, graphite is expensive, and although a graphite rod costs less than a fine bamboo model, it costs substantially more than fiberglass. But now at least there is a medium-priced alternative with many advantages, and graphite rods have captured an important share of the market in the three or four years since their first appearance.

So now anglers have all these materials to choose from, and even though it may be more difficult to love a glass or graphite rod than it is a handsome bamboo model, there is such a wide variety of styles and actions and prices to choose from that any angler, from beginner to expert, is virtually assured of finding what he wants.

163

But regardless of the material, no fly rod is any good if it lacks a sufficient number of guides. Since guides still must be wound to the shaft by hand, some companies have chosen to minimize labor costs by skimping on the number of guides. If a rod does not have enough of them, the line will sag between the few it does have, creating friction that restricts the length of a cast that may be made with the rod. A good 8-foot fly rod should have 10 guides, counting the top guide.

Fortunately, all the major manufacturers now follow the practice of labeling their rods with the recommended line weight. This is especially helpful to beginning fly fishermen, who may be uncertain in their choice of the right-sized line.

In general terms, a rod selected for fishing the Interior lakes should be one capable of making long casts. It is not necessary to make a long cast every time — the exceptions would be when the angler is casting to individual rising fish or to a specific area — but more often than not, the angler will be fishing "blind" over water where no fish are rising. When that is the case, it is a simple matter of logic that the longer the cast, the greater the probability a fish will see the fly when it is being retrieved back to the starting point.

Long casts generally mean a long rod, and one with a good deal of strength, or "backbone." The latter also is necessary to punch a fly into the face of a driving wind, as one is frequently required to do on the Kamloops trout lakes.

To meet these requirements, a rod of at least 8 feet is necessary and 8½ feet is better. Various models of bamboo, glass and graphite all are equal to the task, but the weight of the rod is an important consideration. A long day spent casting a heavy rod with line to match can be extremely tiring to the caster, possibly leaving him with a sore set of muscles prompting him to quit earlier than he would have otherwise. If a rod is well-balanced, comfortable and the angler is in rhythm with its action, the weight may not make much difference; but for handling a long, heavy line on a windy day, graphite may have an edge because of its light weight.

Most anglers who have been at the business for a while will carry more than one rod with them in a boat. One probably will be rigged with a weight-forward sinking line for wet-fly or nymph fishing. It is likely to be the longest, strongest rod he uses, and should be capable of throwing a good-sized fly at least 60 feet. A second rod is likely to carry a floating line, ready to go in case the angler encounters a hatch and the trout begin to rise. It may be a somewhat shorter, lighter rod, offering a little more sensitivity and control in covering a rise and working the fly on the surface. Still a third rod may be rigged with a sink-tip line for fishing over shoals or in weedy pockets, and in strength and length it may fall somewhere between the first two.

164

In my own case, the first rod would be an 8½-foot graphite model matched to a No. 7 weight-forward, fast-sinking line. This outfit is capable of throwing large flies a good distance, even into the teeth of a wind. The dry-fly rod would be a 7½-foot model of either bamboo, glass or graphite, depending upon which one I felt like using that day. All these rods are light, sensitive and accurate and well suited for dry-fly work with either a No. 5 double-tapered line or a No. 6 weight-forward where greater distance is required. The sink-tip line would go on a light, 8-foot fiberglass rod that is comfortable and capable of all the distance usually needed. But these are personal preferences which may not necessarily coincide with those of another angler.

I think there is a place for small rods, even on the open, windy reaches of the Kamloops trout lakes. I enjoy using them because they add a little to the challenge of casting and because it is more exciting to fight a large trout on a 6-foot, 2-ounce rod than it is on an 8-foot, 4½-ounce model. But they are not for everyday use; one must know the lake well, know exactly where the fish will be, and use a cautious, quiet approach to get within the shorter casting range of such a rod. It makes no sense at all to use a small rod to fish blindly, since it is impossible to cover more than half the water a longer rod would reach. A short rod also requires the angler to work harder; he must make twice as many casts because the retrieve will be only half as long as it would be if he were making longer casts with a longer rod. And little rods are almost useless in a strong wind.

But when all the conditions were right, I have enjoyed many exciting days battling Kamloops trout on a 6-foot rod — a thrill that is difficult to describe unless you have experienced it. One should approach the use of such rods with some caution, however; with them, it is very easy to fight a trout to the point where it is exhausted beyond recovery. This is true simply because it is more difficult to land hard-fighting trout on a little rod, and care should be taken to avoid fighting a fish too long so that its survival will not be in jeopardy if it is to be released.

Regardless of its material, weight or length, a good rod will last a lifetime if it is properly cared for. The finish of a rod is vital to its longevity; if the varnish cracks or flakes, allowing water to penetrate, it may ruin a bamboo rod or damage the appearance of fiberglass or graphite rods. Cracked varnish over the windings also can cause damage, although most glass and graphite rod manufacturers now use a nearly-impregnable epoxy dressing to cover the windings. The finish of each rod should be checked carefully at least once a year, and if it is cracking the damaged portion should be carefully sanded and covered with several coats of new varnish.

Guides also may require periodic replacement. Worn guides with sharp edges will ruin an expensive fly line in short order, and even the super-hard new alloys used in rod guides will not last forever.

These measures are especially important when some of your fishing is done from a boat, as much of it is on the Kamloops trout lakes. A wet boat deck will spread tiny bits of sand and gravel from your boots, and these will adhere to any loose coils of line that fall to the bottom of the boat. They make fine abrasives and will wear out guides in a remarkably short time. For these reasons, the fisherman should strive to keep a clean boat and clean his line as frequently as possible.

Finally, a rod never should be put away when it is wet — especially into a cloth bag. Spots of mold will form quickly on the cork grip and the bag, and the latter will soon rot. A mold-covered rod may have to be sanded and refinished, and even then it is likely to retain an unpleasant odor. Take the time to dry your rods carefully before putting them away after a day of fishing.

A good rod is a precision instrument and a dependable tool. It may represent many hours of a craftsman's labor and a sizeable investment of the angler's own resources. It also reflects something of the owner's personal tastes and values, and it will bring him a great measure of satisfaction and reward. It is something to be chosen with care and used and cared for with respect, especially when the quarry is as worthy as the Kamloops trout. There is no single rod, or set of rods, that is "right" for the Kamloops lakes; the choice belongs to each individual angler, perhaps to be made through a long process of trial and error. We have tried here to offer a few general guidelines to make the choice a little easier, but if trial and error still is the result, then at least — because it involves fishing — the experience should be mostly pleasant, and the final choice especially pleasing.

Lines

Developments in fly-line technology have come almost as rapidly as they have in the field of rod manufacture. Today the angler has a choice of a bewildering array of different types designed to cope with almost every conceivable angling situation. But with few exceptions, the Kamloops trout angler will need only the three types already mentioned — a floater, sinker and sink-tip.

In dry-fly fishing on the Kamloops trout waters, where long casts usually are more important than delicacy of presentation, a weight-forward floating line is advisable. Floating lines also are used to fish nymphal or pupal imitations in or just beneath the surface film, and because fish often take such imitations very softly some fly-line manufacturers have begun adding "strike indicators" to their floating lines. These consist of short strips of fluorescent material that are highly visible across the water, and by watching them closely the angler is able to detect the very slight movement that usually occurs when a feeding trout gently sucks in the fly. Many individual anglers have added such "strike indicators" to lines that did not have them by slipping a section of fluorescent-colored fly line over their leader butt and glueing it in place with epoxy glue.

Most modern synthetic floating fly lines are well made and will last a considerable period of time if cared for properly. Proper care means keeping them clean, and a number of different line cleaners are available for the purpose. Synthetic lines rarely require dressing, as the old silk lines did so frequently, but after considerable use the thin tip sections of the modern lines may become slightly waterlogged and will require light dressing to remain afloat.

Color is an important consideration in choosing a floating fly line. The color should be readily visible in twilight, when so much dry-fly and surface-film nymph fishing is done. The fishing often reaches fever pitch in the last few fleeting moments before total darkness, and at such times the fly may be invisible to the angler in the rapidly fading light. If a dark-colored line is being used, the fisherman may not even be able to gain an approximate idea of where his fly is, but if the line remains visible he will have at least a close idea of its location. Fortunately, fly-line manufacturers have taken this problem into consideration. White and ivory-colored lines, first developed for use in fishing motion pictures, proved very good for evening fishing and manufacturers have continued to produce them. Fluorescent pink and yellow lines are even better, and their bright colors seem to have little or no effect on the fish during daylight hours.

Different line manufacturers use different nomenclature to describe their sinking lines, but generally there are four types: the slow sinker, or intermediate; fast sinker; extra-fast sinker and super-fast sinker (Scientific Anglers Hi-Speed Hi-D). Of these, the fast sinker probably is best suited for all-around wet-fly fishing in the Kamloops trout lakes. If kept clean, these lines will sink a fly quickly enough so that the angler does not have very long to wait before beginning his retrieve, and they do not sink so rapidly that the fly will dive toward the bottom between strips of the retrieve. This allows the fly to be retrieved toward the surface at a steady angle and keeps the line relatively taut so that the sensation of a strike is transmitted directly to the angler and he can set the hook with a minimum of slack. Fast-sinking lines are adequate for the depths most often fished in the Kamloops lakes.

However, there will be times — especially on bright, warm days, or during the lazy dog days of late summer — when a fast-sinking line may not be adequate to the task. I once fished alongside an angler who hooked 10 trout to my single fish, even though we both were using the same fly and casting to the same water. The difference was that he was using an extra-fast-sinking line while I was using a fast sinker. It was a warm, August afternoon and the fish were lying deeper than I could reach them with the line I was using. Such occasions are more the exception than the rule, and an angler on a limited budget probably can get along nicely without an extra-fast-sinking line. But if the added cost is not a problem, such a line should be included in a fisherman's kit for those times when only a deep-sunk, slowly-retrieved scud or leech pattern will do the job.

167

While using an extra-fast-sinking line, an angler should expect to "hang up" more frequently on weeds or bottom debris than he would with other types of lines. This, however, is an acceptable hazard since the reward, under certain conditions, is likely to be greater.

The super-fast-sinking lines are a relatively new development and they have not been in use long enough at this writing to gain widespread popularity. They were developed primarily for use in steelhead rivers and certain types of saltwater fly fishing and it seems probable they will prove to have very limited use, if any, in the Kamloops trout lakes.

The weight-forward design is best for any sinking line that is intended for use on the Interior lakes, for reasons already stated. Although there is no firm evidence that trout shy away from a submerged line of any color, anglers prefer somber hues and the fly-line manufacturers have obliged by producing lines that are mostly green or brown.

Sink-tip lines are made so that only the 10 feet on the terminal end will sink while the remainder floats, which makes it an ideal line for certain specialized situations. With a sink-tip line it is possible to cast to deep pockets in shallow weedbeds or to fish a wet fly or nymph over a shallow shoal without much danger of hanging up. The productive weedbed at the extreme south end of Roche Lake or the extensive shoal areas in nearby Plateau Lake are examples of places where sink-tip lines might be employed.

There is one problem inherent in the design of sink-tip lines: The sinking tip submerges at an angle to the floating belly of the line, and the longer it is allowed to sink, the greater the angle. The obvious problem created by this is that when a fish takes the fly the energy of the strike is not transmitted in a direct line to the angler and by the time the shock reaches the rod tip the fish already may have gone. This problem can be overcome by closely watching the end of the floating portion of the line for any tell-tale movement, just as one would watch a "strike indicator" attached to the end of a floating line. If this is done, and an effort is made to set the hook at any sign of movement, the angler will not miss many fish.

The "hinge" where the sinking tip joins the floating line is a vulnerable point and the finish of early sink-tip lines often cracked quickly at this junction. Many anglers soured on sink-tip lines because of this problem, but subsequent development seems to have licked the difficulty and the sink-tip lines in my possession have been in use for several seasons with little sign of wear.

Sink-tip lines are manufactured in a variety of colors ranging from peach to green. The sinking portions generally are a darker color than the floating segment of the line. Again, the color seems to make little difference to the fish.

In fishing the Kamloops trout lakes I use sink-tip lines less than either floaters or sinkers. But I would never be without one; there are situations where nothing else will do, and having a sink-tip line available may mean the difference between a slow or blank day and a productive one.

It is worth reiterating the importance of keeping fly lines clean. Grit picked up from a boat deck will drastically shorten the life of a line and quickly damage rod guides, and it is virtually impossible to keep a line from picking up some of it. The remedy is to periodically wipe down the line or, better yet, apply a commercial line cleaner. It also goes without saying that standing on a fly line does no good at all.

Whatever type of line is used, it should be attached to a long length of backing on the reel spool. A strong, well-conditioned Kamloops trout can take out surprising lengths of line and backing on its initial run and there is a special feeling of consternation in watching the last few turns of backing evaporate from a spool when a trophy-sized trout is making a wild bid for freedom. It is hard to say how much backing is enough. I once watched an angler on Lundbom Lake hook a huge trout that took 35 yards of line and 100 yards of backing without pause, popping the leader when the last turn of backing paid out and the line came up tight against the knot that held the backing to the spool. Few fish will run that far, but the ones that do are the ones you will least want to risk losing.

Braided dacron is the most common type of backing material. Most fishermen choose either 18- or 20-pound test. At a minimum, the reel should be capable of holding 50 yards of backing plus the fly line, and 100 yards or more is better. The fly line may be spliced to the backing or attached by means of a blood knot, nail knot or Albright Special knot. Whatever method is used, the knot or splice should be small and pliable enough to pass easily and quickly through the rod quides, since the slightest friction may be enough to break a strongly-running fish. It also is good practice to periodically strip the line from the reel and test the knot; the penalty for not doing so may be the loss of a fly line as well as a fish.

Leaders

The leader is the weakest length between the angler and the fish. This fact alone dictates that special care should be taken in choosing leaders and making certain that leader knots are tied securely, yet many fishermen neglect to do so. Losing a good-sized fish or two may provide temporary incentive to be more careful — but it also may be a long time before another good fish comes their way.

The purpose of the leader is to disguise the fly's connection to the line, and the choice of a leader therefore involves certain compromises. One must consider the clarity of the water, the size of the fish he is likely to hook and the size of the fly to be used. If he is fishing a lake where large fish are common, a stout leader may be called for; but if the water is especially clear and the day is bright, he may hook nothing at all unless he uses a light leader. Somewhere between these two extremes is a safe middle ground that will result in consistent action and at least a reasonable chance of landing fish. With experience, the angler will enjoy growing success in landing large fish on light leaders, but until this level of skill is reached some sort of compromise is necessary.

A leader with a tippet of 3- or 4-pounds breaking strength is strong enough to handle the fly sizes most commonly employed in fishing for Kamloops trout, although it may be necessary to use 6-pound tippet for large, bulky flies such as dragonfly nymph patterns. Conversely, very small dry flies require very light tippets, but only rarely — if at all — is it necessary to use such small patterns on the Kamloops waters.

Most leaders now are made of nylon. Different brands of nylon material may have different diameters for equivalent breaking strength; for instance, one manufacturer's material may have a rated breaking strength of 6 pounds for a diameter of .011 inches, while another's may have the same rated breaking strength for material with a diameter of .090 inches. In order to avoid the confusion that results from such differences, it seems best to discuss leader material in terms of breaking strength rather than diameter. In fishing for Kamloops trout, I have never used a leader tippet of more than 6 pounds breaking strength, nor do I think it ever would be necessary to do so. In fact, I rarely use leaders as heavy as that unless fishing deep in relatively unclear water where I expect to hook only large fish, or unless I am using a large fly that cannot be delivered properly with a lighter leader. A tippet strength of 3 or 4 pounds seems well suited for most circumstances, but occasionally — in fishing for spooky trout in clear water under bright sunlight — I have found it necessary to go to a tippet of 1-pound breaking strength, or even slightly less. If one is very careful, it is possible to land surprisingly large fish on such cobweb tippets, but the choice of fly sizes that may be used with such light leaders obviously is limited. There also is the constant risk that a fish will strike violently enough to snap the tippet even before the angler has an opportunity to react.

Unless the water is clouded by an algae bloom — in which case the length and diameter of the leader is not so important — a relatively long, fine leader usually brings better results, especially on bright days. But there is no established "correct" length for a leader; the choice of length really depends upon the skill of the caster and whether the leader is properly designed. Neophyte casters often have some difficulty handling a long leader, and for them anything over 9 feet long may be out of the question. Experienced fishermen and proficient casters generally prefer somewhat longer leaders.

My own preference in fishing the Kamloops trout waters is for a leader measuring at least 11 feet with a sinking line and 13 feet with a floater, and the latter may be lengthened to 15 feet for fishing in still, shallow water under bright conditions.

A number of ready-made, tapered leaders are available commercially in various tippet strengths and sizes and usually in lengths of 7½ or 9 feet; the longer length is recommended. The great advantage of these manufactured leaders is that they have no knots that might pick up bits of algae or weed in the water. Their disadvantages are that it is difficult to lengthen them without destroying the careful balance of the taper formula, and if they are weakened by wind knots or tangles it is necessary to replace the entire leader. Many anglers prefer to tie their own leaders, joining together sections of different strengths and diameters to form tapers of various formulae. Leaders of almost any length may be built in this way, and if a section is weakened by a wind knot it is a simple matter to replace it without having to tie on a whole new leader. The disadvantage is that the blood knots used to join the leader sections together may pick up bits of weed.

The choice of a knot to join the leader butt to the fly line is critical. A nail knot is easy to tie but is somewhat bulky and may become caught in the rod guides with disastrous results when one is attempting to land a fish. The needle knot is more difficult, but its slim profile makes it preferable (in this knot, a needle is inserted into the fly line core, the leader is drawn into the line for about half an inch and out the side, then is secured around the outside diameter of the fly line with a couple of turns). Another alternative is the epoxy splice, in which the leader butt is coated with epoxy, inserted into the fly line with a needle and left to dry.

No matter what method is used, the fly line-leader connection is subject to heavy stress and wear and should be inspected periodically and replaced if necessary.

The clinch knot and the single or double turle knot are most often used to attach the fly to the leader tippet. My preference is the double turle; it is easy to tie and permits realistic movement of the fly, and only rarely have I lost a fish to knot failure.

Reels

A fly reel should provide adequate storage space for the line and sufficient backing, and it should have a steady and consistent drag that does not vary in pressure regardless of how fast a fish is running or how much line and backing remain upon the drum. It should do all these things and yet still be light enough that it is not an encumbrance to the fisherman and durable enough to put up with heavy use. It is not easy to find all these qualities in a single reel, and unless one is willing and able to pay for them he must be prepared to sacrifice some.

The Hardy Lightweight series of reels offers all these qualities. These reels are available in a wide variety of models and sizes capable of storing lines of all sizes and various lengths of backing. They are made with a high degree of precision, are light in weight and have a drag system that is usually consistent if the reel is kept clean and well lubricated. They have the added quality of making a delightful racket when a fish is taking out line, and the "Hardy sound" is sweet music to anglers the world over.

171

The Orvis C.F.O. series and the Scientific Anglers System reels are equally as good. All, however, are relatively expensive.

The Pflueger Medalist series is a good lower-priced alternative. These reels are slightly heavier than the Hardy Lightweights, are not quite so pleasing in appearance and are not available in such a wide variety of sizes. They also are relatively quiet reels. But they are sturdy, durable reels with a good drag system, and they are capable of many years of faithful service.

An even lower-priced alternative is the Crown rim-control fly reel. Although available in a limited range of sizes, this is a light, well-made, durable reel that allows the angler to control the drag with finger pressure against the flange of the reel. This takes some practice, but adds a little excitement to the playing of a fish. Although it lacks a drag system, the Crown reel does have a click that provides a pleasing racket when a fish is taking line.

Extra spools are available for all these reels. A single reel with two extra spools, and a different type of line on each spool, is enough to equip an angler for the great majority of situations he will face on the Kamloops trout waters. But any reel, no matter how expensive or well made, should be disassembled, cleaned, oiled and greased periodically to ensure proper function under the sudden stress of playing a strong fish.

Floating Devices

Although it is possible to cast from shore or wade the shallows of many Interior lakes, some sort of floating device usually is necessary to reach the best fishing — shoals surrounded by deep water or productive flats at the far end of a large, wilderness lake.

Float tubes have gained increasing popularity in recent years, although they are still something of a rarity on the Kamloops trout waters. Their great advantage is their ease of portability; they can be conveniently carried in the back seat of a car or easily carried over a trail to a remote lake. They are ideal for small waters, but have limited usefulness on the large, windswept and sometimes dangerous lakes that dot the surface of the Southern Interior Plateau. Perhaps their biggest disadvantage is that the angler who uses one has a poor vantage point because he is necessarily close to the surface of the water. This makes it difficult to see fish rising some distance away, or to detect the subtle take of a nymph fished just beneath the surface at the end of a long cast.

Small, inflatable rubber rafts also are easily portable; deflated, they can be stuffed into a pack and carried on an angler's back. As with float tubes, they are best suited for small waters. A sheet of plywood placed in the bottom of a rubber raft makes it a much more stable craft and may allow an angler to stand up and cast. This also gives him a higher vantage point and a greater range of vision than is possible when fishing from a float tube.

Some fly fishermen prefer to use canoes, although their relative lack

172

of stability makes it difficult to stand up and cast, particularly on windy days.

The majority of the anglers who fish Interior lakes prefer to use boats, and on waters accessible by road, boats unquestionably provide the safest, most efficient means of reaching the fish. For an angler who sometimes fishes alone, a light, durable 8- to 12-foot boat that may be carried on top of a car or light truck is best. An infinite variety of designs is available, but only a few combine all the features that are desirable for a fly fisherman.

A good fly-fishing boat should have a flat or nearly flat bottom and a wide beam for stability. It should have ample freeboard and be relatively free of obstructions inside the hull. These requirements automatically eliminate double-hulled or catamaran fiberglass designs, which are awkward to handle and have a clumsy interior arrangement. It also eliminates round-hulled aluminum boats that tip easily, or aluminum prams with narrow beams which are unsafe for the same reason. Flat bottoms and high freeboards are more common among wooden-hull designs, but a wooden boat with floorboards is an abomination to cast from unless a rubber mat or piece of indoor-outdoor carpeting is placed over the boards.

Fiberglass designs have the great advantages of durability and freedom from maintenance. But fiberglass boats are heavy, and may be too difficult for one man to handle easily, especially if they must be loaded on or off the top of a vehicle. Fiberglass hulls also transmit noise rather efficiently, although this problem may be minimized by laying a mat on the floor of the boat. Relatively few fiberglass designs incorporate the features necessary for a good fly-fishing boat.

Weight also may be a serious problem in wooden boats. Unless one is a professional weightlifter, a light plywood model may be all that an individual angler can handle. Because building a wooden boat requires a good deal of hand labor, wooden designs are less common today than they once were, having yielded much of the market to mass-produced fiberglass or aluminum craft. But some designs are available which incorporate all the features needed by a fly fisherman, and they come without floorboards. But wooden boats require much more maintenance than either aluminum or fiberglass; when new, they may have to be sanded, primed and painted, and they will surely have to be caulked. And they will require periodic repainting and recaulking thereafter. All this may take time away from fishing. The same problems obviously apply to wooden prams, and the slightly V-shaped hull designs of many of these craft may make them too unstable to be a safe casting platform.

Aluminum boats and prams are both light and durable and require little, if any, maintenance. Many designs are available and a good number of them are well suited for fly fishermen. The big disadvantage of aluminum craft is that they transmit sound to the water so readily, and even a small object dropped inside the boat may make a noise loud enough to spook fish in the vicinity. Again, this problem can be minimized by placing a mat or carpet on the floor of the boat and by keeping the oarlocks well lubricated.

After having spent much of my life in small boats, I now own one I consider the best I have ever used for fly fishing. It is a 9-¼ foot aluminum pram that weighs only 68 pounds and can be handled easily by one man. It has a flat bottom, wide beam and high freeboard and is extremely stable even in the teeth of a fierce wind. Its hull design includes a short sloping bow which allows it to plane over the surface and it is extremely easy to row and to handle. The noise problem has been licked by placing a rubber mat on the floor with a layer of indoor-outdoor carpeting on top of the mat. And although I have used it now for many seasons, it has required no maintenance other than a periodic cleaning. Unfortunately, the manufacturer has long since discontinued the model and these prams now are nearly impossible to find. But I have seen others that were similar in size and design which probably would prove to be just about as good.

Anchors are essential in fly fishing from a small boat. Two should be carried, one to be let down from the stern and the other from the bow to prevent the boat from swinging around in a wind. If the boat is allowed to swing after a long cast, a belly will form quickly in the line, making it difficult or impossible to hook a fish. Almost any heavy object will serve the purpose — even a heavy stone in a pinch — and it should be attached to a length of rope that is about the equivalent of twice the maximum depth in which the angler expects to be fishing. The extra length is necessary to provide sufficient "scope" for the anchor to take purchase and hold when a stiff breeze is pressing on the boat.

Various pulley arrangements for anchor ropes are sold commercially, and these are a great convenience. Some are designed to be mounted as permanent fixtures on the transom or the bow; others may be put on and taken off by means of a vise-like arrangement.

There is no justification for using an outboard motor of more than 4 or 5 horsepower on any but the very largest Interior lakes. A motor of that size is sufficient to get an angler to or from the fishing grounds in short order, which is its only legitimate purpose. Larger motors do more harm than good and they have been the source of many problems on the Interior lakes. Both fishermen and resort owners have lobbied for restrictions on their use, but so far with only limited success.

Motors are not necessary at all on smaller lakes. Those who use them merely make life miserable for both fishermen and fish. When fish are feeding in the shallows, an outboard motor may frighten them away into deeper water for the rest of the day, spoiling the sport for fly fishermen. The big wakes left by too-powerful motors operated at full throttle also may be a real threat to an unsuspecting fly fisherman standing up in his boat. Common sense alone should be enough to deter anyone from using an outboard in shallow water, or operating a large one at full throttle on a small lake crowded with fishermen. But common sense seems to be a quality all too often lacking in boatmen whose only exposure to the outdoors is on a weekend away from the city, and it is a sadly common sight to see oversized boats and motors racing around a small lake as if bent on spoiling the sport of everyone else in the area. Oil slicks left by excessive outboard use also may harm the hatches of aquatic insects.

The widespread problems caused by abuse of outboard motors make it seem inevitable that eventually their use will be restricted on the Interior lakes. Until that happy day comes, they should be used only on larger lakes, only when necessary, and only with discretion. At other times, oars are perfectly adequate — and oars always start.

Accessories

A rod, reel, line and leader and some floating device to carry the angler are all that is necessary to fish the Kamloops trout lakes. But fly fishermen are fascinated by gadgetry and countless accessories have been developed to cater to their whims. Some of these are a bit frivolous, but others have real value in convenience, comfort and efficiency.

Flies, of course, are an essential part of an angler's kit and so is something to carry them in. Many types of plastic, leather or metal fly boxes or wallets are manufactured for the purpose. Size, ease of access and storage capacity are the points to consider in choosing one of these devices — and the final choice may boil down to a matter of whether the box or wallet will fit in a jacket or vest pocket. Metal fly boxes should be made of aluminum alloy to inhibit rust and plastic boxes should be sturdy enough to withstand the inevitable knocking about they will receive.

After a lot of experimentation, I have finally arrived at a system for storing flies that suits my purposes. The flies themselves are kept in clear plastic boxes with hinged lids and six compartments in each; the boxes themselves fit nicely into the slots of a container originally designed to hold 16-millimeter film cans. Each box is labeled for easy reference and the whole arrangement is a little like a tiny chest of drawers. It works fine for me, but the choice of a system for storing flies is best left up to the individual angler.

Extra spools of leader material also are a necessary component of an angler's equipment, and these may be carried in boxes or kept on lengths of dowel inserted through holes in the center of the spools. Anglers who tie their own leaders also may wish to carry a small micrometer to measure the diameter of leader material.

In dry-fly fishing still water, it is essential to keep the leader from floating. A floating leader casts a shadow and is highly visible to fish, but if a leader can be made to sink just beneath the surface its connection to the fly is nearly invisible. Various "leader sinks" are sold in tackle shops and in my opinion none is wholly satisfactory. But the best I have found is a product called Gehrke's Xink, a liquid that comes in a small plastic bottle. It should be applied to the leader tippet and allowed to dry before use. It works well enough for awhile, but seems to lose its effectiveness rather quickly and frequent applications are necessary. Even at that, it is better than other preparations.

Keeping the fly afloat is every bit as vital as keeping the leader submerged, and there are many products designed to "dry out" flies and keep them floating. I've tried most of them at one time or another and for many years thought Mucilin paste was the best available. Then along came a new product called Gehrke's Gink, made by the manufacturer of Xink. A small, soft paste that comes in a tiny jar, it is by far the best fly floatant I have ever used. Its one disadvantage is that during extremely warm weather the paste turns to liquid and spills easily — and it leaves a permanent greasy stain on clothing.

A clipper or a small pair of sharp scissors is indispensable for trimming knots or removing flies from leaders. A small pair of pliers also is handy for bending down hook barbs to make it easier to release fish, or to remove the fly the wind has deposited in the back of one's jacket.

I am never without a pair of polaroid sunglasses while fishing. They cut the glare reflected from the surface and keep the eyes from tiring through a long day of fishing under bright sunshine, and they offer protection from an errant cast. They also enable the angler to see through surface reflections, making it easy to spot submerged weedbeds or shoals

176

surrounded by deep water. When fishing shallow water with a marl bottom, a good pair of polaroids also sometimes make it possible to see individual cruising fish, and then it is a simple matter to lead them with a cast and watch the result as the fish comes to the fly. Sighting cruising fish, stalking them and casting to them is, to me, the ultimate excitement in angling. Unfortunately, this is seldom possible in the majority of the Kamloops trout lakes — the water in many of them is not transparent enough, or the bottom is too rocky or covered with weed growth for the trout to be visible. But it sometimes is possible in the shallows at the south end of Roche Lake, or over the flats of Plateau, around the margins of Blue Lake, in parts of Stake Lake, in nearly all of Valentine and doubtless in other waters. However, a pair of polaroids is necessary to see the fish in each case.

Having lost several pairs overboard, I now attach a cord to my polaroids and wear them around my neck. It may make me look a bit like an old-fashioned schoolteacher, but I haven't lost a pair of glasses since I began using the cord.

Other handy accessories include a hook-sharpening file or stone, a thermometer to take water temperatures, a notebook in which to take notes and a scale and measuring tape. Some anglers prefer to carry a net, although these often get in the way and are an unnecessary luxury if one does not plan to keep very many fish.

An ashtray may seem a strange thing to recommend as part of an angler's outfit, but if one is in the habit of smoking while fishing, I would certainly recommend it. There are numerous documented instances of trout having been caught with undigested cigarette filters or matches in their stomachs, and doubtless these items have caused some trout to come to an uncomfortable and untimely end. The same is true for the pull-tabs from beverage cans, and I have seen trout that had become wedged in one of the holes of the plastic web that held a six-pack of cans together. The simple truth is that any angler who has any respect for the fish he seeks or the water he fishes should never throw anything overboard. He should treat a lake as he would his own living room — since the lake is, in fact, the trout's living room, and litter may be lethal to fish or other organisms that live there. An ashtray and a litter bag should be carried in every boat.

All this seems obvious, and yet many fishermen who should know better treat the lakes they fish with casual indifference. In other respects they may be ardent conservationists, working to protect trout habitat while they continue to degrade it with their own litter. The astonishing variety and amount of litter that has been turned up by drag hooks in some of the Kamloops lakes is proof of the seriousness of the problem.

It is hard to enjoy fishing if one is too cold or too warm or too wet, and proper clothing is a critical part of any angler's equipment. Hats are especially important; they shade the eyes and the face, offer protection

177

from flying hooks and offer at least some insulation from rain and hail.
The frequently-changing weather of the British Columbia Interior calls
for a wide variety of other clothing. An angler planning a trip to the
Interior should pack long underwear, a heavy sweater and a warm jacket.
If he has these items he can always take them off if the weather grows
warm; but if he doesn't have them in cold weather, he will regret it.
Good rain gear, capable of keeping an exposed fisherman dry in a torren-
tial thundershower, also is essential.

Insect repellent and a good sunscreen lotion are other items important
to an angler's personal comfort. Mosquitoes around some of the Interior
lakes often are numerous and vicious, especially in the first warm weather
of spring, and some sort of effective repellent is necessary to keep the
annoyance to a minimum. Cutter's and Deep Woods Off both do a good
job, and they should be applied lightly to clothing as well as exposed skin
to keep mosquitoes from biting through shirts and trousers — which they
will do readily.

The sun can do a lot of damage to a fisherman, especially at the relatively high elevations of many of the Kamloops waters. A painful dose
of sunburn, or worse, may be suffered in a surprisingly short time unless
precautions are taken. Numerous effective sunscreen lotions are available;
my personal choice, recommended by a physician, is one called U-Val,
and a single application usually is enough for a full day's protection.

The foregoing represents the minimum list of accessories and clothing
an angler will wish to have if he fishes often on the Interior lakes. And
over a period of time he undoubtedly will accumulate many other items
not mentioned here. The problem then becomes one of how to carry
them. No one yet has come up with a vest containing enough pockets to
satisfy a gadget-loaded fly fisherman, and a tackle bag or box probably
would have to be as large as a steamer trunk for him to get all his gear
comfortably inside. But this is a problem for each angler to approach in
his own way, and — not having solved it for myself — I would not pre-
sume to give advice.

TECHNIQUE

There is something slightly intimidating about the first sight of an un-
familiar lake. Usually there is nothing to indicate what secrets it may
hold, nothing but an opaque expanse of water with perhaps a scattered
random rise. The rocks and wrinkles that are telltale markers of the
hiding spots of trout in streams are lacking, and there is no easy guide to
where the fish may be. Reading the water of a lake is much more difficult than reading a stream.

Yet the requirements for trout in lakes are precisely the same as those
in streams: Food, cover and comfort. In a stream, the food is carried on
the current, cover is obtained beneath an overhanging bank or sagging

limb, and comfort is found in a pocket sheltered from the full force of the flow. But in a lake, the trout must go to the food rather than vice versa, seeking it out in the productive shallows and weedbeds. Cover is found in the camouflaging weedbeds, over dark gravel bottoms or in the sheltering depths, and comfort is available in the zone with the most favorable oxygen and temperature characteristics when a thermocline is present. Some time must be spent in exploration before any or all of these characteristics become apparent.

Generally speaking, the shallow areas of any lake are most productive of the scuds and insects that trout feed on. Some of these may be determined from the lay of the land around the lake; a long, gently-sloping point extending well out into the lake may be assumed to continue its extension beneath the surface, providing a shallow place where trout crusing the shoreline may congregate to feed. Similarly, a bay lying in a gentle, concave hollow may offer a broad expanse of shallow water. But some shallow areas will not be so readily apparent from the surrounding topography, and it is best to cruise the shoreline in search of shoal areas extending well out into the lake. Some shoal areas, or "sunken islands" as anglers often like to call them, may be located far from shore in the center of the lake, and these may be found only by accident or on the direction of anglers familiar with the water.

Once the shallow areas of a lake are found and marked, it is time to try some exploratory fishing over them. If there is no obvious feeding activity over the shallow area itself, the angler should anchor near the edge and cast over it into deeper water in hopes of intercepting trout that may be cruising the edge of the shoal. Almost any shallow area is likely to have trout feeding over or around it at some time of the day, although early morning and late evening are the most reliable times, when the absence of light gives the trout a sense of security that may be lacking during the brightness of the day. Gravel reefs or marl-covered shoals may be equally productive, though fish may feed less cautiously over the former because they somehow sense that they are more difficult to see over a pattern of broken gravel.

The mouths of inlet streams also may be productive spots, both because the current carries food from the stream and the flow carries fine gravel and silt which, over time, builds up a shallow apron at its mouth which may become a good food producer in itself.

The point to remember is that trout in lakes must aggressively seek their food, and because the shallows – depths up to 15 feet – produce most of it, trout are more apt to be found feeding there than in any other area.

The trout's preference for feeding in relatively shallow water is one of the things that makes fly fishing so much more effective than other methods. The shallows are pretty much off limits to anglers using any

179

kind of weight, and by their choice of method they restrict themselves to the least productive portions of a lake.

The wind may play an important role in determining where trout feed in a lake. A breeze blowing from the same direction all day will concentrate hatching or spent insects on one side or in one corner of a lake, and hungry trout will quickly take advantage of the fact. Observant anglers should do likewise. If the wind should become strong enough to stir fair-sized waves all across the surface, there usually will be slicks — narrow patches where the water remains strangely unruffled — extending for long distances, and veteran anglers know from experience that it pays to "fish the slicks." The reason is simple enough; insects on the surface are more easily visible in the calm water of the slick than the broken water around it. "Fishing the slicks" can be especially rewarding during a good sedge hatch or ant flight. And when the wind dies, it may leave drift lines of spent insects and other flotsam, and trout sometimes will rise to spent flies in the drift line.

Cover usually is less important to trout in lakes than in streams. Deep water is an excellent source of cover and trout are quick to take advantage of it if they sense danger. But the security of deep-water cover is left behind when trout penetrate deeply into the shallows to feed, and under such circumstances they are invariably nervous and wary and must be approached carefully. When hooked in shallow water, a trout's first response is likely to be a long run in a frantic bid to return to the safety of the depths.

Cover is likely to be much more important in a clear, shallow lake where food is equally abundant everywhere. This is especially true if the lake should have a marl bottom, over which cruising trout may be highly visible. Under these circumstances, trout are most likely to be found in areas where they are least likely to be seen, such as over weedbeds or rocky reefs. With polaroid glasses it is easy to find such areas, and if a careful approach is used, some good fishing may be had by casting into them.

When trout are not actively feeding, cover becomes their paramount concern and they will spend most of their time in areas where they feel safe. This is true in any type of lake, and whether the best cover is a shallow weedbed or simply a stretch of deep water, the trout will seek it out. Fishing will be slow for as long as the trout remain off the feed, but some may be taken by locating areas of obvious cover and casting to them.

Comfort usually is not much of a problem for trout in the Kamloops lakes. In the early spring and late fall, when oxygen levels and temperatures are uniform throughout the lake, the trout will feel at home anywhere and their movements will be dictated by their requirements for food and cover. But in the hot summer months, when many lakes stratify, the fish will seek the layer of water with most favorable temperature and oxygen characteristics and their movements will largely be confined within those limits. Anglers usually can establish the depth of this layer by the time-honored and tedious method of fishing a sinking line and allowing it to sink for various periods until it reaches a point where consistent action results. Perhaps a quicker and easier way is to use a depth thermometer to determine the level of the thermocline and fish accordingly.

All of the very best fishermen I have known have had one thing in common, and that is the ability to give absolutely total concentration to what they were doing. Some are not especially skillful anglers, but their alertness and involvement more than compensate for any failure of skill. By honing every faculty to a keen edge and using it to focus on everything going on around them, they are able to pick up subtle, helpful clues — the almost invisible surface bulge that may indicate a feeding fish below, a slight shift in wind or light that may indicate a different angling strategy, the behavior of birds or insects that is sometimes a tip-off to the behavior of the fish. Each of these fishermen understands something of the complex ecological interrelationships of a lake and how a change in one element may produce changes in many others, and through observation and interpretation they are able to put such understanding to good use. Perhaps most remarkable of all, each of them is able to maintain a level of fierce concentration for many hours at a time, without losing the edge that gives them a powerful advantage over both fish and their fellow fishermen.

From this description, one might think these anglers are single-minded individuals, one-dimensional characters whose only interest is fishing. But I do not think this is the case at all; they are simply people who find maximum enjoyment through maximum involvement, a quality they frequently bring to many other fields besides fishing. I suspect the ability to totally immerse one's self in an activity is as much an accident of birth as it is an acquired habit, but there is no question that concentration and perception can be sharpened through practice, and anyone who looks upon fly fishing as a full-time hobby would do well to develop these qualities. They are, in my estimation, the most important angling techniques.

Once an angler has familiarized himself with the water, found and marked some likely-looking feeding or sheltering spots and sized up the general situation, he should be ready to choose the method appropriate for the situation: Dry fly, wet fly or nymph.

Dry-fly Fishing

In a stream, the movement of the current provides movement to the fly and also creates the problem of drag. In a lake, the opposite is true; there is no current and no drag and if the fly is to have any movement at all, it must be imparted by the angler. Whether there should be movement depends upon what insects are hatching, if any; how the trout are responding to the hatch, if at all, and the surface conditions at the time.

If a hatch is in progress, the first problem is to determine what it is

181

and then choose a fly that is of the same general shape, size and color of the natural. Good imitations are perhaps even more important in lakes than in streams because the still-water environment gives the trout a more leisurely opportunity to inspect the fly before deciding whether to take it. Once the fly is chosen, some sort of dry-fly floatant should be applied and care should be taken to avoid getting any paste or fluid on the hook itself so that it will not be too slippery to hold in a fish. If the surface of the lake is still, leader sink should be applied to the business end of the leader.

If fish are feeding actively on the hatch, best results usually are obtained by casting to individual rising fish. The angler should watch the rise patterns carefully for a clue to the direction of a cruising, feeding fish and attempt to place his fly in front of the trout. If no pattern is visible, then the fly should be dropped as quickly as possible inside the spreading ring of water from the most recent rise in hopes the fish still will be there to see it.

Then the angler must decide whether to move the fly or let it sit still. This is extremely important; movement, or the lack of it, is probably the most significant factor in dry-fly fishing on lakes. The fisherman should carefully observe what the naturals are doing, and if a traveling sedge hatch is in progress and the majority of the insects are in motion, he should attempt to gently retrieve his fly at a speed approximately equal to that of the naturals. A retrieve that is too rapid, or one that is too slow, may mean the difference between success and failure. This is especially true on a calm surface; if the wind is blowing up a chop, the rate of movement is somewhat less important.

If the day is cold and dark and most of the sedges remain motionless for a time to dry their wings, then the angler should do the same with his imitation. If the trout are slow to respond, the fisherman should then take more time to observe how they are reacting to the naturals. If most of the rises seem to be to moving insects, he should fish his fly accordingly, and vice versa.

Since the sedge hatch involves large insects frequently in motion, it is the most difficult to fish — but also usually the most rewarding. Other hatches pose less complicated problems. Mayfly dun imitations always should be fished dead drift to conform with the behavior of the naturals; ants should be fished half-drowned in the surface film, with perhaps an occasional tiny twitch to imitate the motions of a struggling natural. On the infrequent occasions when Kamloops trout rise to hatching chironomids, some movement of the fly again may be necessary, although an imitation fished dead drift usually gets the best results. The best advice is to keep a close eye on the naturals and try to imitate their motion, or lack of it.

I have frequently enjoyed excellent dry-fly fishing late in the year when no hatch was in progress and there were no rises. The technique is to find a good feeding or sheltering area and cast over it with a high-floating fly, usually a small sedge pattern, and then retrieve it as quickly as possible. The rapid movement of the fly across the surface will bring up fish from considerable depths, perhaps triggering some sort of psychological response. Because the fly is moving so rapidly, it is not always easy to hook the fish, but their spectacular response to the skated fly is a sight to see — especially under conditions that would seem to rule out the successful use of a dry fly.

In fishing a dry fly under any circumstances, it is important to keep a straight line from the rod tip to the fly. If the wind is coming in at an angle, it will quickly blow a belly in the floating line, creating enough slack so that it is nearly impossible to set the hook in a rising fish. If the wind is a problem, the fisherman should anchor with the wind at his back so that the direction of his casts will be mostly parallel to the direction of the wind. Movement of the fly should be imparted by retrieving the line rather than lifting the rod; the rod tip should be held as close to the surface as possible so there is no slack between the rod and the water (the same applies in fishing nymphs or wet flies).

In order to be effective, a dry fly must remain afloat. It can be dried by false casts during fishing, but it is a good idea to apply another coat of dressing after a fish is taken. After several fish have been taken on the same fly, even a new dose of floatant may not be enough to keep it afloat — particularly if it is being retrieved — and it is time then to tie on a new fly.

Concentration is vital in dry-fly fishing. One should never take his eyes off the fly, for it is nearly axiomatic that the moment an angler looks away is the moment a fish will rise. Trust peripheral vision to detect rises away from the fly; then it is a simple matter to quickly lift the floating line off the surface and deliver a cast to the point of the rise.

Fish feeding on a surface hatch frequently will cruise a similar path along the margins of a shoal or weedbed, and by careful observation of rise patterns it is sometimes possible to determine parts of this route. Once one of these "hotspots" is located an angler can often obtain excellent results merely by casting repeatedly to it and waiting for a cruising fish to come along and take. If conditions are such that the fish are at least occasionally visible, the task becomes even easier. As stated previously, one of the ultimate thrills of dry-fly fishing is to sight a cruising fish, calculate its path, cast ahead of it and sit back to watch the results.

The Kamloops trout is a swift riser and the angler's response to a rise must be equally swift. The correct response is to raise the rod swiftly and firmly, tightening the line to set the hook in the trout's jaw. The timing requires some practice; if the response is too swift, the fly may be pulled right out of the fish's mouth; too violent and the leader is almost sure to break; too slow and the fish will be gone. Only with experience will the fisherman be able to judge the correct timing and pressure, and he should always be prepared to make allowances for the strength of his leader.

Dry-fly fishing has a rather weighty and dogmatic tradition that discourages experimentation. The more one reads on the subject, the more aware he becomes of the stifling codes and canons that have been established by the masters of the sport. Yet the individual angler should not allow himself to be intimidated by all these things. He should feel free to experiment freely and frequently. As with most anglers, if given a choice I should rather catch a trout on a dry fly than any other way, and experimentation has given me many rewards I would not have had otherwise. The limits of dry-fly techniques are shaped only by the bounds of men's imaginations, and doubtless there is much that remains to be discovered.

Nymph Fishing

It is difficult to draw a hard-and-fast line between nymph fishing and wet-fly fishing. The generally accepted definition is that a nymph is an imitation of the immature stage of an aquatic insect (or a scud or leech) while a wet fly is not meant to imitate anything in particular. Nymphs also may be fished on either floating or sinking lines.

The techniques of floating-line nymph fishing in lakes are quite different from those of dry-fly fishing. The problems of wind interference and slack are pretty much the same, but there the similarity ends. The biggest difference is that in nymph fishing, both the fly and the take often are invisible.

A floating-line presentation is called for when fish are feeding on nymphs just beneath the surface. Such feeding activity usually is apparent from the characteristic surface bulges left by turning trout in pursuit of a nymph or pupa — although sometimes nymphing fish will leave only a small, delicate surface ring to mark their passage. If the angler, through experience and observation, knows what insect is likely to be emerging, or is able to capture a sample from the water, he should put up an appropriate imitation and begin casting to feeding fish.

The choice of whether to retrieve the fly or fish it motionless depends upon what insect is being imitated. If the imitation is of an emerging sedge pupa or damselfly nymph, it should be retrieved accordingly — although some experimentation is likely to be necessary to establish the correct rate of retrieval. Even when the fly is being retrieved, the take may be surprisingly gentle, so the angler should be prepared to set the hook at even the slightest feeling of resistance. The surface bulge left by the feeding fish will not become visible until after the fish has made its pass at the fly, and by then it is too late to set the hook.

If the imitation is of a chironomid pupa, then it may be necessary to grease all but the point of the leader so that the fly floats almost vertically in or just beneath the surface film. The imitation should be fished without motion, or with no more than a very occasional twitch. If the fly is in the surface film, strikes sometimes may be visible; but more often than not, the fish will take the fly subtly and gently, and the only indication will be a very slight movement of the line. This is where the fluorescent "nymph indicators" come in handy, telegraphing the movement so the angler can set the hook. Again, the fisherman should strike by lifting the rod swiftly and firmly — but not too swiftly, or too firmly.

Damselfly nymph and/or sedge pupae imitations also may be fished on sink-tip lines, which also are very useful for fishing imitations of dragonfly nymphs, scuds and leeches. The sink-tip line is best employed in relatively shallow water or over weedbeds when surface bulges are not apparent. The technique is simply to cast, allow the fly to sink to the desired depth and retrieve at an appropriate rate. Strikes, if they are forthcoming, usually will be felt as a slow, sullen resistance. However, it pays to keep a close eye on the floating portion of the line for any telltale movement that may signal a more subtle take.

Fast-sinking lines frequently are used with scud or leech imitations fished in relatively deep water, usually with a very slow retrieve. Perhaps because they feel somewhat more secure in deep water, the Kamloops trout seem to respond to these deeply-sunk patterns with less caution: a take usually comes in the form of sudden, violent resistance, and in most cases the fish hooks itself even before the angler can react.

It is worth repeating that in fishing with sink-tip or fast-sinking lines, the fisherman should strive to keep his line straight and hold his rod tip close to the surface so there is no sagging belly in his line. The more direct the angler's connection to the fly, the more successful he will be in hooking fish.

Wet-fly Fishing

Wet-fly fishing has been labeled the "chuck-and-chance-it" method, a disparaging term no doubt coined by dry-fly purists to show their contempt for wet-fly anglers. Although its negative connotation may be unnecessarily harsh, it is an essentially accurate description of the method: Wet-fly fishing involves the use of non-imitative fly patterns which are cast more or less at random. In the Kamloops trout lakes, wet-fly fishing usually involves "attractor" patterns, brightly-colored flies designed for maximum visibility and movement.

These patterns may be fished with either a sink-tip or fast-sinking line, depending upon the depth and character of the water. Many veteran Kamloops anglers consider the attractor patterns a sort of last resort when imitative flies have been tried and failed and there is no visible evidence of feeding fish. The attractor patterns are fished at varying depths with varying retrieves until a fish finally takes hold. The fish may yield a stomach sample that will then prompt the angler to change back to an imitative pattern, but if not he will go on using the attractor pattern, fishing it in the same manner that brought results the first time. His casts will be random only to the extent that he cannot see the fish, for surely he will have chosen a spot where he knows fish are likely to be present, or one that has produced results on earlier occasions.

Wet-fly fishing can be surprisingly productive when trout are not actively feeding. The sight of a colorful attractor pattern may stimulate a response when nothing else will. The strike, when it comes, is likely to be strong and abrupt, pulling the line from the angler's fingers, and again the fish usually will hook itself. Wet-fly fishing may lack the high degree of skill and refinement demanded by the dry fly or the nymph, but it gets results — and it should be a part of any angler's repertoire.

Anyone who fishes the Kamloops trout waters, by any method, should not expect uniform success. Very seldom will he have a day where it seems as if a trout came on every cast, and if he does it most likely will be in a lake where small trout are plentiful. Most experienced fly fishermen measure success in terms of size of trout rather than numbers, and in those waters containing large trout a catch of four or five fish a day may be considered excellent. It will be a red-letter day indeed if the number of such trout should rise into double figures, but regardless of the total, each fish is likely to be a memorable one. And inevitably there will be days when even the most skillful anglers will go without a single fish.

The point is that the Kamloops trout lakes, like trout waters everywhere, can be very fickle, and sometimes they will withhold their rewards stubbornly. But over the long term, those who develop their skills, fish patiently and remain intent will find their rewards are more than ample.

Playing and Landing Fish

What happens once the fish is hooked? In that split second even before the angler has felt the exhilaration of contact, the trout already has begun its response. It moves with the speed of instinct and its usual reaction is to run with all its strength, or throw itself recklessly into the air. How quickly the angler reacts in these moments, and how well, often determines the outcome of the struggle. A tangle in the line or the clumsy pressure of a finger against it may result in a smashed leader and a lost fish.

If the trout's initial response is to run, there is little point in trying to stop it unless it is headed for some obstruction. If the fish is a large one, any attempt to slow it down is likely to result in a broken leader. It will quickly take slack line from the angler's hand or the bottom of the boat and pull a great deal more from the reel, and usually there is no harm in letting it go as far as it wants — so long as it does not strip all the backing from the reel. There is potential danger when a large fish runs in a curving direction; a large belly forms in the heavy fly line as it slices through the water behind the fish, and sometimes the line's resistance alone is

enough to cause the leader to part. There really is not very much an angler can do about this. But if the trout runs in a more or less straight direction, the line follows easily and the angler has only to wait until the
run is over, when the fish is likely to turn or jump. And once the fish
has taken all the slack and is "on the reel," it is best to continue to play
it from the reel and avoid retrieving line by hand; the latter method
should be reserved for smaller fish that pose less of a hazard to the leader.

If the fish jumps – either at the moment of the strike or any time
later – the correct response is to instantly lower the rod tip to ease the
strain on the line. A violent leap against the pressure of a taut line may
tear the hook out, or increase the chance that the leader will be broken
if the fish should fall on top of it. Dipping the rod usually will create
enough instant slack to cushion the shock of a strong leap.

A favorite tactic of the Kamloops trout – particularly when it has
just made a long run away from the angler – is to run straight toward
the source of resistance. This move may trick even an experienced angler into thinking he has lost the fish; when the trout reverses direction
and begins running toward the fisherman, it creates an instant belly in
the line and there is no longer any feeling of resistance. The slack line
may enable the fish to escape before the angler realizes what has happened. One way to guard against this is to watch the line carefully; even
though all feeling of resistance has disappeared, if the line is still moving
it is a sure sign that the fish is still hooked. The problem then is to recover line quickly enough to get a straight connection with the fish.
Sometimes a reel simply can't keep up with a fast-running fish, and it
then becomes necessary to strip line rapidly by hand. This is the only
exception to the rule of thumb that a large fish always should be played
from the reel, and once the fisherman has again tightened up on the
trout it is a good idea to reel in the slack and get the fish back on the
reel.

The Kamloops trout will spend its strength freely on a long run or a
series of jumps immediately after it is hooked, but once these fireworks
are over it will settle down to slug it out. It may run several more times,
but usually none of these will be as long or as strong as the first; it may
jump repeatedly or thrash the surface, but as its energy ebbs each one of
these demonstrations will be less violent than the last. A large trout will
shake itself like a wet Spaniel, trying to dislodge the hook – a tactic
that is frequently successful. Sometimes a trout will roll itself up in the
leader, or get the tippet tangled around a ventral fin, and usually it will
then come meekly to the angler – although the strain placed on the
leader is dangerous and the trout may suddenly free itself and catch the
angler unprepared to counter a sudden run or jump.

The key to success during this phase of the fight is to keep a steady,
unrelenting pressure on the fish so that it has no chance to rest or regain
its strength. The rod should be kept at an angle and direction sufficient

to keep a steady strain, and if the fish should change direction the angler should change the direction of his rod. Line should be recovered at every opportunity. The continual pressure of the rod will soon tire the trout enough for the fisherman to gain control.

The "end game" is as crucial in fishing as it is in chess. Probably more fish are lost alongside the boat than at any other stage of the game. Any number of things can go wrong: The fish may tangle the leader around the anchor rope if the angler is not attentive, or the sight of a net thrust too quickly toward it may cause it to bolt and break the leader. The angler may pressure the fish too much and pull the hook out of it, or allow it to break the leader on a sharp corner of the hull.

All these things are more likely to occur if one attempts to land a trout too soon. The fish should be played until the angler is confident he has control of it (but not too long, or it will jeopardize the trout's chances for recovery if it is to be released). Then, if the fish is to be netted, the net should be placed in the water and the fish should be led gently over it.

The growth of the "catch-and-release" ethic among sport fishermen has prompted many anglers to stop using nets. On the rare occasions when they decide to keep a fish, most play it to the side of the boat and then take a firm grip on its lower jaw with their thumb and forefinger. This grip seems to momentarily paralyze the trout, making it possible to lift even a very large fish out of the water and into the boat. But obviously it takes practice and must be done with care.

Careful handling is required for trout that are to be released. The fishing regulations published by the British Columbia Fish and Wildlife Branch now contain an excellent statement on the technique of release that seems well worth repeating here:

"There is a growing trend among anglers to release, unharmed, a portion of their allowable catch. The Fish and Wildlife Branch heartily endorses this philosophy of voluntary 'catch and release.' By following a few simple rules you can be certain that released fish will live to be caught again. Remember that a fish that appears unharmed when released may not survive if not carefully handled:

"1. *Time is of the essence.* Play and release the fish as rapidly as possible. A fish played gently for too long may be too exhausted to recover.

"2. *Keep the fish in the water* as much as possible. A fish out of water is suffocating and, in addition, is twice as heavy. He may pound himself fatally if allowed to on beach or rocks (or in the bottom of a boat – S.R.). Even a few inches of water under a thrashing fish acts as a protective cushion.

"3. *Gentleness in handling* is essential. Keep your fingers out of the gills. Do not squeeze small fish . . . they can be held easily by holding them by the lower lip. Nets may be helpful provided the mesh does not

This 15-inch Kamloops was returned to the water to grow larger. The "catch-and-release" philosphy is growing ever more common on the Kamloops trout waters.

become entangled in the gills. Hooks and lines catching in nets may delay releasing, so keep the net in the water.

"4. *Unhooking.* Remove the hook as rapidly as possible with long-nose pliers *unless the fish is deeply hooked.* If deeply hooked, cut the leader and leave the hook in. Do not tear out hooks roughly. Be gentle and quick. Small fish, especially, may die from shock from tearing out a hook.

"5. *Reviving.* Some fish, especially after a long struggle, may lose consciousness and float belly up. Always hold the fish in the water . . . Move it forward and backward so that water runs through the gills. When it revives, begins to struggle and can swim normally, let it go to survive and challenge another fisherman."

To which I would append only the thought that using barbless hooks makes it even easier to release a fish and adds a bit to the challenge of fly fishing.

Etiquette

In these days of ever-growing numbers of anglers, there is bound to be conflict as waters grow more and more crowded. This is particularly true with the presence of so many casual "weekend" anglers who remain

189

largely ignorant of the traditions and niceties of the sport. Unfortunately, there is no easy way for them to learn the rules of courtesy that all anglers should follow; these rules are not written down in the regulations published by the Fish and Wildlife Branch, and where they are mentioned in angling literature they deal mostly with fishing in streams and only seldom with fishing in lakes. So they are not easily accessible, and the most an unsophisticated angler on the Kamloops water can hope to do is learn through observation — or through the pointed comments of another angler whom he has unwittingly offended.

British Columbia fishermen would do well to follow the system that has been established in New Zealand. Waters there are posted with signs explaining the basics of angling etiquette, and the rules are rigidly enforced by peer pressure.

But "etiquette" really is just a $64 word for common courtesy, and a fisherman who follows his best instincts is not likely to have any trouble. In fishing lakes, that means giving a wide berth to an angler who already has anchored and begun casting, to avoid disturbing the water he has chosen to fish; it means refraining from operating a motor in a shallow area where trout may be frightened easily, and it means throttling down to a slow, safe speed when passing another fisherman. It means offering advice only when asked to do so, or asking another angler's permission to fish close by or to pass through water within his casting range (and the latter should be done only when there is no other route to take). It means not getting in the way of another angler who has chosen to drift and cast before the wind, and it means keeping a clean and quiet camp on the lakeshore. Altogether, it means doing nothing to interfere with the sport of any other angler, or his enjoyment of the surroundings and the day.

Most fly fishermen who have been at the business for awhile become aware of all of this, and seldom do conflicts arise between fly fishermen. The problems, when they do occur, usually involve anglers of different persuasions — frequently fly fishermen and trollers. The latter usually are an unsophisticated lot, and in their more or less aimless perambulations around a lake it seldom occurs to them that they may be spoiling a whole day's sport for a fly fisherman by intruding on the water he has chosen to fish. All too often I have seen trollers steer their outboards into shallow areas where fly fishermen were at work, prompting all the fish to flee, or coming so close to anchored anglers that they were unable to cast. There is a certain element of danger in this; more than once I have seen unwary trollers hooked by a fly fisherman's backcast — and more than once I have seen fly fishermen purposely aim a cast at an encroaching troller to frighten him away.

Such incidents often lead to angry words or sometimes worse, and each party leaves the incident with unhappy feelings that may spoil the enjoyment of the day. There is little reason why such conflicts should occur; at any given moment, a fly fisherman may be using only 60 feet of water or a little more while a troller has all the rest of the surface of the lake to explore. Perhaps it is some sort of primeval territorial imperative that impels the trollers — who usually are the majority — to encroach upon the area staked out by a lonely fly fisherman or two. Whatever the motive, trollers often are guilty of inexcusable behavior, and some sort of educational program is sorely needed to set them straight.

Not that trollers have a monopoly on bad manners; there are bad apples among the fly fishing fraternity as well. Usually these are individuals whose eagerness and enthusiasm gets in the way of their judgment, to the point that they make life miserable for other fishermen around them. Fortunately, there are not many of them, and usually peer pressure is enough to straighten them out.

Finally, a word about ethics: Any angler who does not himself faithfully observe fishing rules and regulations has no right to expect any other angler to do so. And rules should not be considered targets; numerical and size limits are not established as goals, but as maximums. Anglers who observe the rules and keep less than a limit catch do themselves and others a great favor.

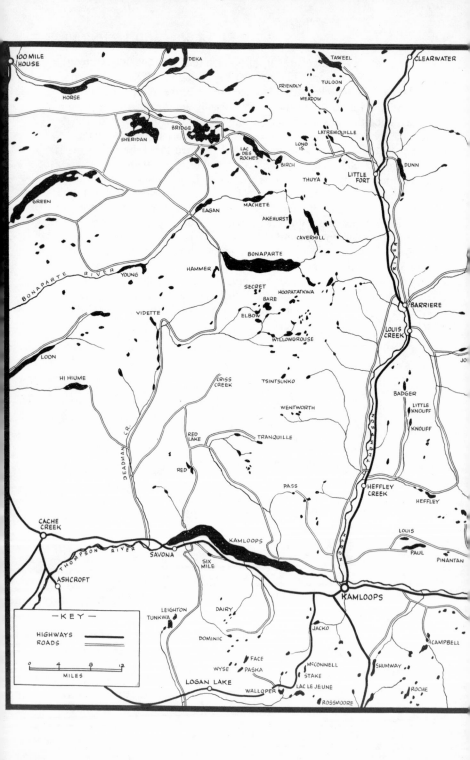

Chapter Eight
Favorite Waters

The Kamloops trout lakes are within the economic reach of almost any angler. There are lakes with posh resorts that cater to an angler's every whim; lakes with fishing camps that range from comfortable to primitive; lakes with developed campsites, and lakes with no development at all. Some lakes lie next to highways; others are reached over dirt roads that range from good to tortuous; some lakes are accessible only on foot or by horseback, and some are reached only by air. Within this broad range there are bound to be at least a few waters to suit the taste and pocketbook of any fisherman.

The problem, of course, is to find them. And to someone who is not familiar with the country, this can be a formidable task, with thousands of waters to choose from. Fortunately, the government of British Columbia — recognizing the value of fishing to its tourist industry — has done some things to make the task easier, with help from private businessmen. Tourism is a very important part of the provincial economy, and even though the government has ignored its responsibility to care for fish and wildlife resources, it nevertheless has done a good job of promoting what is left of them.

One of the most useful things it does is to publish annually a directory of tourist accommodations, listing virtually every hotel, motel or lodging place in British Columbia. Fishing camps are included, along with a brief description of where they are located, the services they provide, the rates they charge and how to get in touch with them. The directory also includes maps of major highway routes, information on air, bus and rail service and a good deal of other useful data. It is free to anyone who asks for it and may be obtained by writing to Tourism British Columbia, Ministry of Tourism and Small Business Development, Parliament Buildings, Victoria, B. C. V8W 2Z2. Ask for the "Directory of British Columbia Tourist Accommodation" for the current year.

This handy publication will save a visiting angler a good deal of time and legwork in finding a place to go. But virtually all the Interior fishing camps require reservations in advance, so it is essential to write or telephone well ahead of time.

The maps in the accommodations directory are not large enough to show the locations of smaller lakes, and of course the directory does not describe the many waters that lack fishing camps or resorts. Of these, a good number have developed or primitive campsites that are made to order for anglers who prefer to stay in tents or campers instead of lodges or resorts. So good maps are absolutely essential, and they must be of a scale large enough to show the smallest lakes and the side roads that lead to many of them.

Such detailed maps are available from the Geographic Division of the Department of Lands, Forests and Water Resources in Victoria. These are published in various scales and may be obtained at reasonable cost, but it is necessary first to write for an index from which to order.

Good as these maps are, they very quickly become out of date as new roads are built or old ones are washed out or grown over. Still, they may be relied upon as accurate guides to the general area and more recent maps showing the latest road changes usually may be obtained at sporting goods stores in the Interior. For instance, the Kamloops & District Fish & Game Association publishes and sells a "Fishing and Hunting Map of the Kamloops Area" which shows all the important lakes and contains advertisements from many fishing camps and resorts. The 100 Mile Fly Fishers publish a Cariboo area fishing map which may be purchased in 100 Mile House. And the Tourist Bureau of the Merritt & District Chamber of Commerce publishes a somewhat less elaborate but still useful map of waters around the Merritt area, and these are available in Merritt-area sporting goods stores.

These local maps usually are not to scale and may be totally lacking in topographic detail, but they usually are accurate in showing the best roads to take. For best results they should be used in combination with the more detailed government maps.

At least two fishing guides to British Columbia waters now are published annually in paperback format, and these also provide useful information. Their chief value is in their capsule descriptions of many individual lakes and how to get to them. But these guides, like most of their genre, suffer from one serious defect: Too often no attempt is made to update the information for years on end, with the result that it may become badly obsolete. Before heading off into the bush in search of a remote lake described in one of these publications, it is advisable to verify the information locally. The guides are sold at most sporting goods stores and bookshops.

Compared to many areas of the world, British Columbia has made it easy for visiting anglers to obtain information about its fishing. But getting a fishing license is not so easy. At one time they were widely available, at border crossings, government-operated tourist information centers on major highways, many service stations and at nearly every sporting goods store. But in recent years they have become much more difficult to obtain; no longer are they sold at border crossings or tourist information centers or at most service stations. They are still available at most sporting goods stores, but some stores do not have licenses for non-resident anglers. Correct licenses can be obtained at any regional office of the Fish and Wildlife Branch, but these are not always conveniently located — nor are they always open when an angler is passing through on a tight schedule. However, most fishing camps and resorts make it a point to have the right licenses on hand.

Once the angler has obtained a license, he must carry it with him while fishing — and sooner or later, he is bound to be checked by a conservation officer. When buying a license, the fisherman also should pick up a copy of the current angling regulations and study it carefully.

Even after he has gained the best advice and information it still will take some time for a newcomer to learn the country, the waters and the fish, and to establish favorite lakes to which he will want to return. This should not be a discouraging prospect; rather, it is the sort of challenge that excites most anglers. Even those who have spent a lifetime fishing the Kamloops trout lakes still take keen pleasure in exploring untried waters.

But a word to the wise: Those who are accustomed to doing most of their driving on city streets may find the side roads of the Kamloops area a bit more than they bargained for. It is always advisable to inquire locally about the condition of secondary roads, and it is a wise policy for an outsider to conclude that the road probably is a bit worse than it is reported to be; what a native of the area would consider a "good" road may seem anything but good to a visitor from outside the province. The same logic should be applied in reading maps. Unsurfaced roads that look good in dry weather may become nearly bottomless quagmires after a hard rain, and it is a good idea to carry chains, axe, shovel and a power winch or "come-along" (hand winch) if one plans to travel the back roads of the Interiors. Many roads also are impassable to vehicles lacking high center clearance.

This point cannot be overemphasized. A good number of the roads leading into the Kamloops trout lakes are marginal at best, particularly in the spring, and one who never has driven them has no concept of what he is likely to encounter. It is difficult to get help if one should get stuck or broken down on a little-traveled dirt road 10 or 20 miles from the nearest paved highway. The natives who drive these roads are used to them and it is sort of a rule of the road that they will always stop to help someone in trouble; but it may be a long time before one of them comes along.

This should not discourage anglers who are unaccustomed to such conditions. Many resorts provide their own transportation from the nearest highway or community, and there are many excellent lakes within easy reach of the angler driving the family car.

Train, plane and bus service to the Interior also is available and service is frequent. Arrangements sometimes may be made for an angler to be met at the terminal and taken to a nearby resort or fishing camp. Air charter service also is available at Kamloops to take fishing parties into remote lakes or fly-in camps.

There are so many Kamloops trout waters that one could not reasonably hope to fish them all in a lifetime. The number of lakes and the difficulties involved in reaching some of them also complicate the task of preparing a descriptive list that is in any way comprehensive and accurate. The list that follows therefore is necessarily limited to those waters about which I have personal knowledge or recent information from sources I consider reliable. The list also largely reflects my own angling experiences, which have been mostly on waters located along the Merritt-Kamloops-North Thompson axis. So the list is by no means a complete catalogue of all the Kamloops trout waters, and no lack of merit is implied for those waters which are not included. The reader also should bear in mind that the list is accurate only at the time of preparation and the descriptions given here are subject to rapid and frequent change. It is always advisable to try to obtain up-to-date information locally before starting a trip to a remote lake.

Kamloops Area

It seems appropriate to begin our list with the lakes of the Kamloops area, where the story of the Kamloops trout began. Kamloops is strategically located in the center of a large region of lakes but it is a region that recently has undergone many changes. The city has grown rapidly up the steep slopes of its valley walls and spilled over the ridgetops into the country beyond, and many of the old, rutted roads have been replaced by asphalt highways. South of Kamloops a new town, Logan Lake, now stands where once there were meadows and pine thickets. The added population and improved transportation corridors have combined to change the character of many of the lakes close to Kamloops; visited by ever-growing numbers of anglers and other recreationists, they have lost their pristine qualities, and some now are even ringed by summer cabins or subdivisions. But even though some have lost their best aesthetic qualities, many still provide surprisingly good angling opportunities.

The Lac le Jeune Road leaves the Trans-Canada Highway just west of Kamloops and climbs steeply into the pine-dotted hills. The first time I traveled it, in the days shortly after World War II, it was only a pair of ruts with grass growing high in the center, and the journey as far as Lac le Jeune seemed long and arduous. But as travel increased over the years, the center strip was worn away and the road even became wide enough in spots for vehicles traveling in opposite directions to pass one another without leaving the roadway — if the drivers were careful. Later still, the road became an all-weather gravel route and construction crews removed many of its curves and switchbacks. Today it is a two-lane blacktop highway and drivers find it easy to exceed the posted speed limit. The trip to Lac le Jeune, which once took hours, now takes only minutes.

The first lake accessible from the road is **Jacko**, only about 10 minutes' travel time from downtown Kamloops. A dirt road, often very slippery in wet weather, extends eastward about a mile from the blacktop, climbing over a low ridge to the lake. Late in the spring afternoons, when the shops close in Kamloops, there often is a small parade of vehicles over this road as anglers head out to catch the evening rise.

A small lake of about 100 acres, Jacko nevertheless produces very well at times. It lies at an elevation of about 2,900 feet so that it becomes warm early in the summer; early spring and late fall are the best times to fish it. Located in mostly open country, the lake is rimmed with broad banks of tules and a gently sloping shoreline; the bottom is mostly a soft, black ooze of decaying organic material. There is no natural spawning and the trout population in the lake is maintained by stocking.

In years past, Jacko Lake yielded trout as heavy as 9 or 10 pounds, but that is no assurance that any more such fish will be caught in the future. The average weight of Jacko Lake trout now probably is about 1½ pounds with an occasional larger fish. It is a pleasant lake to fish with a fly, and in the evenings the trout often cruise the edges of the tule beds where a well-placed nymph will take them. Overnight camping is not permitted at the lake, but cartop boats may be launched without difficulty.

Beyond Jacko Lake, about 16 miles from Kamloops, lies **McConnell Lake**. Just off the highway, it is an attractive lake with unusually clear water and a marl bottom visible at considerable depths. Surrounded by thick timber, McConnell is at an elevation of 4,242 feet — high enough so that its water remains cool for fishing well into late spring or early summer.

Easily explored in a day of fishing, McConnell has a surface area of 80 acres and a maximum depth of 84 feet. It is fed by a small, seasonal stream, probably without sufficient flow to support a run of spawning fish in most years. In any case, relatively heavy angling pressure makes stocking a necessity.

McConnell has fairly abundant populations of all the usual orders of insect life and gammarids, but it is not particularly well suited for the fly. Except for a shoal area along the eastern shore, the lakefloor shelves off rapidly. The water level in the lake may fluctuate considerably from one year to the next and low-water years probably are best for fly fishing. The maiden fish I have taken from this lake always have been in peak condition, exceptionally heavy for their length. There is a small campground on the lake with easy launching for cartop boats.

Two miles farther south, the highway skirts the western end of **Stake Lake**, a fine, shallow lake that is perfectly suited for fly fishing. The lake is at an elevation of 4,323 feet and its water temperature often remains low enough through the summer to assure consistent surface feeding. In fact, Stake is an excellent dry-fly lake. While it is not noted for a sedge hatch, it does produce heavy and consistent chironomid hatches through-

197

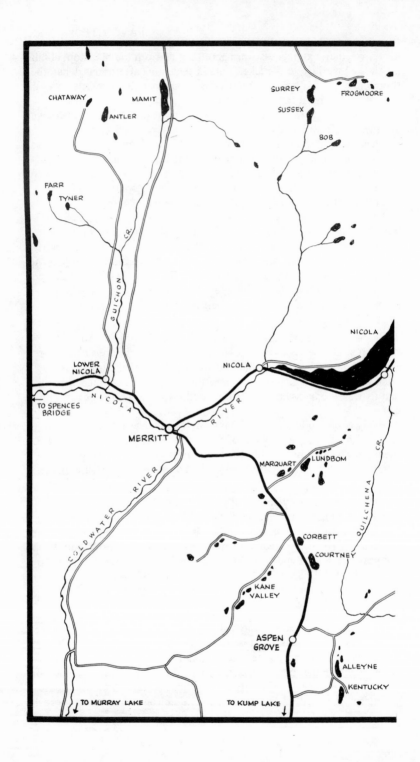

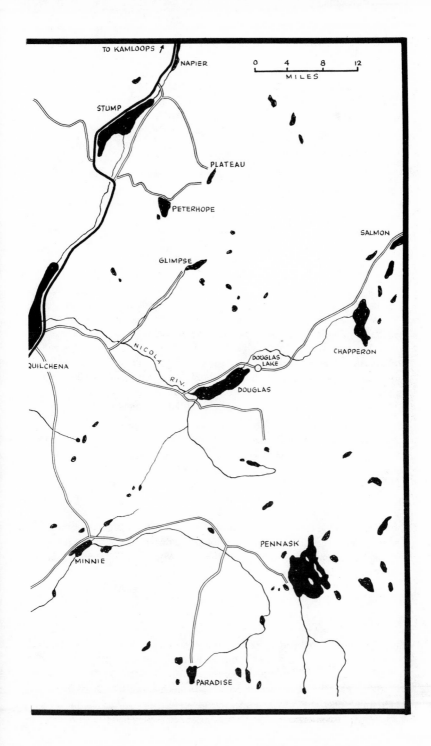

TO KAMLOOPS

NAPIER

STUMP

PLATEAU

PETERHOPE

SALMON

GLIMPSE

CHAPPERON

QUILCHENA

NICOLA

RIV.

DOUGLAS
LAKE

DOUGLAS

PENNASK

MINNIE

PARADISE

0   4   8   12

MILES

out the season and the trout seem especially willing to feed on the adults before they leave the surface.

Surrounded by thick timber, Stake Lake has a surface area of 57 acres and a maximum depth of only 30 feet. The best fly water is in the western end, near the highway, where the lake bottom slopes gently to a depth of 10 to 15 feet. The clear water and marl bottom sometimes make it possible to see cruising fish when the light is right, although there also are some dense patches of weed in which the trout can lose themselves. But Stake is one of relatively few waters where it is possible to spot a fish, cast a dry fly in its path and see everything clearly as the fish rises through as much as 10 feet of water to take the fly — a pleasing and exciting sight.

There is no natural spawning in Stake Lake, so stocking is necessary to maintain the trout population. Decades ago, after it was first stocked, the lake produced trout averaging 8 pounds, but as with so many other waters the size of the fish declined rapidly as surplus food stocks were consumed. Today the lake produces trout in the 2- to 2½ pound class with an occasional larger fish and many smaller ones.

Stake Lake receives tremendous pressure because of the easy access provided by the highway and usually there are plenty of bait fishermen and trollers competing for space on the water. Noise from the constant flow of traffic on the highway also is a distraction. There is a small campground, but its location next to the highway means little peace and quiet for those who stay overnight. Boat launching is easy, but the lakeside soil is soft and one must take care to avoid getting stuck.

Beyond Stake Lake the road forks, with the southern fork continuing toward the town of Logan Lake and the eastern fork leading a mile or so to **Lac le Jeune**. Needless to say, there have been a great many changes to this lake since the turn-of-the-century days when it was known as Fish Lake and Lambert reported daily catches of trout numbering into the hundreds. The once-primitive fishing camp at the western end of the lake has developed into an elaborate resort that now caters to skiers in the winter as well as fishermen and other recreationists in the summer. There is also a very large and comfortable provincial campground on the lake and summer cottages rim the shoreline. With all this, there is always plenty of traffic on the lake, and fishing pressure is intense.

Still, the fishing can be good at times, and the sedge hatch in late June and early July often is excellent. The lake is at an elevation of 4,200 feet with a surface area of about three-quarters of a mile. It is a long, relatively narrow lake with an irregular shoreline, points and bays and some good shoal water. Its maximum depth is about 80 feet. There is some natural spawning in tributary streams, but heavy angling pressure requires stocking to supplement the population.

From Lac le Jeune a difficult dirt road leads eastward to **Ross Moore Lake**, a rectangular lake of about 200 acres with a silty bottom and

Lac le Jeune, seen from the lodge.

brushy shoreline. While not particularly well suited for fly fishing, this lake has yielded catches of trout to 3 or 4 pounds in recent years. A spur road leads to smaller **Fred Lake** nearby.

Walloper Lake lies east of the highway to Logan Lake about two miles south of the Lac le Jeune turnoff. It is a shallow, irregularly-shaped lake with a silty bottom and dark, amber-stained water. Walloper is surrounded by heavy timber at an elevation of 4,300 feet; its maximum depth is 25 feet and its mean depth is only 9 feet. It has especially abundant populations of scuds and leeches and from all outward appearances it ought to be an excellent fly fishing lake. Unfortunately, it is subject to extremely heavy blue-green algae blooms starting as early as June and continuing into September. The bloom restricts visibility and often is so thick that a wet fly or nymph becomes coated with scum after the first couple of pulls of each retrieve.

Walloper also has suffered from frequent winter kills, although the Fish and Wildlife Branch now has a pondmill in operation on the lake in an attempt to alleviate that problem. In past years, after remaining free of winter kill for several seasons, Walloper has produced trout as heavy as 4 pounds, but on my last visit few trout larger than 10 inches were in evidence.

There is a small resort with cabins on the north end of the lake and a campground on the north shore between the highway and the lake. A number of private cabins also have been built on the lakeshore in recent years.

The highway between Lac le Jeune and Logan Lake also provides access to two other chains of lakes. A fishing camp on **Surrey, Sussex** and **Bob Lakes** provides 4-wheel-drive transportation over a slippery road from the highway. A good gravel road leads to the Mile High Lodge on **Face, Paska** and **Wyse Lakes**, three pleasant little timbered lakes that offer fishing for trout to 3 pounds.

Another road leaves the Trans-Canada Highway at Cherry Creek about eight miles west of Kamloops. This dirt road forks a short distance south of the highway; the western fork is a steep, rough and rocky road that leads to **Duffy Lake** at an elevation of about 3,850 feet. Duffy is a clear lake of about 200 acres, deep in the middle with extensive shoal areas around the shoreline. It is an enigmatic lake but produces trout of good size when it "turns on." However, because of its relatively low elevation, it becomes warm enough in the summer to prevent good fishing.

A spur road leads eastward from Duffy to the four small **Dairy Lakes** at an elevation of 4,500 feet. A pickup truck or some equivalent high-centered vehicle is required to get as far as Duffy Lake and a 4-wheel-drive rig is necessary to travel the next three miles to the Dairy chain. But even with 4-wheel-drive, the road is a very uncertain prospect in wet weather.

The road ends at Dairy Lake No. 1, largest of the four. It lies in heavy timber, a pleasant little lake about a mile long that offers reasonably good fishing for trout in the 3-pound class. Because of the high elevation, dark fish are likely to be found in this lake well into late June. The other lakes in this chain are reached over trail. Dairy Lake No. 2, really just a large pond, offers good fishing for trout up to a pound or so; the others are rumored to contain larger fish.

The other fork of the Cherry Creek Road, traversible by car, leads to **Dominic Lake**, a mile-long lake at an elevation of 5,000 feet. A fishing camp at this high-elevation lake offers housekeeping cabins and campsites. Trout are reported plentiful but not large.

Highway 5 heads south from Kamloops toward Merritt, and about 23 miles from the city a good gravel road leaves the pavement and heads in an easterly direction up into the hills for seven miles to **Roche Lake**. This lake, about 2½ miles long and no more than a quarter of a mile wide, lies in rolling, timbered country at an elevation of about 3,700 feet. Poisoned to remove scrap fish, it was stocked with Kamloops trout and reopened to fishing in 1968. Immediately it became popular with Kamloops-area fly fishermen.

One of its chief attractions is a fine sedge hatch, usually beginning about mid-June and continuing at least through the first week in July. The lake also produces abundant chironomid and damselfly hatches and

Afternoon shadows creep over Jacko Lake.

has good populations of scuds and leeches. The trout stocked after the lake was poisoned grew quickly to an average weight of about 2 pounds by the time the lake was reopened. That remains about the average weight, although some fish of 8 pounds or better have been taken and trout of 4 to 5 pounds are not uncommon.

Roche has a marl bottom, extensive shoal areas, large underwater weedbeds and four rocky islands. As with so many lakes in the area, it is used as a source of water for irrigation and a lock on the outlet stream controls the water level. Usually this means high water in the spring, while the lock is kept closed to store water for later use. If the water is high enough, trout move into the long, shallow bay at the extreme south end of the lake, offering some very interesting fishing. The water in this bay is never more than about four feet deep and large trout often are clearly visible over the bright marl bottom. They cruise around and over a dense mat of weed that grows in the center of the bay at its southern-most tip; sedges hatch here in incredible numbers, and the dry-fly fishing sometimes is first rate. When the hatch is off, a scud imitation fished on a sink-tip line also can be very effective. But a very cautious approach is necessary because the fish are wary in the shallow water, and handling large trout can be difficult because of the remains of an old rail fence, submerged when the level of the lake was raised. A lot of good fish have been broken off on the fence posts and rails.

The fishing in this area is not always dependable; if the water is too

Casting a dry fly on Stake Lake.

low, as it often is in dry years, trout simply will not enter the bay. More
dependable is the fishing around the edge of the wide shoal at the mouth
of the bay and the island just north of it. Sedges also hatch abundantly
in this area and it provides consistent dry-fly fishing. Unfortunately,
trollers – of which there usually are large numbers on this lake – often
penetrate the area, and the disturbances caused by their outboard motors
may scatter the trout for hours at a time.

A wide shoal area around the long, narrow island at the northeast end
of the lake also is a reliable spot for fly fishermen, especially in the evening.

There is a large government campground at the north end of the lake
as well as a large private resort with cabins and campsites. The resort has
become as famous as the lake itself because of its large bar and dining
room with picture windows overlooking the lake. The dining room spe-
cializes in fine Mexican cuisine and has gained such a reputation that
many persons come from Kamloops or elsewhere to eat rather than to
fish; some even fly in by float plane for dinner. A fine restaurant may
seem a bit out of place on the shore of a lake surrounded by forest, but
it is all quite tastefully done and detracts little from the surroundings.

A creek draining out of nearby **John Frank Lake** flows into Roche
Lake and apparently there is some movement of fish between the two.
Roche Lake trout also spawn in this creek, and their continued spawning
has been assured for at least the next few years by members of the Kam-

loops Flyfishers Club. Members keep a close eye on Roche Lake and its environs and moved in to clean up and restore the creek after it had been damaged by heavy-equipment operators.

John Frank Lake itself is much smaller and shallower than Roche and winter kills with distressing frequency. It is heavily populated with scuds, however, and its trout grow rapidly; unfortunately, they seldom have more than a couple of years to grow before they are victimized by winter kill.

Other nearby lakes include **Frisken, Bulman** and **Ernest**. The latter, reached over a poor dirt road, is managed as a trophy fishery and produces some very large trout.

North of Kamloops, Highway 5 — known here as the North Thompson Highway — follows the North Thompson River 57 miles to the village of Little Fort, and many lakes are accessible from this route. Just north of Kamloops, the Paul Lake Road leaves the highway and heads east toward **Paul, Pinantan, Pemberton** and **Hyas Lakes**.

Paul Lake, already extensively described, is about 12 miles northeast of Kamloops at an elevation of 2,542 feet. It is a long, fairly narrow lake lying in an east-west direction with a surface area of 985 acres. Because of its proximity to Kamloops, it receives heavy use from a variety of recreationists and numerous cabins have sprouted on its shores. But it remains an attractive lake and produces an occasional trout to 4 or 5 pounds.

Pinantan Lake lies about four miles beyond Paul. It has a surface area of 161 acres and is situated at at an elevation of 2,859 feet with a small resort and cabins at its western end. Unlike Paul Lake, it has a dark, silty bottom. **Little Pinantan** is a shallow, tule-rimmed pond connected to the main lake and sometimes offers exciting fishing in the evening.

Beyond Pinantan the road forks and a northern spur leads seven miles uphill to Pemberton and Hyas Lakes at an elevation of 4,060 feet. The road is likely to be slippery in wet weather. Hyas Lake has a surface area of 159 acres; nearby Pemberton covers 31 acres. A resort on Hyas serves both waters. Both lakes are well suited for fly fishing, and in its very early days Hyas yielded a 16-pound Kamloops to a dry fly. Those days are gone, however, and a 5-pound trout would be a good one now.

Across the North Thompson, a spur of the Lac du Bois Road reaches into **Pass Lake** about 15 miles northwest of Kamloops. Pass is a small, productive lake managed under trophy fishery regulations. It yields some large trout to patient fishermen. There is a small, informal campsite at the lake, but no developed facilities.

About 14 miles north of Kamloops at the community of Heffley Creek a road leaves the highway and extends 12 miles eastward to **Heffley Lake**. This long, narrow lake lies on an east-west axis at an elevation of 3,095 feet with a surface area of 501 acres. Its maximum depth is 77 feet. There are two resorts on the lake as well as numerous cabins. Heffley offers good dry-fly fishing at times, but trout much over 2 pounds are uncommon. Nearby **Little Heffley** — not much more than a pothole — has a few larger trout.

About midway between the highway and Heffley Lake is a turnoff to the north which leads about 10 miles to **Knouff Lake**. Few lakes are located in a more attractive setting. Knouff is at an elevation of 3,768 feet, lying amid rolling hills cloaked in pine and aspen. It has clear water, a gravel bottom and broad reaches of shoal water, covered with weed and broken by patches of marl. There are five small islands, four of them in line like a small fleet of sailing ships with living pines for masts. Knouff has a surface area of 254 acres, a maximum depth of 79 feet and a mean depth of 32 feet.

The early history of this lake already has been related. The great hatches of traveling sedges are gone, never to be restored, and the immense trout that once rose to floating imitations are gone with them. Nevertheless, it remains a pleasant place to fish, and its points and bays, shoals and "sunken islands" are ideal spots to cast a fly. Its trout still are firm and bright, even if much smaller than in the old days.

The old resort still stands at the north end of the lake, its log cabins nestled in the timber, and a new campground has been added. The lake is fed by a stream which flows out of **Little Knouff Lake** on a hill just to the north. Little Knouff is a shallow, oval-shaped lake with a marl bottom. From time to time it has produced large trout, but fishing is limited to a small area of deeper water in the center of the lake — most of it being too shallow for the wary trout to enter.

Just before the Knouff Lake Road reaches the resort, a sign marks the access to **Badger** and **Spooney Lakes**. The three-mile dirt road becomes greasy in wet weather but usually is traversible. These lakes lie at an elevation of about 3,750 feet. Badger is about 1½ miles long and perhaps half a mile wide; Spooney, a much smaller lake, is immediately west of Badger. Both lie on a north-south axis.

Compared to Knouff, neither of these lakes is especially attractive. Both have brushy shorelines and dark, silty bottoms. Badger has two small islands, but lacks the visible shoals that make Knouff such a pleasant lake to fish. But although Badger and Spooney may be lacking in looks, their productivity provides more than ample compensation. Both are rich with a wide variety of aquatic fauna and both produce heavy chironomid hatches in the spring. Best of all is their sedge hatch, which sometimes begins as early as the end of the first week of June. The sedges are abundant, and once the adults are on the water the dry-fly fishing often is extraordinary. The trout are large, with fish of 5 pounds not uncommon. Both lakes are managed under trophy regulations and are ideally suited to the purpose.

There are two campgrounds on Badger. One, in an open meadow at the south end of the lake, is privately operated under control of the re-

sort at Knouff Lake. The other is a B. C. Forest Service campground recently carved out of the timber on the east side of the lake at about its
midsection. It was, as of this writing, still a raw and muddy site with
fierce mosquitoes in the spring, but should improve with a few more seasons of use.

It probably is safe to say that when they are "on," Badger and Spooney produce some of the finest fly fishing to be found in the Kamloops
area.

Thirty-six miles north of Kamloops the Squam Bay Road leaves the
North Thompson Highway at Louis Creek and heads east. This road provides access to **Johnson Lake**, which is 23 miles from the highway. The
last nine miles are steep and slow. This lake, about 3½ miles long, is
noted for its clear water and its fine dry-fly fishing. Trout to 5 pounds
have been taken in recent seasons, although most are a bit smaller. There
is a fishing resort with housekeeping cabins, a store and a campground on
the lake.

A number of fishing camps on remote lakes are served by aircraft
from Kamloops. These include:

— Akehurst Lake Resort on **Akehurst Lake**, about 48 miles north of
Kamloops in Nehaliston Provincial Forest. Akehurst, slightly more than
two miles long, is at an elevation of about 4,600 feet. Several smaller
lakes nearby also hold trout. The resort has housekeeping cabins.

— Alpine Fishing Resort on **Elbow Lake**, 38 miles northwest of Kamloops at an elevation of about 4,600 feet. From the lodge and housekeeping cabins on the lake, trails lead to four other nearby lakes; the resort keeps boats on each.

— Bare Lake Fishing Camp, Ltd., on **Bare Lake**, is just over the hill
from Elbow Lake about 40 miles northwest of Kamloops. Five other
lakes are accessible from the camp, with boats on each.

— Caverhill Fishing and Hunting Camp on **Caverhill Lake**, just east of
Akehurst Lake about 46 miles north of Kamloops. Caverhill, about four
miles long, has an irregular shoreline with many points and bays and a
large island at its northern end. It is at an elevation just under 4,600
feet. There are cabins at the fishing camp with access to many other
lakes nearby.

— Rainbow Chain Lodge on **Hoopatatkwa** ("Hoopy") **Lake**, about 32
miles north of Kamloops at an elevation around 4,600 feet. Access from
the lodge and cabins to six other nearby lakes, with boats on each.

Just south of Hoopatatkwa lies **Willowgrouse Lake**, a long, narrow
lake where fishermen sometimes fly in and camp on the shore.

Bonaparte Lake is about 45 miles northwest of Kamloops. The Bonaparte Fishing & Hunting Resort at the west end of the lake now is accessible by car, but the lake also remains a popular target for float planes.
The attraction for fly fishermen is not 10-½-mile-long Bonaparte itself so
much as nearby **Hammer Lake**. Hammer also is accessible by a slippery

207

road about two miles southwest of Bonaparte. The 1¼-mile-long lake gets its name from its shape. Situated at an elevation of about 3,900 feet, it has a fine sedge hatch and once was almost legendary for the huge trout that rose to feed on the adult insects. Today, trout of 4 or 5 pounds are about tops, and there are many smaller ones.

Little Fort-Clearwater

The country around Little Fort is rocky, steep and rugged. From the village on the banks of the North Thompson the ground rises steeply to a labyrinth of ridges covered with dense thickets of pine. The creases and folds between these ridges hold hundreds of lakes. The Bridge Lake Road, a major east-west route, comes in to meet the North Thompson Highway at Little Fort; the highway itself continues north to Clearwater.

Most of the many lakes west of Little Fort have not held trout for long. As with the lakes farther south, these waters grew trout rapidly when first stocked and some fish of spectacular size were caught. But as is always the case, the average size of the fish in most waters began to decline as abundant food stocks were whittled down. Many of these lakes are interconnected by small streams in which spawning runs quickly became established, and some lakes soon became overpopulated with small trout.

Although the aquatic fauna of the lakes in the Little Fort area is much the same as it is in the waters around Kamloops and Merritt, the clearwater, marl-bottom lakes that are common farther south are mostly lacking. The majority of lakes in the hills west of Little Fort have dark or amber-colored water and trout from them tend to be more heavily spotted and somewhat darker in color than fish from the lakes farther south. But this is only a sign of their adaptation to the local environment and has nothing to do with their condition; if anything, a healthy, maiden trout from these waters fights at least as well as its silvery counterparts from the lakes around Kamloops or Merritt.

There are so many lakes in this area it would be impossible to do justice to them all. The following description includes most of the better-known fishing camps and waters:

— Aurora Lakes Resort, a chain of eight lakes including **Latremouille**, **Lynn** and **Moose**, accessible from Little Fort via the Bridge Lake Road, a total distance of about 13½ miles. These lakes are at an elevation of around 4,000 feet. The resort includes cabins and a central lodge.

Meadow Lake Fishing Camp, a chain of 10 lakes about 18 miles west of Little Fort. Housekeeping cabins are located on **Meadow Lake** with other waters accessible within walking distance. Jeep transportation to the camp is arranged from Little Fort. The lakes are around the 4,500-foot level.

— Rock Island Lake Fishing Camp, Ltd. on **Rock Island Lake**, about 14 miles northwest of Little Fort at about 4,500 feet elevation. The camp offers housekeeping cabins and there is access to six other lakes in the area.

— TaWeel Lake Fishing Lodge and Nehaliston Fishing Camp, both on **TaWeel Lake**, about 15 miles northwest of Little Fort. This famous lake, about four miles long at an elevation of 3,939 feet, has been a consistent producer of trout for more than 40 years. Both resorts on the lake provide jeep transportation from Little Fort and there is walk-in access to smaller lakes nearby.

— Thuya Lakes Fishing Resort on **Thuya** and **Island Lakes** about 18 miles west of Little Fort, south of the Bridge Lake Road. Other lakes in this chain include **Dot, Disappointment, Young's, Summit** and **Trail's End**, plus others nearby. One of these, a pothole named **Bitchey Lake**, yielded a trout of 16 pounds in the years after it was first stocked; in another, **Pearl Lake**, I landed a 7½-pound Kamloops which — so far as I can determine — may be the only trout ever caught in this little lake.

These lakes vary in elevation from 4,300 to 4,700 feet. Some have gravel bottoms; some have dark, silty bottoms, and at least two — Summit and Disappointment — have extensive rocky shoal areas. None is more than a mile long, all are shallow and lily pads are common around their margins. The area also abounds in beaver ponds, some of them connected to the lakes through a network of small streams. Spawning occurs in many of these streams, and as a result of it two of the lakes, Thuya and Island, became so overpopulated that at one time the Fish and Wildlife Branch lifted the catch limit on them in hopes that anglers would thin out the population. The last time I fished these waters some years ago it was easy to catch 20 trout an hour on dry flies, although 15 inches was about the maximum size.

Because of their elevation, these lakes generally fish well through the summer. The resort provides housekeeping cabins and campsites.

Farther west, toward 100 Mile House, are many more worthwhile waters, including **Bridge Lake** itself, **Hathaway, Fawn, Sheridan** and others, offering a wide variety of fishing. Fishing camps and resorts are located on these and a large number of other waters throughout the area. However, due to fluctuations in the provincial economy over the past few years, many of these resorts have changed hands and a few have closed. Anglers planning trips into the area should write or call ahead to ensure the accommodations and services they want are still available.

The town of Clearwater is about 21 miles north of Little Fort on Highway 5. A road heading west out of Clearwater extends another 21 miles to Moose Camp, with access to **Rioux, Dubee, Coldscaur** and other lakes. These lakes are at elevations between 4,500 and 5,000 feet in the high country southeast of **Canim Lake**, a great, sprawling lake more than 12 miles long.

Herbie McNeil, a Michigan native, homesteaded a ranch at the east end of Canim Lake after working as a freight hauler in the Cariboo and

209

opened a 125-mile trapline along Canimred Creek, a tributary of Canim Lake. In 1935 McNeil and his brother caught some trout in the creek, kept them alive in buckets of water and hauled them upstream above a waterfall that historically had kept trout from gaining access to the upper reaches. There they released the trout back into the stream, and from that initial stocking fish eventually stpread throughout the Canimred drainage and into several lakes, including Rioux.

Ralph Bell, a judge in Everett, Washington, was from the same Michigan town that had been McNeil's former home. In 1946 Bell, his son, Lew; George Duwe and his son, Sam, and Knut Kravik and his son, Gerald, traveled to the area and found wonderful fishing in both Rioux and Coldscaur Lakes. But the small lake north of Rioux still was barren of fish, so they caught some small trout in the creek and carried them to the lake, where they were released. They named the lake Dube — a contraction of the first syllables of the names Duwe and Bell (over the years common usage has added a second "e," accounting for the present name of Dubee).

Lew Bell, now an attorney in Everett, recalls that they returned each year for the next decade, restocking Dubee Lake each year (there are no tributary streams suitable for spawning). Later they built a pump and fitted it to a milk can, using the pump to oxygenate water in the can and keep trout alive. The trout were caught from Rioux Lake, placed in the can and carried by horseback to other barren lakes in the area, where they were released. Some of the stockings were successful; others were not. But in this way fish were introduced to the lakes now served by Moose Camp.

For most of the past decade, the camp has been operated by Dave and June Jones. With accommodations for only a limited number of guests, fishing pressure has remained light and the fishing good. As with most of the lakes in the area, Rioux Lake is shallow with stained water and many lily pads. Trout are plentiful, if not especially large, and the lake produces consistent dry-fly fishing throughout the summer. Under the stewardship of the Joneses, the camp won an excellent reputation for its comfort and cuisine. The camp changed hands in 1979 and it is to be hoped that the new owners will continue in this tradition of excellence.

Savona Area

Savona, once known as Savona's Ferry, is a sleepy little town on the north shore of the western end of Kamloops Lake. The new Trans-Canada Highway now bypasses the main part of the town and most motorists see it as a passing blur of houses capped by a sawmill at its eastern end. Within a mile of the town the Thompson River flows out of the lake and into its wild canyon, a favorite haunt of steelheaders downstream. And in the hills around Savona are some of the very richest of the Kamloops trout waters.

The potholed pavement of the old highway climbs a steep hill just

east of town and passes through a gate onto the Six Mile Ranch. There
it continues several miles, past a barren little lake, until it literally disappears under the water of **Six-Mile Lake**, which has risen to cover the
old highway. It is a shallow lake with a silty bottom and lies in a fold
between hills at an elevation of slightly more than 2,000 feet. Because
of its low elevation, it fishes well early in the spring and receives most of
its pressure in May while the trout still are spawning in the higher lakes.
Occasional large fish have been taken, but the usual trout ranges from 1½
to 2 pounds.

Before the old highway enters the Six-Mile Ranch gate, a good gravel
road goes off to the south, slowly climbing about 16 miles to **Leighton**
and **Tunkwa Lakes**. These are two natural lakes that have been raised
and enlarged to provide water for irrigation. They are at an elevation of
about 4,000 feet in rolling country, surrounded by meadows and thick
stands of pine. Tunkwa, the larger of the two, is about 500 surface acres;
Leighton is perhaps half that size.

Surely these two are among the very richest of the Interior lakes.
Every common type of trout food is present in abundance, and partly
because of this abundance the trout in these two lakes — especially in
Tunkwa — sometimes are very hard to catch. The natural fauna are so
numerous that an artificial fly faces stiff competition.

Yet this same abundance also produces very large trout. In fact, surveys showed Kamloops trout in Tunkwa Lake had a higher growth rate
from their first to second years than those in any other lake studied.

Tunkwa Lake has a very irregular shoreline with many small peninsu-
las and bays and broad shallow reaches around its north and south ends.
It is fed by several small streams entering from the south, and one of
them has been used by the Fish and Wildlife Branch as an egg-taking station. Tunkwa Lake Fishing Camp, on the east side of the lake, has both
cabins and campsites, and there are a number of private cabins on the
lake. The fairly easy access to this lake has led to mob scenes on holi-
day weekends, but at other times it is a quiet, pleasant place to fish. But
there is little shelter from the wind, and Tunkwa can become very rough
at times; this is one lake where an outboard motor may be justified.

In late May Tunkwa produces an incredible hatch of chironomids.
The insects are so numerous they become an irritant, flying into the
eyes and ears and sometimes the mouths of anglers. Emerging pupae are
so numerous that it is an easy task for a trout to cruise along beneath
the surface with open mouth, capturing many pupae with little effort.
At such times the odds against success for the angler are very great, but
sometimes — especially in the evening — a chironomid pupa imitation
fished on a floating line and stripped at an extremely fast and totally
unrealistic rate of speed will prove very effective. The response of the
trout to a rapidly-moving imitation under these circumstances defies
rational explanation, but it does occur.

211

KAMLOOPS

The outlet of Tunkwa Lake at its north end is controlled by an irrigation lock. Below the lock a short but spectacular waterfall plunges into
Leighton Lake. In the spring it is a common sight to see ripe trout trying vainly to ascend the falls, sometimes stranding themselves on the
rocks. Leighton also has a number of shallow bays and flats and there
are two small islands along its eastern shore when the water is high in
the spring. Its smaller size makes it easier for a fly fisherman to cover,
and it is somewhat more protected from the wind than Tunkwa. Both
lakes have relatively dark water, silty bottoms and thick growths of
underwater weeds.

Leighton also has a heavy early hatch of chironomids and an excellent hatch of damselflies in early June. A good damselfly nymph imitation works wonders then. Both Leighton and Tunkwa are drawn down
for irrigation during the summer so that the water level always is low in
the fall. A realistic bloodworm imitation fished over the weedbeds in
shallow water produces very well in late September and early October.

The trout in these two lakes average 2 to 4 pounds, with occasional
fish of 6 or 7 pounds. Tunkwa fish, on the average, may be a little larger than those in Leighton. But maiden fish in either lake are unfailingly
as bright as polished chrome and fight with unusual vigor and violence.
My ratio of fish hooked to fish landed in these lakes is not very good —
testimony, perhaps, to their special strength.

Leighton drains through a culvert into a creek and there is little, if
any, natural spawning. There is a campground on the eastern shore and
a few private cabins, but no other facilities.

Of the two, Leighton is my favorite. It is somewhat easier to fish and
always has yielded trout a little more generously than Tunkwa — although
that is not to say that they always come easily. But I have many pleasant memories of both lakes, going back many years, and by any measure
they are among the most rewarding of all the waters that harbor Kamloops trout.

Just north of Kamloops Lake, the Trans-Canada Highway crosses
Deadman Creek where it flows out of the hills to join the Thompson River. A good gravel road leaves the highway to parallel the stream through
its spectacular narrow valley, rimmed with colored bluffs and hoodoos —
strangely-shaped sandstone formations. About 12 miles up the valley
from the highway is the headquarters of the Circle W Ranch, with access
to **Hihium Lake.** Truck service from the ranch carries anglers up a steep
and slippery road to the lake, four miles long and a mile to a mile and a
half wide at an elevation of 4,480 feet.

From the time I first fished it as a small boy, this lake has been among
my favorites. Its trout never have been of trophy size, but always there
have been many of them from 2 to 3 pounds and they come eagerly
across the rocky shoals to take a fly. Hihium is one of relatively few
mountain lakes to have a natural population of Kamloops trout, the fish

apparently having originally gained access from the Bonaparte River via Loon Creek, Loon Lake and Hihium Creek, which flows into Loon Lake. Spawning both in the outlet stream and several small tributaries, these fish have perpetuated a population of strong, wild Kamloops trout. Only in recent years, after several poor spawning seasons and intensive angling pressure, has it been necessary to augment the wild population with stocking.

The maximum depth of the lake is about 60 feet, though most of it is much shallower. It has a silty bottom with many underwater weedbeds and numerous rocky shoals, some close enough to the surface so that tules sprout from them. The weedbeds harbor a teeming population of scuds and late June and early July bring a sporadic but sometimes excellent sedge hatch. The phantom midge, Chaoborus, also is present and is taken by trout in great numbers; spring brings a heavy hatch of chironomids and fall brings the flying ants, and the damselfly and dragonfly nymphs emerge in their seasons. Altogether, the fly fisherman at Hihium has a wealth of creatures to imitate in an environment that is particularly well suited to the fly.

The lake has several long points, some with gravel bars extending far out toward deep water, and there are several shallow, sheltered bays. Heavy algae blooms in July and August sometimes put a damper on the fishing, but there are nearly always some trout to be found.

The Circle W maintains remote housekeeping cabins around the lake, reached by boat from the roadhead. The lake lies on an east-west axis and sometimes is swept by strong and dangerous winds. An outboard is essential here, both for safety and to save time moving between fishing spots located far apart.

The Circle W has had three sets of owners since it was founded by Bud Walters. Bill and Bea Comeaux were the owners on my first boyhood visit when we climbed the moutainside in an old British Army ambulance that looked as if it had seen hard service since the days of El Alamein. For many years afterward the ranch was operated by Pat and Harriet Kirkpatrick of Mercer Island until Harriet's untimely death. Now it is owned by Bob Bendzak, a Seattle dentist and fly fisherman.

There is another resort, Hihium Lake Fishing Camp, at the west end of the lake, accessible via Loon Lake, and a public access of sorts over a marginal road following a natural gas pipeline that runs from the Deadman Creek Valley to a point near the lake. In the past decade an increasing number of private cabins also have been built on the lake — a saddening thing to see in this once wild and unspoiled area.

I have fished this lake off and on for more than 30 years, sometimes as early as the third week of May — when there was four inches of snow on the ground and the creeks were filled with spawning trout — and sometimes as late as the third week of September when we were the last to leave before the cabins were closed for the winter. Of all the times I

213

have fished there, early September is my favorite — when the nights are crisp and clear, the mornings are calm and frosty and the trout strong and eager. Inevitably, the fishing is no longer what it once was — ever-growing angling pressure has seen to that — but it remains surprisingly consistent, and last year the lake produced some of the largest trout seen there in years. Hihium is an old friend and a good one and never once have I left it feeling disappointed.

Merritt Area

The town of Merritt occupies a broad valley where the Coldwater River flows down from Coquihalla Pass to join the sluggish Nicola. Hills rise steeply on every side of this natural basin and the air hangs heavy with smoke and ash from the wigwam burners at the Merritt mills. Compared with most Interior towns, Merritt has a long history, with the old Coldwater and Adelphi Hotels offering evidence of its longevity. It also is an important road junction; Highway 5 comes in from Princeton to the south and continues north to Kamloops, and Highway 8 comes in from Spences Bridge to the west. From the Indian town of Lower Nicola, just west of Merritt, a partly-paved road follows Guichon Creek north past Mamit Lake toward the town of Logan Lake, where it connects with a paved road running west toward Ashcroft and a dirt road that runs through to Tunkwa Lake. And on every side of Merritt, the hills are speckled with lakes of every size, shape and description.

Driving north from Princeton toward Merritt on Highway 5, one follows a narrow, scenic valley, the roadway trading places with a chain of small lakes. One of the largest of these lakes is Allison and about three miles north of it a tiny pothole known as Steve's Lake lies west of the highway. At that point a dirt road turns west about half a mile to **Kump Lake**. This fine little lake, about half a mile long, lies in a pocket about 3,700 feet above sea level. It is a shallow lake, with amber-stained water over a silty bottom and an ample crop of lily pads. At its south end is a shallow lagoon rimmed by a spectacular cliff with pines clinging to its edge.

Kump has a decent sedge hatch and provides interesting dry-fly fishing at times for trout up to about 3 pounds. There is an undeveloped camp-site on a bluff on the east side of the lake, but boat launching is rather difficult because the access is at the foot of a steep incline at the base of the bluff.

About 12 miles north of the Kump Lake turnoff and three miles south of the community of Aspen Grove a dirt road leaves the east side of the highway, climbs over a hill and drops down into a valley containing another chain of lakes — **Crater, Alleyne, Kentucky** and **Bluey**, from north to south.

These lakes are at an elevation of about 3,250 feet, surrounded mostly by pine and aspen groves. Crater has a surface area of about 50 acres;

Alleyne, just to the south, covers about 135 acres. Kentucky, about half a mile south of Alleyne, has an area of 108 acres with a maximum depth of 120 feet and a mean depth of 53 feet. Bluey lies about a mile south of Kentucky and has a surface area of about 100 acres. All these lakes are fairly deep and relatively lacking in shoal water, so they are not very well suited to fly fishing. But they are fished heavily by trollers and produce good numbers of trout in the 2- to 2½-pound class. Crater and Bluey also have produced some trout of exceptional size in past years.

The water in Kentucky Lake is quite clear and it is possible to see trout cruising over the light-colored, mostly barren bottom at considerable depths. And although the general conformation of the lake does not lend itself to fly fishing, there is a shallow, sheltered bay at the south end that sometimes offers exciting fishing because it is one of those rare places where it is possible to see the trout, cast to them and watch their response to the fly.

There are small camping areas at all these lakes and boat launching is not difficult. Kentucky Lake also is noted for the bears that are frequently in evidence around its shores.

About 13 miles south of Merritt, Highway 5 skirts the western edge of **Courtney Lake.** This beautiful lake, slightly more than a mile long and about half a mile wide at its widest point, is surrounded by gently rolling hills that are covered with golden grass in the dry summer months. Scattered groves of pine, fir, aspen and wild rose huddle in the hillside watercourses where the snowmelt runs off in the early spring. The lake itself, at an elevation of about 3,300 feet, is made to order for fly fishing. It is shallow throughout, with many submerged weedbeds and broad shoal areas that anchor the roots of tules. The margins of the shoals are easily visible through the clear water so that it is a simple task to find a likely spot.

Courtney was poisoned some years ago to remove a large population of scrap fish. Since it was restocked with Kamloops trout it has produced spectacular fishing for trout to 6½ pounds, with good numbers in the 2- to 4-pound class. All the usual aquatic fauna are present, although Courtney's sedge hatch is not especially prolific. Because of its elevation, the lake does not fish well during the summer months, but the fishing is excellent in the spring and fall.

Due to its location at the edge of a major highway, the lake receives heavy use — although its shallow character makes it a difficult lake for trollers. There is a large public access on the western shore, but the boat-launch area is small and constricted by boulders along the shoreline. There is no campground and that and the presence of the highway are the only drawbacks. If Courtney were not so close to the highway — if it were hidden just a slight distance back in the hills — it would be ideal.

215

Even as it is, the lake ranks as one of the most outstanding in the Merritt area.

Just a mile north of Courtney is **Corbett Lake**, a pretty 100-acre tarn that also lies on the east side of the highway. It is a rich, shallow, weedy lake, also ideally suited for fly fishing, and next to those in Paul Lake, its trout probably have been studied more than those in any of the other Kamloops trout waters. Undoubtedly there are a good many sound biological and practical reasons for this: The lake is easily accessible and small enough so that its trout population can be controlled without much difficulty and accurate creel censuses can be obtained without much trouble. But I have a suspicion that one compelling reason biologists have chosen to do much of their work on this lake is the presence of Corbett Lake Country Inn and its reputation for setting one of the finest tables in the province, backed up by one of the finest wine cellars.

The current proprietor and chef-in-residence is Peter McVey, who trained in France and held several very prestigious positions in England before moving to British Columbia to indulge his first love, which is fly fishing. On any given night his guests may include anglers from several provinces and states, come to sample the culinary artistry which McVey continually performs over the big gas range in the old kitchen at the inn.

McVey is a small, round man, possessed of boundless energy and enthusiasm and an impulsive, inquisitive mind. Nearly always he is involved simultaneously in several projects to improve the fishing in Corbett Lake and any number of others nearby. And he is himself an accomplished fisherman, one of the finest casters in the province, and so often did his name appear on the Merritt Fish & Game Club trophy for the season's largest fish that the club finally simply gave him the trophy to keep. After a stint as chef at the Grasslands Hotel in Merritt, a short span as operator of the Thuya Lakes fishing camp and an abortive attempt to open a camp on Minnie Lake, McVey settled down at Corbett Lake, where a frantic schedule permits precious little fishing time. In the winter months, when the pace eases a bit, he retreats to a workshop behind the inn and turns out hand-made bamboo fly rods for a growing list of customers. Under the tutelage of Bob Southwell, master English rod builder who is a periodic visitor to Corbett Lake, McVey's skills have increased steadily until now his reputation as a bamboo artisan rivals his reputation as a chef, and there is a long waiting list of buyers for his excellent rods.

In addition to its famous host and dining room, Corbett Lake Country Inn has a number of comfortable cabins, some with handsome stone fireplaces, and maintains a small fleet of rowboats for rental to cabin guests or drop-in customers. There is no campsite on the lake, and despite its proximity to the highway there is no developed public access.

The lake itself was poisoned in 1973 to remove scrap fish. Kamloops trout were restocked, but the lake's recovery was delayed by a recurring problem of winter kill which was not completely solved even by the in-

Corbett Lake, with boats from the lodge in the foreground.

stallation of two pondmills. But an electrically-driven compressor seems finally to have licked the problem. It is operated around the clock for six weeks during the height of winter, and in the winter of 1979 Corbett Lake had the highest oxygen content of any lake sampled in the area. Its trout now have survived several consecutive winters and fish up to 3 pounds were taken in the spring of 1979. With another year or two of growth the lake should produce fish of 5 pounds or better, as it did in the days before the scrap fish infestation.

The lake has the usual wide assortment of aquatic life and there is an especially fine evening hatch of small mayflies in the spring. With its many weed-covered shallows and shoals it is an intriguing lake to fish, and its apparent recovery and addition to the list of fly-fishing-only waters is welcome news to anglers.

About half a mile north of Corbett Lake, or 11½ miles south of Merritt, a gravel road leaves the west side of Highway 5 and extends about 3½ miles to the first of the Kane Valley Lakes, which include **Harmon, Kane, Menzies** and **Englishman**. These scenic little lakes are at an elevation of about 3,700 feet; Harmon Lake, the largest, covers only 53 acres. There are campsites around these lakes, but no other facilities.

These waters once produced very pleasant angling and were popular with some fly fishermen, but for a number of years they have contained an enormous population of shiners. Although they have continued to produce some trout, much of their productivity necessarily has been used

217

up by the shiners. These lakes were scheduled for poisoning in the fall of 1979 in an effort to rid them of shiners, but because they are connected by streams flowing through marshy areas it seems unlikely that a total "kill" could be achieved. The future of these waters therefore remains in some doubt.

Five miles north of Corbett Lake, or seven miles south of Merritt, a dirt road on the east side of the highway reaches about three miles through rolling hills and timber to **Lundbom Lake**. This attractive lake, slightly more than a mile long and about a quarter of a mile wide, lies in a fold between hills at an elevation of about 3,600 feet. Thick pine forest grows down to the lakeshore on the southern side while open grassland rolls away to the north.

Lundbom surely is one of the most fertile of the Interior lakes. It is a fine, clear lake with a gravel bottom and shallow, weedy bays. It hosts a tremendous scud population and one of the finest traveling sedge hatches in the province. A small, seasonal creek flows into its eastern end, but there never is enough water for spawning and the trout population is maintained by careful stocking. This lake has produced trout as heavy as 14 pounds and one of 12½ pounds was taken in the spring of 1979. Of course there are not very many of these, and the average size probably is about 1½ pounds — although 4- to 6-pound fish are not uncommon.

With such obvious attractions, and lying as close to Merritt as it does, Lundbom receives very intense fishing pressure. This was not always the case; a decade ago, before the lake was "discovered," it was possible to stay there several days without seeing more than one or two other anglers. But the word got around, the road to the lake was improved and sport shop owners in Merritt began steering their customers there. In the past five years I have never once seen fewer than 10 parties camped in the numerous campsites around the lake, and usually there are several times that number. Such pressure inevitably has brought with it a great deal of abuse; motor homes park on the lakeshore and drain their sewage into the lake, and careless campers have strewn garbage along the shores. Trollers pound the lake mercilessly, and although they seem to catch few fish, the constant thump of their motors and the oil slicks they leave on the surface seem to prevent the larger fish from feeding on the surface as they once did freely. Obscenely large boats and motors race up and down the lake, posing a serious safety hazard to fishermen in smaller boats, and the summer air vibrates constantly with the annoying whine of trail bikes. The wildlife that once was abundant around the lake has long since been driven off, and a colony of rare wildflowers on a hillside above the lake has disappeared in the trail bike ruts. In the absence of any regulations or enforcement to curtail these abuses, Lundbom's days as a productive fishery are definitely numbered. Much of its charm already has been destroyed and it no longer is a very pleasant place to fish. And this is a tragedy of the first magnitude, because very few lakes possess all the attri-

Sun dapples the water while a fly caster is at work on a fall day at Lundbom Lake.

butes that Lundbom has in abundance. It is a priceless resource, and if it is destroyed there will be nothing to take its place.

Some fly fishermen continue to return to Lundbom despite the hazards and distractions. The lake fishes well in late May and early June when there is a fair mayfly hatch and damselfly emergence. The sedges begin about mid-June and continue through the first week of July, but only rarely do the large fish seem to seek them on the surface anymore. Late September also is a good time to fish Lundbom, and a deep-sunk, slowly-retrieved scud pattern does well then. The lake sometimes is slightly clouded in September by a late algae bloom.

The lake lies on an east-west axis and there is no shelter from the prevailing westerly wind. The lack of shelter makes Lundbom a dangerous lake despite its relatively small size, and a west wind blowing down the mile-long reach of the lake often builds waves of three feet or more. On one such day I witnessed the capsizing of four boats; fortunately, all the anglers were saved, but most of their equipment was lost. Local anglers complain that the wind blows at Lundbom four days of every seven, and my experience confirms their observation. In an ironic way, this probably is a good thing for the lake because it provides the only respite from the steady pressure.

Lundbom once was one of my favorite lakes, and it has provided me with many memorable days. Pressure from local residents killed a proposal to make it a trophy lake, and that may have killed the lake as well. I grow very sad when I think of what has happened to this beautiful lake, and I very much hope that something may yet be done to reverse its decline while there is yet time to save it. But I am not at all confident that this will happen, and it seems likely that Lundbom Lake will soon be only a memory in the minds of those fortunate enough to fish it in its golden days.

Marquart Lake is an equally rich water that has fallen on hard times for different reasons. Its future, however, may be brighter than that of its companion, Lundbom.

A dirt road — really just a pair of ruts — leaves the northwest shore of Lundbom and climbs over a hill past a barren pothole to the shore of Marquart about a mile to the west. Marquart also is accessible from Highway 5, but driving in from that direction involves fording the outlet stream. The ford is very slippery and often impassable without a 4-wheel drive.

Marquart has a surface area of about 60 acres and its silty bottom is thickly carpeted with weed. A long, tule-covered shoal occupies the middle of the lake. As with Lundbom, it has a pine forest on its southern shore and open grassland with a few groves of cottonwood and aspen on the hillside to the north. The lake lies at an elevation of about 3,700 feet and an irrigation lock controls its westward-flowing outlet stream. There is no natural spawning.

Marquart is very rich in most forms of aquatic life, although it lacks the superlative sedge hatch found on Lundbom. Nevertheless, it grows very large trout in a short time. Shallow throughout, it has suffered occasional winter kill, but after one five-year period without a kill it produced trout weighing more than 11 pounds. Again, such trout were few in number, but Marquart fish are always heavy. Occasionally it has been planted with Eastern brook trout as well as Kamloops trout.

Several years ago shiners appeared in Marquart Lake and the trout fishing began to decline. The fishing, never fast, grew slower still, and the fly fishermen who had patiently probed the lake for its large fish returned to it less and less often. Finally, in the spring of 1979, it was poisoned. Reports are that it will be restocked with Kamloops trout and managed as a fly-fishing-only lake with a reduced limit.

If this turns out to be the case — and assuming winter kill is not a frequent problem — then Marquart should again offer fishing for large trout in the future. It is an excellent fly-fishing lake, and a slowly-fished scud

220

A fly fisherman in a rubber raft works the weedbed in Marquart Lake. The remains of the season's first snow are on the hillside behind him.

pattern is always reliable. There are several good campsites around the lake, but no other facilities.

At the southern outskirts of Merritt, the Coldwater Road leaves Highway 5 and follows the Coldwater River Valley to the southeast. After 19 miles of gravel a right turn crosses the river to connect with the Coquihalla Pass Road. After another 12 miles, at the old railroad station of Juliet, a dirt spur leads off at a sharp right angle to the north. This spur is a steep, rough, rocky road that climbs the side of a mountain about 1½ miles to **Murray Lake**. Murray is slightly more than a mile long, perhaps little more than a quarter of a mile wide. It is a clear, relatively shallow lake with a grayish marl bottom and not much weed growth. It is not a particularly rich water but does have a good sedge hatch that continues into the second week of July. Dry-fly fishing can be excellent when the hatch is on, although the trout seldom exceed 2½ pounds and most are a good deal smaller than that. Mature fish also tend to remain dark well into the summer in this lake.

There is a small camping area and access at the south end of the lake and a number of private cabins have been built on the shoreline around the north end.

From the village of Lower Nicola just west of Merritt on Highway 8, the Aberdeen Mine Road heads north into the high country, providing access to the Chataway Lakes, a distance of about 16 miles. These lakes, which include Chataway, Gypsum, Dot, Antler, Billy, Echo and Roscoe, also are accessible via a dirt road that leaves Highway 8 about 14 miles east of Spences Bridge.

These small lakes — Dot and Roscoe, the two largest, are no more than a mile long — are scattered at elevations ranging from 4,500 to 5,300 feet. They offer a variety of fishing that holds up well through the summer. Chataway, Gypsum and Roscoe all produced small trout in quantity during the 1979 season; fish in Dot Lake ranged to about 2½ pounds, and those in Echo and Antler ran from 3 to 7 pounds. The access road to Antler is rough and muddy and there is about a five-minute walk from the road end to the lake. Antler has good sedge and chironomid hatches and imitations of the pupae of either insect work well, as do floating imitations of the sedge adults. Access to Echo Lake requires a two-mile hike.

There is a lodge with housekeeping cabins at Chataway and campsites also are available.

Gordon Lake is about 7½ miles southeast of Chataway, accessible via a maze of logging roads from either Highway 8 or the Aberdeen Road. Located at an elevation of about 4,200 feet, it was a "hot" late several years ago — one that local fishermen never mentioned to tourists — and produced some large trout. But, as usually is the case, word eventually got around, pressure increased and the population of large fish was quickly harvested. Since then one seldom hears much about this hard-to-reach lake.

From Merritt, Highway 5 angles to the northwest, skirting the long eastern edge of Nicola Lake on its way toward Kamloops. At the old community of Quilchena on the lakeshore a gravel road leaves the highway and winds south into rolling grasslands about 12 miles to Minnie Lake. This sprawling, two-mile-lake lies between grassy slopes at an elevation of about 3,500 feet. Timber is very sparse in the area and there is no protection from the strong winds that frequently sweep the length of the lake, making fishing very difficult.

Minnie is a shallow, rich, weedy lake with an extremely heavy chironomid hatch in the spring. It grows large trout in a short time but winter kills with disconcerting frequency. Whenever two or three mild winters occur in succession, permitting trout to survive, Minnie usually produces fish in the 6- to 8-pound class. A stream flowing into the eastern end of the lake permits these fish to spawn.

Less than a mile down the road lies Stoney Lake, another shallow weedy lake about a mile long. This lake historically has been unable to

222

support trout through the winter, but during the time he was attempting to establish a fishing camp on Minnie Lake, Peter McVey spent long hours with a bulldozer diverting a stream to flow into Stoney Lake. His hope was that the stream would provide sufficient circulation in the lake to allow trout to survive through the winters. Fish were stocked after the diversion began flowing into the lake and they survived the first winter and grew rapidly on the abundant natural feed. But when McVey abandoned the fishing camp idea there was no one to look after the stream and beavers built dams that soon blocked its flow. The following winter the fish all died and on my last visit to Stoney Lake it was again barren. Potential may exist for a good fishery on this lake, but it seems likely that winter kill would always be a problem even if the diversion were kept free of beaver dams.

About 25 miles south of Quilchena on the same road is the Paradise Lake chain. The last 10 miles of the road are steep and rough. The lakes, at an elevation right around 5,000 feet, include **Paradise, Island, Boot, Elkhart, Bobs, Boulder** and **Johns**. Some are accessible by road and others by trail.

One man's paradise is not necessarily another's, and it always has seemed to me that whoever named this chain of lakes must have been either an incurable optimist or an incorrigible promoter, or perhaps both. These small lakes — Paradise, the largest, is about a mile and a quarter long — are raw and rocky with dark, amber-tinted water. Most of them produce large numbers of small trout, although Island Lake has a decent sedge hatch and sometimes offers interesting dry-fly fishing for trout up to 18 inches. Another lake, Boot, has a history similar to that of Gordon Lake; word got around that some large fish were present in Boot and local fishermen soon moved in and caught them all.

A fishing camp, Paradise Lakes Resort Ltd., maintains housekeeping cabins and campsites on Paradise Lake.

The road south from Quilchena also connects with a back road that provides access to **Pennask Lake**. However, this is a difficult, sometimes impassable road and much better access is available from Peachland on Okanagan Lake, about 40 miles east. The lake, restricted to fly fishing only, is at an elevation of 4,500 feet. It has a surface area of about three square miles, an irregular shoreline and a number of islands. Its maximum depth is slightly less than 70 feet and its mean depth is a little more than 30 feet, but there are broad reaches of shallow water made to order for fly fishing. The trout in Pennask tend to be small, however, with 1½ pounds about the maximum size. There are campsites at the lake.

About three miles northwest of Quilchena another gravel road leaves Highway 5 and heads east toward Westwold, with access to **Glimpse** and **Salmon Lakes**. About four miles east of the highway a turnoff to the north leads eight miles into Glimpse, a fine fly-fishing lake at an elevation of about 3,800 feet. The lake, about a mile and three quarters long, of-

fers an interesting variety of water with extensive shoals and weedbeds.
Once a very popular lake with fly fishermen, Glimpse has declined somewhat in recent years — undoubtedly due in part to Indian netting of the
spawning tributary — but still is well worth a visit. The Glimpse Lake
Fishing Camp maintains housekeeping cabins and campsites and the camp
operator forbids the use of outboard motors — a practice that makes the
lake all the more attractive to fly fishermen.

Salmon Lake, one of the first waters to be limited to artificial flies
only, lies about 30 miles east of the Highway 5 turnoff through the Douglas Ranch. It is at an elevation of 3,070 feet with a surface area of 304
acres. Its maximum depth is 39 feet and it is mostly shallow with a silty
bottom and extensive weedbeds, especially at its west end where the best
fly fishing is found. Trout range to 4 pounds, although most are somewhat smaller. A heavy algae bloom limits fishing success during the summer months.

A resort at the east end of the lake offers housekeeping cabins and
campsites.

About six miles north of Nicola Lake a well-marked road leaves the
east side of Highway 5 for **Peterhope Lake**. This five-mile road once was
a formidable obstacle, but recent improvements have made it possible to
reach the lake in a matter of minutes.

This famous lake once furnished some of the most exciting fishing for
Kamloops trout to be found anywhere. It is oval-shaped, about a mile
and a quarter long, with clear water and a rich marl bottom. Wide shoal
areas reach out from the shoreline and a couple of "sunken islands" provide ideal water for the fly fisherman. The lake is at an elevation of
3,650 feet with a surface area of 287 acres and although its maximum
depth is a surprising 108 feet, more than half the lake is less than 30 feet
deep. All the usual orders of aquatic life are present, though the sedge
hatch has declined over the years — as it has in many other lakes.

Peterhope once yielded trout of 8 to 16 pounds, many on dry flies,
although the size of the fish varied from year to year. As described
earlier, the size fluctuations were due to the success, or lack of it, of the
spawning runs in both the inlet and outlet streams. In dry years, the inlet
sometimes is incapable of sustaining eggs or fry, and the flow of water
through the irrigation lock at the outlet often is insufficient to allow recovered spawners or their offspring to return to the lake. Growth is very
rapid in those years when the number of trout in the lake is small.

In recent years, however, Peterhope has had a large population of
small trout. There are still a few lunkers, but they are not nearly as numerous as they once were. Chosen as one of the first three lakes to be restricted to the artificial fly, Peterhope has become the usual site of the
annual "Totem Trophy Fishout," in which fly fishing clubs from all over
the Northwest compete for a trophy presented by the Totem Flyfishers
of Vancouver. This event often brings the region's most expert anglers

Fly casters explore the edges of a shoal on a windy day at Peterhope Lake.

together around the third week in June, but the results — few fish larger than 3 pounds have been captured in this competition — are indicative of the lake's decline. Still, Peterhope remains one of the most beautiful fly fishing lakes to be found anywhere, and the annual Totem Trophy competition sustains its tradition as one of the Interior's most popular lakes.

A fishing camp on the northwest shore of the lake has housekeeping cabins and boats and there is a large government campground on the northern shore. During the past few years a number of private cabins have been built along the eastern edge of the lake.

A main logging road also runs along the eastern shore of Peterhope Lake and beyond the lake, at the 11 mile post, a logging spur leads into **Blue Lake.** This tiny, round lake, at an elevation of about 4,000 feet, is managed as a trophy fishery. Shoal areas covered with cream-colored marl reach out all around the shoreline, sloping out of sight into a deep hole in the center of the lake. The water is extremely clear and trout are very cautious when they enter the shallows. The trout are large — fish of 7 or 7½ pounds are not uncommon — and the fishing is not easy. In fact, it may be nearly impossible, except during the sedge hatch when an appropriate dry fly may seduce an occasional fish. Sometimes, when conditions are right, it is possible to see and stalk individual fish, lay a dry fly in their path and watch them take it. But a careful approach is necessary and the trout do not allow the angler to make even a single mistake.

To assure a continuing population of large fish, stocking of this little lake is limited by the Fish and Wildlife Branch to only a few hundred trout at a time. The lake is surrounded by heavy timber and the road access may be slippery after rain. There is a raw camping area but no other facilities.

The 101 Ranch gate off Highway 5 offers access to the **Frogmoore Lakes**, a pair of mile-long waters at an elevation around 4,700 feet. The last eight miles of the road are little more than a Jeep trail. These lakes usually provide fast fishing for smaller-sized trout. Cabins and boats are available at the lakes.

Highway 5 parallels the western shore of **Stump Lake**, a sprawling lake more than five miles long at an elevation of 2,460 feet. For many years, after it was poisoned to remove scrap fish, Stump Lake was famous as a producer of king-sized trout, some over 15 pounds. It is a rich, shallow, weedy lake, with clear water and several small islands — some of which become shoals when the water is high. Broad shallow areas at both the north and south ends of the lake are especially attractive to fly fishermen.

The size of the trout has been due to limited stocking and the richness of the lake itself. All the usual aquatic fauna are present in abundance, along with an unusually large snail population. But fishing in Stump Lake often is much like fishing for steelhead; the prospects are not very certain, and it is possible to put in many long hours with very few fish to

226

show for the effort. That, plus the difficulty posed by the strong south wind that blows up the lake nearly every afternoon, has made Stump Lake less popular than it otherwise might be. The best fishing also is limited to early spring and late fall; due to its relatively low elevation, the lake's water becomes quite warm during the summer.

There are access and camping spots on both the western and eastern shores of the lake. The old mine on the eastern shore, long a well-known landmark in the area, burned to the ground a few years ago — victim of a fire that started when a party of graduates from the local high school got out of hand. Also within the past few years some ambitious entrepreneur — whose desire for proft surely exceeds his taste — has subdivided "recreational" lots on the eastern side of the lake, built an asphalt road to them and posted a sign along the highway to advertise them. They have not sold well, but each year sees the construction of a few more cabins on them, and their presence adds nothing to the aesthetic quality of the surroundings.

At the north end of Stump Lake a road leading through the Stump Lake Ranch offers access to **Plateau Lake**, a distance of about six miles from the highway. The road is narrow and rocky and may be difficult in wet weather, but the trip is worth it: Plateau is a fly fisherman's dream. Slightly less than a mile long and only a few hundred yards wide, Plateau has an ideal conformation for fly fishing. A deep trench runs through the middle of the lake with broad, shallow shoals extending from its edges to the shoreline, and at either end of the trench — which is to say at both ends of the lake — are round, shallow, weedy bays. The bottom is rich golden marl and the lake is fed by springs which may be seen boiling up through the marl in the shallows at the north end. The lake is at an elevation of about 4,100 feet and has a good population of all the usual orders of aquatic fauna, including a good sedge hatch. Late spring evenings offer very exciting dry-fly fishing when large trout penetrate the shallows to feed on sedges hatching over the shoals.

Unfortunately, Plateau has been subject to occasional winter kill, which makes it an uncertain prospect from one season to the next. At its best, after several winters of survival, it has produced trout up to 10½ pounds, but fish of this size are very rare. On my last visit the lake was generous with trout in the 15-inch class and occasional larger fish to 3½ pounds.

There is a pleasant campsite and boat-launching area on the western shore where the road comes in. The lake also is accessible by a spur from the Peterhope Lake Road, but this is a notoriously bad route that frequently is impassable after rain.

Beyond Stump Lake Ranch Highway 5 continues north to the Roche Lake access and then to Kamloops.

Ashcroft Area

The town of Ashcroft is on the Thompson River about two miles east

227

of the Trans-Canada Highway and about five miles southeast of Cache Creek, a major highway junction. The main street through the portion of Ashcroft on the east bank of the Thompson continues south on an asphalt road that soon begins climbing into a series of switchback turns as it ascends the steep benchland southeast of town. About six miles from town a good gravel road leads off to the north and skirts the edge of **Willard Lake**, visible from the main road, and **Barnes Lake**, just to the north of Willard. Barnes is the larger of the two, slightly more than 1¼ miles long, while Willard is barely a half mile long. Both are shallow, weedy lakes with silty bottoms, and both are controlled for irrigation purposes (with the outlet from Barnes flowing into Willard). They lie at an elevation of about 2,250 feet, which makes them a good bet for early spring and late fall fishing.

Five years ago Willard held many large fish that came willingly to a fly cast into the weedy pockets at its north end. That winter ice fishermen made short work of the large trout and the following spring anything much over 15 inches was unusual. Although it is a rich lake, Willard is so easily accessible in either summer or winter that it receives intense pressure and still has not returned to its former stature.

Barnes Lake, perhaps because it is a little larger, has proven slightly more resistant to heavy angling use and is a relatively consistent producer of trout up to 2½ pounds.

There are campsites on both lakes. Boat launching is easy in the spring when the lakes are full but can be a problem after they have been drawn down in the fall.

Beyond Willard Lake the asphalt road continues southeast where it becomes known as the Highland Valley Road and runs through country devastated by strip-mining until eventually it connects with the dirt road running north to Tunkwa Lake, the pavement running northeast toward Logan Lake and the partly-paved, partly-gravel road that heads south for Lower Nicola and Merritt. But before it reaches these important junctions, the Highland Valley Road also intersects with the O. K. Mine Road, a good gravel road that winds into the timbered hills to the south. About four miles up the O. K. Mine Road a small sign points to the **Island Lake** access, a rough dirt road that drops about a quarter of a mile to the lakeshore.

Island is a natural lake whose water level has been raised by construction of a dam along its western shore. A pumphouse stands on the shoreline and the lake serves as the water supply for a nearby mine. It is surrounded by dense timber, except that everything below the high-water mark was cut before the lake was raised so that it has an ugly "artificial" look when less than full. The lake covers about 250 acres and apparently derives its name from a large, rocky shoal that undoubtedly was an island before the water level was raised.

Now managed as a trophy fishery, Island contains abundant scud,

228

leech and chironomid populations. It also produces some very large trout, with fish of 6 to 7½ pounds not especially uncommon, but as is usually the case in such situations the fishing is never very fast. The lake also blooms heavily, which puts a damper on the fishing after late June and until early fall.

There are rough, informal campsites along the northern shore of the lake. Aesthetically, it is far from a pleasing place, but it does provide some angling of high quality.

Other Areas

From the Kootenay to the Cariboo, there are hundreds of other lakes that hold the Kamloops trout. The Balfour Arm of **Kootenay Lake** itself offers a unique fishery for huge trout of the Gerrard Kamloops strain, and many are taken there on a dry fly. The Okanagan has many outstanding lakes, including the **Dee Chain, Beaver, Hatheume Lake** and its surrounding waters, the **Headwaters Chain** and **Oyama Lake.** The country east of Kamloops has many interesting waters, including **Pinaus Lake** and its surrounding waters, **Pillar Lake, Arthur** and **Bolean Lakes, Niskonlith Lake** and **McGillivray Lake.** The area around 100 Mile House offers **Gustafsen** and **Howard Lakes** and fly-only **Valentine** among many others.

To mention only their names does little justice to them, and of course there are many more excellent waters not named here at all. But the number and variety of waters holding Kamloops trout is one of the chief attractions of the fishery, giving each angler the opportunity to assemble a personal list of favorites, adding and subtracting over the years as familiar waters decline and new discoveries take their place.

And there are other waters whose names never are mentioned, except perhaps in whispers to a trusted friend. These are legendary lakes with monstrous trout whose poundage is never measured in less than double digits. They appear on maps only as anonymous blue images lost among hundreds of their kind. Perhaps they are real and perhaps they are only imaginary, or perhaps they are a little of both. Whatever the truth about them, they add a sense of excitement to the search for a place to fish. What fisherman has not dreamed of finding such a Shangri-La? There is both mystery and strong appeal in the notion of discovering a shining lake, well hidden in the hills, known only to a chosen few; a lake whose waters hold trout that are the stuff of legend. Some men spend a substantial portion of their lives in search of such a place, and though they may never find it, they still find satisfaction in the search.

And who knows? There is always the chance that a few of them will find what they are looking for.

Chapter Nine
The Future

I n the first edition of this book, I suggested that the future of the
Kamloops trout fishery would depend largely on how capably the
people of British Columbia could deal with the problems of population
growth and industrial development in the Interior. It was a safe thing to
say; the growth trends already were well established and gaining momentum, and it was obvious that the province soon would face the same kinds
of problems that had damaged or destroyed productive sport fisheries in
many other parts of the world.

But at the same time I expressed optimism that the people of British
Columbia would be able to handle those problems, going so far as to say
that "the nobler aspects of man's character will emerge to preserve those
things that are most beautiful and meaningful in his world," of which the
Kamloops trout surely is one. Now, with the benefit of a decade's worth
of hindsight, it is apparent that optimism was sadly misplaced.

The explosive growth of population and development in the Interior
has taken place without any intelligent planning or direction. It has become a metastasizing cancer whose ugly tumors are now painfully visible
wherever one chooses to look. The general, hypothetical problems that
were discussed in the first edition of this book are now specific and real
and their impacts are everywhere being strongly felt.

Most of those problems already have been described in some detail.
Development of the mining and forest-products industries stimulated
rapid population growth in parts of the Interior and subsequent transportation improvements made it more easily accessible to visitors from
outside population centers. The influx of new residents and new visitors
has led to increased traffic on the highways and the lakes, pollution of
Interior rivers and proliferating lakeside cabins and real-estate developments. It also has crowded the Interior lakes with a new class of recrea-
tionalist — people frequently infatuated with big boats, bigger motors,
off-road vehicles, snowmobiles and other mechanical contrivances, and
people often lacking knowledge of the outdoors, or respect for it, or for
the rights of others who use it.

These changes have occurred while the provincial government was
mostly bent on following a policy of maximum resource exploitation
and minimum protection. Fisheries and wildlife management problems
have been treated either with indifference or hostility and budgets have
been cut at a time when management and enforcement needs are greater

and more urgent than ever. The inevitable result has been a serious deterioration in the quality of at least some parts of the Kamloops trout fishery. Many lakes have been damaged by overuse and abuse and some have been altogether lost for fishing or any other recreational purpose.

It need not have been so. With a little planning and foresight the Interior easily could have accommodated all its growth without serious strain on its natural or social systems. If development had occurred in a controlled, rational manner, there would today be room for even more of it. But that opportunity has been lost, and additional growth now will only add to the problems.

There is no sign that growth is slowing down, and some developments now pending or already under way will have consequences that are potentially far more serious than anything that has gone before. They include the strip-mining in the Highland Valley, the proposed coal-fired generating plant at Hat Creek and the building of the Coquihalla Highway. Each of them is worth a closer look:

Strip-mining: There are, as we have seen, a number of productive lakes in the Highland Valley between Kamloops and Merritt and these have become important and traditional parts of the Kamloops trout fishery. This has been true even though for many years the valley also has been the scene of mining activity for massive deposits of copper and other minerals. However, nothing in the past was even remotely comparable to the huge Bethlehem and Lornex copper strip mines opened between Logan Lake and Ashcroft in the past few years.

It is difficult to describe the incredible size of these mines to anyone who never has seen them. Thousands of acres of topsoil and timber have been removed and whole mountains are being leveled; the awesome scars probably could be seen by an observer on the moon. The loss of wildlife habitat is incalculable, and although there have been promises that the land will be restored, there is considerable doubt that successful reclamation is possible in an area of such limited rainfall.

Except for Divide Lake, a once-pleasant trout water that has become a receptacle for mine tailings, the lakes of the area have mostly escaped direct impacts from the mining. But the indirect impacts have been enormous: Ten years ago there were no paved roads in the area; now there are paved highways from Kamloops and Ashcroft and the road to Merritt is paved over most of its length. Ten years ago the area was inhabited only by a few ranchers and Indians; now there are 400 family homes in Logan Lake, a "company town" built by Lornex. The improved access has brought the Highland Valley lakes and surrounding waters within easy reach of many more people, and they are virtually in the backyard of the residents of Logan Lake. In the absence of any effort to control the increased use or exploitation of these lakes, many of them have suffered. The decline of the waters along the Lac le Jeune Road, now the most heavily traveled route to Logan Lake, is one example.

The presence of the town of Logan Lake is an especially sore point to other residents of the area. The town was built to provide mineworkers a nearby place to live; it is about 15 minutes driving time from the major mine sites. But Ashcroft is only about 30 minutes away, and Merritt 45, and the citizens of both communities have argued that it would have been almost as easy for mineworkers to commute from their towns. They contend there never was any need to build a town in the Highland Valley, and they resent the use of tax money to pay for services in the new town that duplicate those already in existence in the old ones. Aside from the economic arguments, a very good case also could be made that the Highland Valley was an extremely inappropriate place to build a town and the whole region would have been better off without it. An intelligent regional plan, had there been one, almost certainly would have prevented it.

But the town is there and it will not go away. In fact, it promises to get much larger. As of this writing Lornex was planning an expansion that will bring more workers and their families to Logan Lake. Another company, Highmont, had announced plans to begin mining on property it owns in the Highland Valley, and still another, Valley Copper, was considering opening yet another mine. If all these developments take place the population of Logan Lake will grow by at least 4,000 persons. The added population will place additional strains on the environment while the expanded mining operations will continue to whittle away the land base and wildlife habitat of the area.

The mining activity has provided badly-needed jobs and added greatly to the local economic base and most Interior residents seem to support it — or at least seem reconciled to it. Apparently they are willing to accept the environmental costs (although many probably do not yet realize what these will be) and it is within their rights to make such a decision. But the distribution of the added population brought by the mining is another matter, one that could have been handled with much less impact on the social and recreational amenities of the region.

In retrospect, building a town at Logan Lake was a bad mistake, and as expanded mining activity attracts more people to the area the consequences of that mistake will become ever more obvious. The surrounding lakes, already heavily used, will be subjected to even greater use, and unless more are placed under trophy management — as Island Lake has been — and are protected from waterfront development, the future of the fishery in and around Highland Valley appears in great jeopardy.

Hat Creek: B. C. Hydro, the province's electric utility, long has had its eye on the enormous coal deposits in the Hat Creek drainage west of Ashcroft. Although no firm decisions have been made, the utility has proposed building a giant thermal generating plant that would burn coal strip-mined from the area.

The project would be huge. The mine and plant together would consume up to 8,000 acres of land, most of it for the mine. The generating plant would bring an estimated 2,500 new permanent residents to the communities of Ashcroft and Cache Creek. Water for the generating turbines and for cooling would come from the nearby Thompson River, and the plant would consume up to 2.6 percent of the average low flow of the river. That does not seem like very much water, but the Thompson already is under stress from the industrial and domestic sewage dumped into it at Kamloops and the withdrawal would make it even more difficult for the river to assimilate those wastes. The reduction in flow would mean a higher concentration of pollutants which might be enough to tip the balance against the river's priceless salmon and steelhead runs.

But the real threat from the Hat Creek plant would be its atmospheric emissions. Cooling towers would give off large quantities of water vapor that would create additional precipitation; sulfur dioxide in the stack gases would combine with that and natural vapor to form sulfuric acid that would fall as "acid rain." The prevailing winds would carry most of this to the east — directly over the watersheds of some of the richest Kamloops trout waters.

Acid rain from industrial fallout already has destroyed some freshwater fisheries in Scandinavian countries and damaged others; similar damage is becoming increasingly apparent in some waters of the Northeast United States and the Canadian maritime provinces. The damage is greatest in waters that are naturally neutral or slightly acidic; the acid rain increases their acidity, which reduces their productivity and eventually may make them incapable of supporting fish life at all.

Most of the Kamloops trout lakes are strongly alkaline, which accounts for their high productivity. They would be better able to withstand the impacts of acid rain than lakes in other areas. Nevertheless, acid rainfall would reduce their productivity so that they no longer could support trout populations of the same average size or numbers that they do now. Over time, the fisheries in some lakes almost certainly would be lost and many others would be severely damaged. It is impossible to estimate how quickly the damage would occur or how widespread it would be — except that it would affect a very large area. Indeed, in weighing the environmental consequences of the Hat Creek proposal, the question is not whether there will be adverse impacts, but how great will be the scope of the disaster.

British Columbia now has sufficient generating capacity to be able to satisfy its own needs and have some power left for export, and there are serious questions whether a project the size of Hat Creek will be necessary in the foreseeable future — especially when there has not yet been any real effort to conserve electricity in the province. However, such considerations never have troubled B. C. Hydro very much and in the past it has embarked on a number of ambitious schemes of dubious necessity. Ideas such as the Hat Creek generating plant also have a very long life, and even if practical and environmental considerations should block

the development for now, the scheme undoubtedly will surface again in
the future.

The Hat Creek coal deposits almost certainly will be developed at
some future time – if not by B. C. Hydro, then by someone else. The
coal also could be used to produce synthetic fuels, or its high alumina
content could be extracted to make aluminum, or it could be shipped to
other areas for use. Any of those alternatives would cause environmental
difficulties, but none would be likely to pose as great a threat to the Kamloops trout fishery as the generating plant. If it is built, a significant number of the region's most important lakes are almost certain to be eventually damaged or destroyed.

Coquihalla Highway: Though the Highland Valley mining and the
Hat Creek generating plant would cause extremely serious problems,
they are minor compared to the potential impacts of the Coquihalla Highway. The four-lane highway is planned to follow the Coquihalla River
upstream from Hope, over the Coquihalla Pass and northeast along the
valley of the Coldwater River to Merritt. Construction already has begun
at the southern end near Hope. Eventual plans call for a four-lane extension from Merritt to Kamloops, following either the existing route of
Highway 5 or a new route to the west that would skirt the eastern rim
of the Highland Valley.

Even without the Merritt-Kamloops connection, the highway from
Hope to Merritt would radically change the whole transportation pattern of the southern Interior. The present main route is Highway 1, the
Trans-Canada Highway along the Fraser Canyon. Traffic flowing along
this artery into the central Interior now bypasses Merritt through Spences
Bridge 40 miles west. The Fraser Canyon route has been vastly improved
in recent years, but it remains a two-lane route over much of its length,
with many twisting turns and steep grades. The Coquihalla Highway
would be four lanes all the way, a virtual freeway, and would cut at least
30 miles from the Fraser-Thompson Canyon route from Hope to Kamloops. Much of the traffic that now bypasses Merritt would switch to
the new Coquihalla Highway, completely altering the character of the
Coldwater and Nicola Valleys and of Merritt itself.

Merritt's "off-the-beaten-track" location always has been a sore point
with local businessmen, who have lobbied many years for the new highway. They see it as a great stimulus to the area's economy, which it
surely will prove to be. But theirs is a narrow, short-term view which has
not considered the adverse impacts of the project. Once the flush of new
economic activity has worn off and the tremendous environmental costs
of the highway begin to become apparent, the people of Merritt almost
certainly will deeply regret their support for it. Merritt always has been
a destination, but with the new highway it will become a way station, a
fuel-and-fried-chicken stop on the route to Kamloops. The great influx
of people the new highway is bound to bring to the area will include

many casual visitors who undoubtedly will have even less appreciation and regard for its environment than those who use it now. Pressure on the surrounding lakes, already intense, will grow enormously, and abuses like those already described on Lundbom Lake will multiply a hundred-fold.

Highway development has turned the community of Cache Creek into an ugly little strip town, its crowded streets lined with gas stations and fast-food franchises, and there is no reason to expect that things will happen any differently in Merritt. In fact, the cancerous growth that follows major highway construction is a fact of life all over North America, and even the strongest zoning or planning ordinances have proven to be paper tigers, powerless to stop it.

There still is a possibility that the enormous financial cost of the new highway — perhaps coupled with a slowly dawning awareness of its environmental costs — will stop it short of completion. But this seems unlikely since such projects, once begun, develop an almost irresistible momentum of their own, and if the highway is finished on schedule in a few years the changes will begin with the first traffic that rolls into Merritt. Within a few years after that, or a decade at most, I fully expect that the fishery in the rich lakes surrounding Merritt and in all the lakes along the route between Merritt and Kamloops will be gone, and serious fishermen will turn their attention to the relatively undisturbed waters farther north around Little Fort, Clearwater and 100 Mile (a switch that already is beginning even without the new highway). Merritt's economy will suffer from the change, and residents of the area will suffer the loss of one of its most important amenities.

Although the Coquihalla Highway, the Hat Creek generating plant and the expansion of mining in the Highland Valley are the most serious immediate threats to the fishery, there are other potential problems. One is the development of energy corridors — rights-of-way for oil or gas pipelines or electrical transmission lines. Rather than confining these to existing highway corridors, which in many cases would have been less costly and less environmentally destructive, the government has permitted new and unnecessary swaths to be cut through rich forests and grasslands. The most obvious impact of such development is visual; they are ugly and they have spoiled some of the aesthetic qualities of lakes such as Roche, Peterhope and Lundbom. But they also may cause more subtle problems; for instance, no one has studied the effects on fish of the defoliating agents sprayed on some of these rights-of-way and carried by runoff into spawning streams or lakes. Perhaps there are no significant effects, but if there are they will show up only after the damage already has been done. That possibility could easily have been avoided if the energy transmission lines had been more logically located.

Commercial trout farming is another potential problem. The huge Douglas Ranch has begun experimenting with trout farming in two lakes.

236

Local residents seem not to have recognized the implications of creating a commercial market for what historically has been a game fish, but they would not have to look very far for an example. In Washington State, a commercial Indian fishery for steelhead made possible by a court interpretation of old treaties has all but destroyed steelhead sport fishing on a number of famous rivers. And the commercial market for Atlantic salmon has made them a target for widespread poaching, which has become an extremely serious problem in Canada's maritime provinces. With proper controls and rigid enforcement, trout farming need not become a problem. But so far the anglers of British Columbia seem not to have recognized that a problem may exist, or that controls might be necessary.

From the foregoing discussion, it might seem that the author is opposed to any economic growth or development in the Kamloops region. Unquestionably, the Kamloops trout fishery would be better off if there were no further growth, but obviously that is not a realistic attitude. Economic growth is both necessary and desirable and people have an inherent right to expect it. But uncontrolled growth often is more destructive than beneficial, and the headlong rush to use the resources of the Interior already has deprived its future citizens of a large measure of their birthright. Economic forces are not so sacred that they should not be subject to controls necessary to preserve resources and amenities that are the common heritage of all the citizens of the province. By controls, I mean intelligent planning, and that is precisely what has been lacking in the economic development of the Interior. It is more sorely needed now than ever if the projects just described, and others like them, are to be developed without destroying the fisheries and wildlife of the area, the environment that supports them — and the lives and aspirations of the people of the region.

Fortunately, there are a few positive signs. Entities such as the Thompson-Nicola Regional District have begun efforts to draft a regional plan that would confine industrial, residential and transportation growth to appropriate defined areas and regulate the use of lakes so that those important for their wilderness and/or fisheries values would be preserved for those purposes. But the success of such an enterprise depends upon widespread public and governmental support — and there are few signs that this will be immediately forthcoming.

Other groups are becoming more and more outspoken in their concerns for the fishery and the environment. These include fly fishing clubs, other sportsmen's groups and the B. C. Interior Fishing Camp Operators Association, as noted earlier. They also include various environmental organizations. By themselves, however, none of these groups has enough political influence to accomplish very much, and there is little liaison or community of effort between them. But they have many interests in common and by joining together they probably could play a significant role in the direction of future development of the province. Unfortunately, these groups still are ruled by old attitudes and rivalries and there seems little prospect they will get together very soon.

The establishment of more trophy lakes is another positive step. At least these waters will be partly protected from growing angling pressures and there will likely be more and more of them. Elsewhere in the province, catch-and-release regulations have been imposed on a number of rivers to protect their dwindling steelhead runs, and it may be expected that similar rules will be applied to some of the Kamloops trout waters as a protective measure.

So far, however, all these things are only very minor obstacles in the way of the socio-economic juggernaut that threatens to overrun the Interior. In the final analysis, there must be a full-scale shift in public attitudes before any real progress is made toward the intelligent use and conservation of the area's resources. People must recognize that fish and wildlife also have economic value that makes them worth saving, and that they have extremely important personal and spiritual values as well. Only when the people of British Columbia demand better management of their resources will the government be compelled to respond. But unless those demands are made very soon, there will not be very much left to manage.

In all, the future of the Kamloops trout fishery does not appear very promising — although I would like nothing better than to have future events prove that assessment wrong. Even if it proves correct, there always will be some waters where big trout will prowl the shallows in the evening, searching for awkward sedges fluttering on the surface, and in them the long and colorful traditions of the fishery will be continued. But very probably there will be many fewer such waters than there are now, and the fly fisherman of the future will face sharply limited opportunities. This means, in a very real sense, that for the Kamloops trout fisherman the future is now. For at least the next few years there will be many lakes filled with strong, bright trout that will come as eagerly to a fly as they always have; lakes where one may still go to hear the high, lonely, shivering cry of a loon, or to sit in solitude and silence and marvel as the fleeting, milky glow of evening steals from the water and the cold light of countless stars gleams down over unbroken ranks of pine.

Such sights and sounds and places are to be savored and remembered, for they may not come again.

Acknowledgements

A long with every other Kamloops trout fisherman, I owe a debt to those patient and persevering scientists whose research over the years has uncovered so much information about the habits and life history of the Kamloops. Much of this information has been applied to management of the fishery, with obvious and lasting benefits. Without the work of men like Charles Mottley, Peter Larkin, Stuart Smith and so many others, there would not be nearly as many Kamloops trout to fish for as there are today — nor would there be nearly as much to write about. And it is in writing about the Kamloops trout that I owe a special, personal debt to these men, most of whom I know only from having read their work in the pages of scientific journals.

There is a wealth of information about the Kamloops trout in such journals, but most of it is not readily accessible to the casual fisherman. Thus I am especially grateful for permission to use some of that information in this book: To the Fisheries Research Board of Canada for permission to quote from its Journal and the Journal's predecessors, the Bulletin of the Biological Board of Canada and the Progress Reports of the Pacific Biological Station; to the American Fisheries Society for permission to quote from its Transactions, and to the Canadian Department of Fisheries for permission to quote from the Canadian Fish Culturist. A complete listing of the references used will be found in the Bibliography.

The late Letcher Lambuth of Seattle provided a great deal of help and encouragement in the preparation of the original edition of this book. It is proper to again acknowledge his kind assistance, for without it the original edition might never have come into being — and without the original, this revised edition obviously would not have been possible. I shall always remember Letcher's help, and I am glad that I was able to assist in the belated publication of his own important work, *Angler's Workshop*. My only regret is that he could not live to see it.

George Stringer, former regional biologist at Kamloops, was most helpful in preparation of the original edition; Dr. Bill McMahon of Seattle shared his memories of the last days of Bill Nation, and Enos Bradner, former outdoor editor of *The Seattle Times*, provided thoughtful criticism of the manuscript and wrote the foreword to the original edition. To each of them I again express my thanks.

I have shared many good times and many good waters with Alan Pratt, chief artist for *The Seattle Times*, and I am happy and fortunate to be able to share these pages with him. His maps from the original edition have been revised and updated for this one. His lifelike paintings of Kamloops trout fly patterns were the centerpiece of the first edition; unfortunately they could not be used again because of the many changes in fly-pattern preferences over the past decade, and they have been replaced by photographs. However, the original paintings still hang on the walls of my home where I still admire them, and I shall always be grateful to Al for his help.

A very special note of thanks is due to Lee Straight, former outdoors editor of *The Vancouver Sun*, now sport fisheries advisor for the Canadian Department of Fisheries and Oceans. Lee is one of British Columbia's most knowledgeable anglers and certainly one of the province's most entertaining writers. It had been my plan to ask him to read and criticize the manuscript of this edition, but he volunteered to do so before I could even ask. For that I am grateful, and I deeply appreciate his thoughtful comments and suggestions.

Some men are fortunate enough to have families who also enjoy fishing and the outdoors, and I am one of them. In fact, I'm certain that Joan, my wife, and Stephanie and Randy, my daughter and son, would have preferred more fishing trips in the past year instead of staying home to watch me write about fishing. Their understanding and support — and their tolerance — are largely responsible for the completion of this manuscript. And to Joan belongs the credit for many of the photos that appear in this book.

Finally, my thanks to all the anglers with whom I have shared the waters of the Kamloops trout. With them I feel a bond of common experience that will not be easily understood by one who never has sampled the excitement of the Kamloops. The fellowship of angling is one of its greatest rewards, and through the Kamloops trout I have made many good friends. I hope that both the fishing and the friendships will long endure.

Bibliography

Adamson, W. A. *The Enterprising Angler*; William Morrow & Co., New York, 1945.

Almy, Gerald. *Tying & Fishing the Terrestrials*; Stackpole Books, Harrisburg, Pa., 1978.

Carl, G. Clifford; Clemens, W. A., and Lindsey, C. C. *The Freshwater Fishes of British Columbia*; British Columbia Provincial Museum Handbook No. 5, Victoria, B. C., 1967.

Clemens, W. A.; McHugh, J. L., and Rawson, D. S. *A Biological Survey of Okanagan Lake, B. C.*; Fisheries Research Board of Canada, Bulletin LVI.

Coker, Robert E. *Streams, Lakes, Ponds*; Chapel Hill, University of North Carolina Press, 1954.

Crossman, D. J., and Larkin, P. A. *Yearling Liberations and Change of Food as Effecting Rainbow Trout Yield in Paul Lake;* Transactions of the American Fisheries Society, Vol. 88, No. 1, January, 1959.

Dibblee, G. *Effects of the Mining Industry on Fresh Water Fisheries of British Columbia*; Canadian Fish Culturist, Issue 25, October, 1959.

Dymond, J. R. *The Trout and Other Game Fishes of British Columbia;* Biological Board of Canada, Bulletin No. XXXII, 1932.

Essig, E. O. *Insects of Western North America;* Macmillan Co., New York, 1929.

Gordon, Sid W. *How to Fish from Top to Bottom;* Telegraph Press, Harrisburg, Pa., 1955.

Haig-Brown, Roderick L. *A River Never Sleeps;* William Morrow & Co., New York, 1944.

Haig-Brown, Roderick L. *The Living Land;* produced by the British Columbia Natural Resources Conference, William Morrow & Co., New York, 1961.

Haig-Brown, Roderick L. *The Western Angler;* Derrydale Press, New York, 1939; 2 vols.

Haig-Brown, Roderick L. *The Western Angler,* revised edition; William Morrow & Co., New York, 1947.

Hartman, G. F. *Reproductive Biology of the Gerrard Stock Rainbow Trout;* Symposium on Salmon and Trout in Streams, University of British Columbia, February 22, 1968.

Hartman, G. F.; Northcote, T. G., and Lindsey, C. C. *Comparison of Inlet and Outlet Spawning Runs of Rainbow Trout in Loon Lake, B. C.;* Journal of the Fisheries Research Board of Canada, Vol. 19, No. 2, March, 1962.

"Huge Rainbow Trout;" British Columbia Wildlife Review, December, 1968, pp. 24-25.

Hutchison, Bruce. *Rivers of America: The Fraser;* Rinehart & Co., New York, 1950.

Inland Empire Fly Fishing Club, Spokane, Wash. *Flies of the Northwest,* fourth edition, 1979.

Johannes, R. E., and Larkin, P. A. *Competition for Food Between Red-side Shiners and Rainbow Trout in Two British Columbia Lakes;* Journal of the Fisheries Research Board of Canada, Vol. 18, No. 2, March, 1961.

Kilburn, Jim. *The Caddis Larvae;* Western Fish & Game, Vol. 6, No. 2, March, 1971.

Kilburn, Jim. *The Caddis Fly;* Western Fish & Game, Vol. 6, No. 3, May, 1971.

Kilburn, Jim. *The Damselfly Nymph;* Western Fish & Wildlife, Vol. 6, No. 5, August/September, 1971.

Kilburn, Jim. *The Dragonfly;* Western Fish & Wildlife, Vol. 7, No. 2, March, 1972.

Lambert, T. W. *Fishing in British Columbia;* Horace Cox, London, 1907.

Larkin, P. A. *Introduction of the Kamloops Trout in British Columbia Lakes;* Canadian Fish Culturist, No. 16, August 16, 1954.

Larkin, P. A. *Management of Trout Lakes in British Columbia;* Tenth Annual Game Convention, Prince George, B. C., May 23-26, 1956.

Larkin, P. A., and Northcote, T. G. *Indices of Productivity in British Columbia Lakes;* Journal of the Fisheries Research Board of Canada, Vol. 13, No. 4, July, 1956.

Larkin, P. A.; Parker, R. R., and Terpenning, J. G. *Size as a Determinant of Growth Rate in Rainbow Trout;* Transactions of the American Fisheries Society, Vol. 86, 1956.

Larkin, P. A., and Smith, S. B. *Some Effects of the Introduction of the Redside Shiner on the Kamloops Trout in Paul Lake, B. C.;* Transactions of the American Fisheries Society, 1953.

KAMLOOPS

Lloyd, J. T., and Needham, James G. *The Life of Inland Waters;* Charles C. Thomas, Baltimore, 1930.

McMynn, R. G. *Activities and Problems of the Fisheries Management Division;* Address to the Tenth Annual Game Convention, Prince George, B. C., May 23-26, 1956.

McPhail, J. D. *Effects on Fresh Water Fisheries of Agricultural Development in British Columbia;* Canadian Fish Culturist, Issue 25, October, 1959.

Merritt, Richard W., and Cummins, Kenneth W., eds. *An Introduction to the Aquatic Insects of North America;* Kendall/Hunt Publishing Co., Dubuque, Iowa, 1978.

Migel, J. Michael, and Wright, Leonard M., Jr., eds. *The Masters on the Nymph;* Nick Lyons Books, Doubleday & Co., Inc., New York, 1979.

Mottley, C. McC. *A Biometrical Study of the Kamloops Trout of Kootenay Lake;* Journal of the Fisheries Research Board of Canada, Vol. II, No. 4, 1936.

Mottley, C. McC. *The Classification of the Rainbow Trout of British Columbia;* Progress Reports of the Pacific Biological Station, No. 27, 1936.

Mottley, C. McC. *The Effect of Increasing the Stock in a Lake on the Size and Condition of Rainbow Trout;* Transactions of the American Fisheries Society, 1940.

Mottley, C. McC. *Fluctuations in the Intensity of the Spawning Runs of Rainbow Trout at Paul Lake;* Journal of the Fisheries Research Board of Canada, Vol. IV, No. 2, May-July, 1938.

Mottley, C. McC. *The Kamloops Trout;* Progress Reports of the Pacific Biological Station, No. 7, 1930.

Mottley, C. McC. *Loss of Weight by Rainbow Trout at Spawning Time;* Transactions of the American Fisheries Society, 1937.

Mottley, C. McC. *The Origin and Relations of the Rainbow Trout;* Transactions of the American Fisheries Society, 1934.

Mottley, C. McC. *The Production of Rainbow Trout at Paul Lake, B. C.;* Transactions of the American Fisheries Society, 1939.

Mottley, C. McC. *The Propagation of Trout in the Kamloops District, B. C.;* Transactions of the American Fisheries Society, 1932.

Mottley, C. McC. *The Spawning Migration of Rainbow Trout;* Transactions of the American Fisheries Society, 1933.

Mottley, C. McC. *Temperature and Propagation of Trout;* Progress Reports of the Pacific Biological Station, No. 8, 1931.

Mottley, C. McC. *The Trout of Streams and Small Lakes in Southern British Columbia;* Progress Reports of the Pacific Biological Station, No. 19, April, 1934.

Mottley, C. McC., and Mottley, Jean C. *The Food of Kamloops Trout;* Progress Reports of the Pacific Biological Station, No. 13, 1932.

Needham, Paul R. *Trout Streams,* revised by Carl F. Bond; Winchester Press, New York, 1969.

Northcote, T. G. *An Inventory and Evaluation of the Lakes of British Columbia, with Special Reference to Sport Fish Production;* Fifteenth British Columbia Natural Resources Conference.

Northcote, T. G. *Migratory Behavior of Juvenile Rainbow Trout in Outlet and Inlet Streams of Loon Lake, B. C.;* Journal of the Fisheries Research Board of Canada, Vol. 18, No. 2, 1962.

Pennak, Robert W. *Fresh-Water Invertebrates of the United States;* Ronald Press, New York, 1953.

"Planting Fish in the Early Days;" British Columbia Wildlife Review, September, 1967, p. 21.

Rawson, Donald S. *Productivity Studies in Lakes of the Kamloops Region, B. C.;* Biological Board of Canada, Bulletin No. XLII, 1934.

Read, Stanley E. *Tommy Brayshaw, The Ardent Angler-Artist;* University of British Columbia Press, Vancouver, B. C., 1977.

Richardson, Lee. *Lee Richardson's B. C.;* Champoeg Press, Forest Grove, Ore., 1978.

Shaw, Jack. *Fly Fish the Trout Lakes;* Mitchell Press, Vancouver, B. C., 1976.

Smith, S. B. *The Non-Tidal Sport Fishery;* Fifteenth British Columbia Natural Resources Conference.

Smith, S. B. *Survival and Growth of Wild and Hatchery Trout in Corbett Lake, B. C.;* Canadian Fish Culturist, August, 1957.

Usinger, Robert L., ed. *Aquatic Insects of California;* University of California Press, Berkeley, Calif., 1956.

Whitehouse, Francis C. *Sport Fishing in Canada;* privately printed, Vancouver, B. C., 1948.

Williams, A. Bryan. *Fish and Game in British Columbia;* Sun Directories, Ltd., Vancouver, B. C., 1935.

Index

249